LEGENDARY LOCALS

OF

DRACUT
MASSACHUSETTS

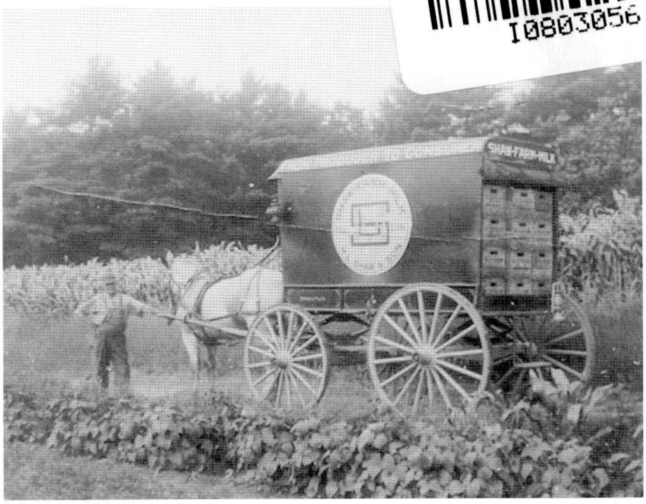

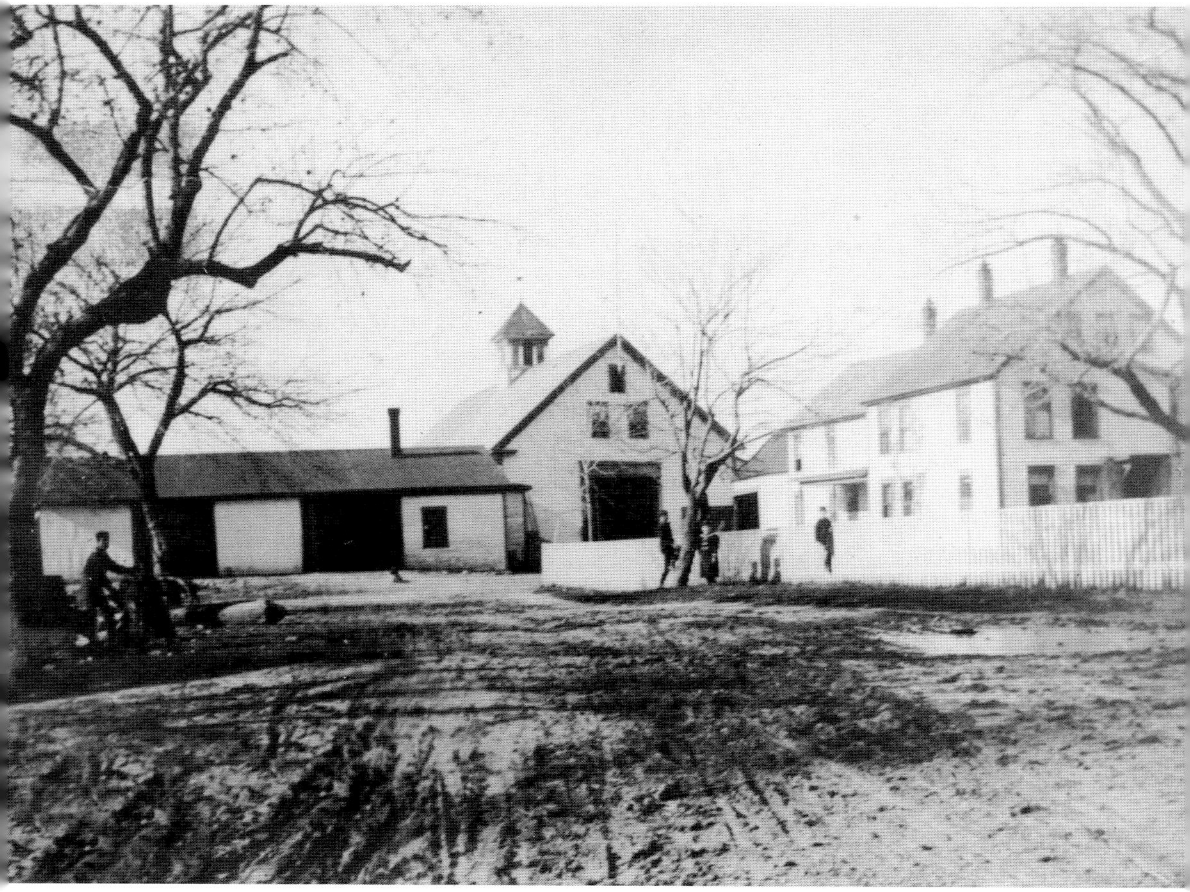

Oliver J. Coburn Farm

Located along Lakeview Avenue, the Oliver J. Coburn Farm was one of many dairy farms in Dracut. First established in 1790, the farm extended from Primrose Hill to the Merrimack River. When hoof and mouth disease devastated the farm's herd of dairy cows in the early 20th century, the Richardsons purchased the land, adding to their Beaver Brook Farm. During the 1940s, the Richardsons used the land as an airport, and eventually, they donated it to the town for the School Department in 1953. Now home to the Dracut Historical Society, the Oliver J. Coburn house still stands at 1660 Lakeview Avenue. (Courtesy Dracut Historical Society.)

Page 1: Shaw and Prince

M.L. Shaw Sr. and his faithful horse, Prince, get ready for their daily home deliveries. Shaw established Shaw Dairy Farm in 1908, and home delivery service is still offered. Prince retired in 1927. (Courtesy Warren Shaw.)

LEGENDARY LOCALS

OF

DRACUT

MASSACHUSETTS

REBECCA A. DUDA

FOREWORD BY MAJ. EVERETT HENRY

LEGENDARY LOCALS

ISBN 978-1-4671-0155-4

Legendary Locals is an imprint of Arcadia Publishing
Charleston, South Carolina

Printed in the United States of America

Library of Congress Control Number: 2013955455

For all general information, please contact Arcadia Publishing:
Telephone 843-853-2070
Fax 843-853-0044
E-mail sales@arcadiapublishing.com
For customer service and orders:
Toll-Free 1-888-313-2665

Visit us on the Internet at www.arcadiapublishing.com

Dedication
This book is lovingly dedicated to my mother.

On the Front Cover: Clockwise from top left:
Edmund Murphy, high school coach, and Armand Sancartier, high school student and athlete, (Courtesy Edmund Murphy; see pages 44 and 45), Dennis Piendak, town manager, and Edward M. Kennedy, senator, (Courtesy Dennis Piendak; see page 25), Arthur Beaudry, longtime volunteer in Dracut youth athletics, (Courtesy Edmund Murphy; see page 48), Edna Cutter, horticulturalist and library trustee, (Courtesy Craig Mahoney; see page 16), Harvey Gagnon, businessman and civic volunteer, Dr. Christos Daoulas, school superintendent, Myrtle Crow, teacher, F. Bradford Morse, congressman, and Pauline Varnum, high school principal and assistant principal, (Courtesy Dracut Historical Society; see page 38), Michael Collins, mill owner, (Courtesy Dracut Historical Society; see page 90), Colleen Garry, state representative, and Bruce Hutchins, high school principal, (Courtesy Garry family; see page 24), Christos Daoulas, seen in Europe during World War II, (Courtesy Arthur Daoulas; see page 80), Michael Monahan, Marine, (Courtesy Eleanor Duda; see page 78).

On the Back Cover: From left to right:
M.L. Shaw Sr. of Shaw Dairy Farm (Courtesy Warren Shaw, see page 101), Larry Zimmerman, pastor at the Old Yellow Meeting House, and Esther Garland and Norma Taplin, Dracut Historical Society volunteers, (Courtesy Larry Zimmerman, see page 110).

CONTENTS

FOREWORD

On December 20, 1884, the Salvation Army first unfurled its tricolored flag in a second-floor hall at Weir's block on Market Street in Lowell. In the 130 years that have followed, the Salvation Army has enjoyed a strong presence in the Merrimack Valley and has continued its mission of meeting spiritual and physical need wherever it is found. Many notable heroes of the faith have visited Lowell, including founder William Booth's daughter Catherine and the colorful character "Joe the Turk," who spent time in the city jail for street preaching. Lowell native Alexander M. Damon began his service with the Salvation Army around 1889 and rose in the ranks of the Army to be the first American-born commissioner and territorial commander of the eastern United States.

Every day, in more than 126 countries around the world, people enter our facilities seeking food or utility assistance, a listening ear, or a safe place for their children to grow, learn, and develop. In the process of seeking help, they discover the Salvation Army is much more than just a place to get a handout, but rather a shield from the world and a hope for a better tomorrow.

The success of our efforts in the greater Lowell area comes in part through the generosity of our many donors. For more than 25 years and counting, the annual radiothon on 980 WCAP has been a key event in raising funds to accomplish our mission. From early days of raising several thousand dollars at the mobile van to recent years of raising more than $100,000, this partnership helps provide kids with toys and clothing for Christmas, fills funding gaps in our various programs, and makes utility and food assistance possible for people in need.

Through the passing years and changing conditions, the Salvation Army, with ever-improving techniques and increased public support, has humbly endeavored to serve humanity at the point of need. The proceeds from the sale of this book will be donated to the Salvation Army in Lowell.

—Maj. Everett C. Henry

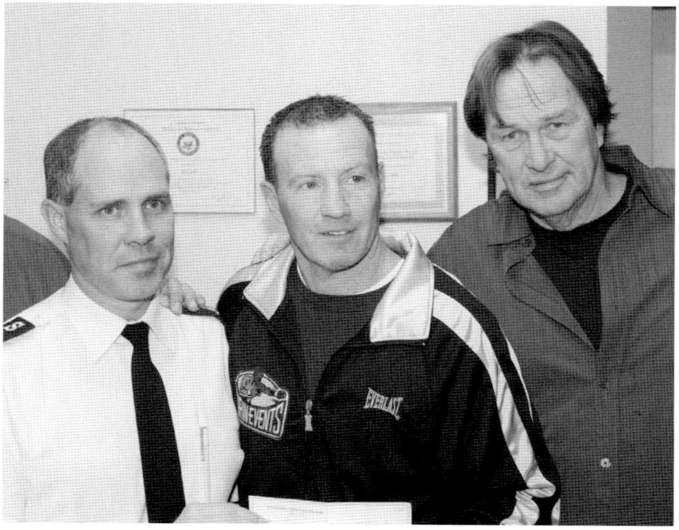

WCAP Salvation Radiothon, 2011
Pictured at the 2011 WCAP Salvation Army Radiothon are, from left to right, Maj. Everett Henry, Micky Ward, and Warren Shaw. The Micky Ward Foundation has been a significant radiothon partner for years. (Courtesy Shawn Ashe.)

ACKNOWLEDGMENTS

Legendary Locals of Dracut focuses on the people of the community, which has always seemed an appropriate topic for me to write about having been a teacher in the Dracut Public Schools since 2004. Over the past 10 years, I have had the pleasure, and honor, to meet hundreds of students and parents. Now, with the publication of this book, they will be able to meet the people who have created the town in which they live. Researching and writing a book is no small undertaking, and regardless of the topic, there are numerous people who contribute to the final product. First, William Dumont deserves a very special thank-you for the countless e-mails he has answered regarding photographs and technical issues. He has, in one form or another, looked at or edited virtually every image in this book. I cannot thank him enough. In addition, he has shared his own family photographs for inclusion in this latest history of Dracut. Brian Duff once again helped with technical issues. Warren Shaw was very generous with his time when it came time to researching land preservation efforts in the town. His firsthand knowledge of this subject was invaluable. Dr. Michael F. McNamara provided help throughout the entire project in a variety of ways, by providing me with names of people to potentially consider and research, to sharing his brother's life story, and finally, to proofreading the text. His help has been appreciated throughout the duration of the project. Harvey Gagnon also reviewed the text. The Dracut Historical Society was most gracious by mentioning my research and desire for photographs in their monthly newsletter. Because of them, I have been corresponding with Martha K. Wolfe in Canada, who has been a wealth of information and most generous with sharing her father's and grandfather's photographs and memorabilia. There are far too many other people throughout the town and beyond who have helped contribute to this book to mention them all by name. However, I was always humbled whenever a family allowed me to bring home personal photographs and effects of their loved ones. I hope their trust in sharing their stories has culminated in a product of which they can be proud.

INTRODUCTION

Where the Beaver Brook Apartments and shopping area is located on Lakeview Avenue today has long been a site of industry and commerce in Dracut. Waterpower from Beaver Brook was harnessed for Dracut's early textile mills, and as early as 1840, according to Silas R. Coburn in his 1922 *History of Dracut*, Scottish immigrants John and Peter Lawson established a thread mill, where Martha Little Davidson would spin the first spool of cotton thread in the United States. Later that century, in 1862, construction began on the Merrimac Woolen Mills in the Navy Yard district. The Merrimac Woolen Mills were so successful they had an exhibition at the 1893 World's Fair in Chicago, where they displayed the first plaid textiles produced in the United States. As with many New England towns in the 19th century, the textile industry helped to shape Dracut and its history. Yet the true fabric of the town is the people of the community. The tapestry of their stories and actions forms the basis for the town known as Dracut.

Prior to the white settlers' settlement of Dracut, the Pennacook inhabited the area from the northern Merrimack River to the St. Lawrence River. Passaconaway (1570?–1679?) was the *sachem* (chief) of the Pennacook nation until turning leadership over to his son Wannalancit. His name meaning "child of the bear," Passaconaway lived along the Merrimack River at the Pawtucket Falls during the summer. By the 1660s, white settlers had begun to inhabit the area of the Pennacook.

John Evered Webb was the town's first white settler. He purchased land on the northern side of the Merrimack River from Jonathan Tyng but did not attempt to establish a permanent settlement. He built a home on what is now called Old Ferry Road, then returned to Boston. His widow sold his land to Samuel Varnum and Edward Coburn, both of Ipswich. They began a permanent settlement in the 1670s, and by 1701, the Massachusetts General Court officially incorporated Dracut as a township. The Varnums and Coburns built their town on the frontier, and the settlers who encountered fighting during King Philip's War (1675–1676) built a garrison house for protection. Samuel Varnum lost two sons during King Philip's War. The garrison stood on what is now Riverside Street in Lowell until 1887, when it was torn down. A replica of the settlers' garrison can be seen at the Dracut Historical Society.

Where the Coburns and Varnums settled along the Merrimack River was the first permanent white settlement north of the Merrimack River, although no longer part of Dracut. Lowell annexed this Dracut neighborhood, Pawtucketville, in 1874. The cemetery they established, the first in Dracut, can still be visited. The Claypit Cemetery is the final resting place for some of Dracut's earliest settlers, including Revolutionary War veteran Moses Bradstreet Coburn.

It did not take long for Dracut to establish its place in history books. During the American Revolution, the town sent a third of its population to fight, and there were numerous Dracut residents who distinguished themselves with their service. Among those who served were Joseph Bradley Varnum, who fought at Lexington and Concord and later served as the speaker of the House of Representatives; African Americans Barzillai Lew, who fought at Bunker Hill, and Tony Clark, who fought at the Battles of Monmouth and Saratoga; Moses B. Coburn, who was injured during the Battle of White Plains New York; and Col. Louis Ansart, a French nobleman who helped improve American artillery and, after the war, renounced his French title of nobility and settled in Dracut. Ansart died in 1804 and is buried in Woodbine Cemetery. His house still stands on Varnum Avenue in Lowell.

With the end of the American Revolution, Dracut residents returned to their lives as farmers, and the town's population grew gradually. In 1790, there were 1,217 residents, then 1,407 in 1820, and by the outbreak of the Civil War in 1861, Dracut's population was 1,881. The outbreak of the Civil War gave Dracut another opportunity to fight on behalf of the country, and many Dracut residents enlisted. Most notable among the enlisted was Moses Greeley Parker, a Dracut native who enlisted as an army doctor in 1864 after graduating from Harvard Medical School. During the war, he helped supervise the construction of an army hospital. The town's library was first established by town meeting in 1900 and was housed on the second floor of town hall. With the $10,000 that Parker donated just prior to his death in 1917, a new permanent home was built for the town's library, which was named the Parker Memorial Library, in 1923.

With the end of the Civil War, Dracut residents began to see their farming community industrialize. On March 31, 1880, Collins purchased the Lawson brothers' mill and built the Collinsville Mills, now known as the Beaver Brook Mills. At its peak, Collins's mills employed 260 workers and produced approximately 230,000 yards of cloth annually. It was Collins who rebuilt the mills into a six-story brick building after a fire destroyed the original wooden structure. Collins sold his mill to the American Woolen Company in 1899. Today, the Beaver Brook Mills are home to local businesses, restaurants, and apartments. The homes along Mill Street and Primrose Hill were originally built for Collins's employees.

Dracut did retain its farming roots, however, and there were still numerous farms in town as the 20th century approached. Today, few of those farms remain. However, most notably Shaw Farm and Brox Farm are still in operation and are very successful.

When the people of Dracut were not working on their farms, in their mills, or at other businesses, they had Lakeview Park, the premier regional resort destination established on the shore of Lake Mascuppic in 1889. Even though there was already the Willow Dale Park on Lake Mascuppic, the Lowell and Suburban Trolley Company wanted to attract more riders, and building a second resort on the lake would help achieve this goal. Lakeview Park had an ideal location, with trolley connections that extended as far south as Boston and as far north as Nashua. The park proved to be a very popular destination, and in 1893, a theater was built at Lakeview, along with the addition of other attractions and activities. Available to visitors were swimming, boating, bowling alleys, restaurants, and a dance hall. In 1928, the dance hall burned, but owner Harry Kitteridge replaced it, as well as a large new roller coaster. In 1935, the last streetcar ran from Lowell to Lakeview, marking the end of an era. Gradually, Lakeview Park received fewer and fewer visitors and eventually closed in the 1970s. The famous carousel, however, has been preserved and is still in operation in New York. The history of the famous park has also been preserved at the Dracut Historical Society; in fact, there is an entire room dedicated to Lakeview Park at the town's museum. As the 20th century progressed, other recreational areas appeared in Dracut. In the 1930s, Belle Grove provided picnic areas as well as boating and swimming along the Merrimack River. Just after World War II, Alex Benoit established the Dracut Speedway at the corner of Loon Hill and Broadway, and it remained a popular spot until it was finally closed in the 1950s.

As the town grew in the 20th century, so did the need for an expanded school system. The town had several one-room schoolhouses. The Collinsville Grammar School, built in 1891, received honorable mention at the 1893 World's Fair as an "ideal country school and grounds." Students who continued with their secondary education were sent to Lowell High School until 1936, when Dracut High School was established. Today's Greenmont Elementary School was the home to Dracut's first high school. Dracut has taken great pride in its school department, and the 20th century has seen some remarkable accomplishments in the town's schools. A native of Dracut, Dr. Christos Daoulas was the longest-serving superintendent in Massachusetts, holding this position from 1962 until his retirement in 1998. To honor him for his remarkable service, the school on Lakeview Avenue was dedicated as the Dr. Christos Daoulas Education Complex in 2005. In addition to having an icon head the schools, Dracut established something unique to the town to help students who wished to continue their education after graduation—the Dracut Scholarship Foundation. In 1957, the first two scholarships, amounting to $350, were awarded to graduating students to help with college expenses. The foundation was incorporated in 1959 and, since then, has awarded $2 million to over 1,300 graduates. A board of 29 volunteers runs the foundation, and the highlight of the year's fundraising efforts is the annual Telethon, which began in 1984. With the help of board members and students, longtime Dracut High School principal Bruce Hutchins produced the first telethon. One of those students, Gary Meuse, now serves on the current board of directors for the scholarship foundation.

Support for the schools continued with Dr. Daoulas's successor, Elaine Espindle. Under her leadership, the town voted to build a new junior high school, Lakeview Junior High School, which opened in

September 2001. During the 2013–2014 school year, Supt. Steven Stone led the district through a major reorganization, and the junior high was renamed the Justus C. Richardson Middle School. Born in 1880, Justus C. Richardson operated Beaver Brook Farm on Mammoth Road for 60 years. He was famous for his innovative farming techniques and blue Hubbard squash. In 1953, he donated the land where the school complex on Lakeview Avenue now sits. He died at age 88 in 1968. The reorganization also created four elementary schools (kindergarten through fifth grade), a middle school (grades six through eight), and a high school (grades nine through twelve).

In addition to supporting academics, Dracut has a storied sports history best known for its football program. Legendary coach Ed Murphy headed the football program from 1946 to 1994. Coach Murphy was a 1937 graduate of Lowell High School who then went on to graduate from College of the Holy Cross. Before coming to Dracut, Coach Murphy served in the Marine Corps during World War II. In 1946, he became the head football coach at Dracut High School, winning the Division 2 Super Bowl against Beverly in 1988. Dracut won the Super Bowl again in 2008.

Dracut played a major role in the American Revolution, and its citizens continued to serve their country as the nation engaged in other conflicts. Those residents who served have been remembered and honored with memorials throughout town. In the 1920s, a monument was erected in Hovey Square to honor those who served during World War I, and in Collinsville Costello Square was dedicated to Collinsville resident James Costello, who was killed in France in early October 1918. During World War II, the residents of Collinsville created an honor roll in 1943 for their loved ones serving overseas. The general chairman of the honor roll committee was Peter J. Boutselis. Gold Star mothers Mrs. Herbert Morse and Agnes Tymula participated in the unveiling. By May 26, 1944, there were 200 names on the honor roll. Later, that honor roll was taken down and replaced with a memorial at the high school to honor all Dracut servicemen and women. During the Vietnam War, Dracut lost Michael Monahan, and to honor his sacrifice for the nation, Monahan Park on Pleasant Street was named for him. Most recently, Dracut lost Capt. John Ogonowski during the attacks on the Twin Towers on September 11, 2001.

The people of Dracut have a history of which they should be proud. In his 1982 book *The Photographic History of Dracut*, Donat Paquet wrote, "The town of Dracut has had from its infancy hard working and most patriotic citizens who have contributed a great deal to their country, their state, to this whole area, and to their town while establishing a foothold here in order to survive, to eke out their existence, then to provide for the well-being, the education, and the future of their children." Those words are as true in 2014 as they were in 1982. This book is just a small sampling of those who have contributed to creating the vibrant community of Dracut.

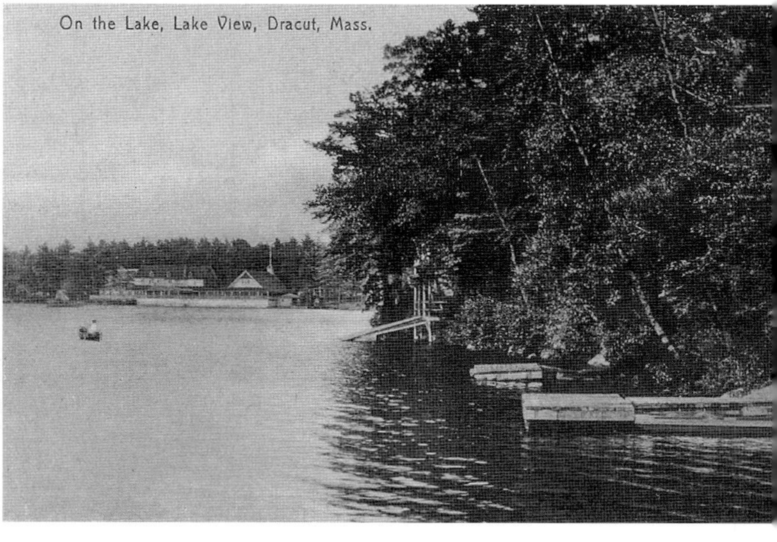

Lakeview Ballroom
This postcard shows the original Lakeview Ballroom on Lake Mascuppic. It burned and was rebuilt in 1928 by Harry Kitteridge. Mascuppic is an Algonquin word meaning "place of the large rocks." (Courtesy the Paul Dumont family.)

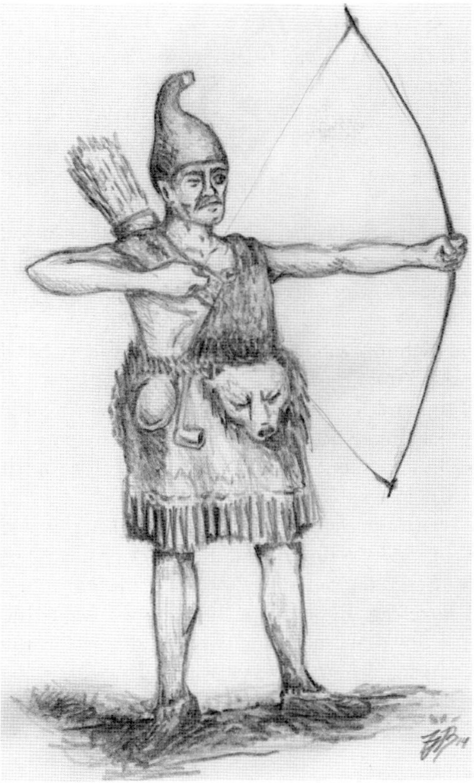

Sachem Passaconaway
This sketch of Sachem Passaconaway was based on an image from Chandler Potter's *A History of Manchester*. Passaconaway made his home along the Merrimack River at Pawtucket Falls. (Courtesy Tyler Bettencourt.)

Field of Blue Hubbard Squash at Beaver Brook Farm on Mammoth Road
For 60 years, Beaver Brook Farm was operated by Justus C. Richardson, who became widely known for his blue Hubbard squash. (Courtesy Dracut Historical Society.)

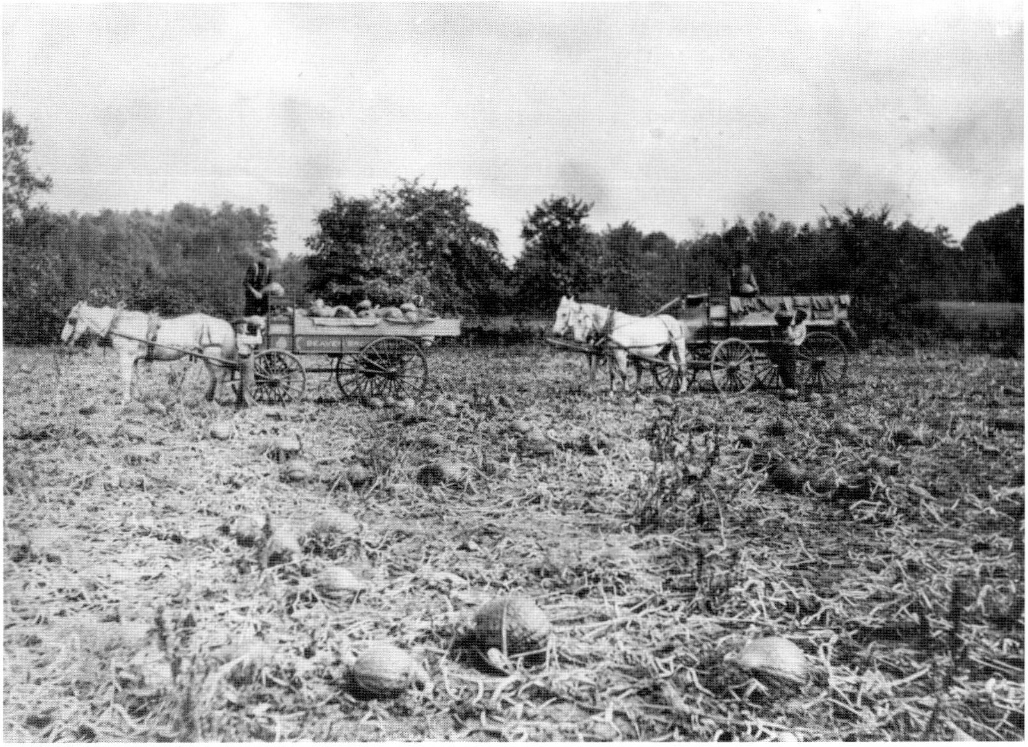

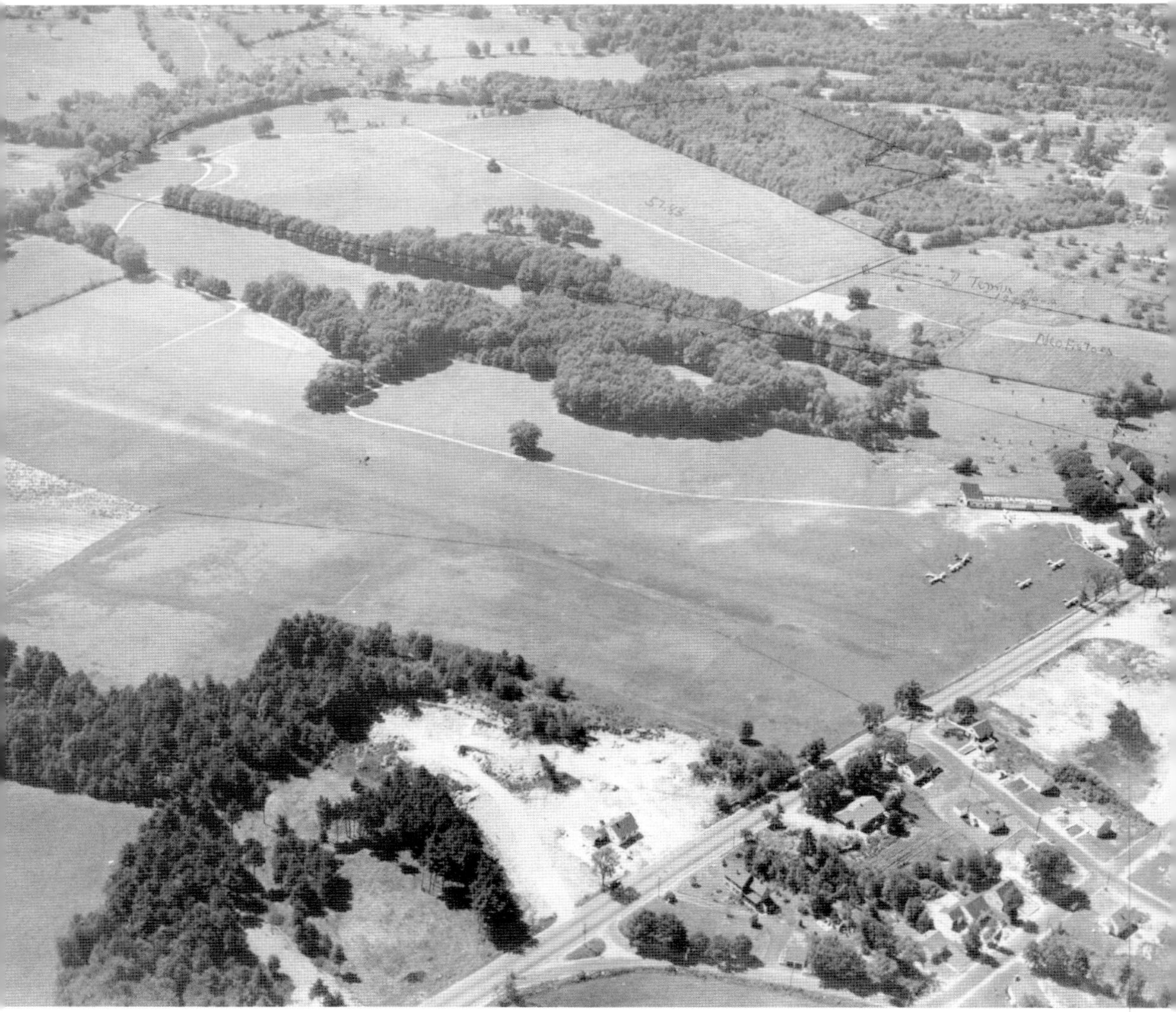

Lakeview Avenue
This aerial view of Lakeview Avenue around 1955 shows construction of the new Dracut High School and the neighboring Richardson Airport. (Courtesy Peter Richardson.)

CHAPTER ONE

Community Builders

Establishment and Growth

Dracut was incorporated as a town in 1701 when the inhabitants petitioned the Massachusetts General Court in Boston to separate from Chelmsford. This request was a result of the difficulty Dracut inhabitants had in attending town meetings in Chelmsford. There were no bridges connecting either side of the river; ferries were the only way to cross. Old Ferry Road bears its name from the ferry landing at that location—the Webb-Coburn Ferry. It was not until 1792 that a bridge was constructed due to the efforts of the Pawtucketville residents. Dracut brothers Parker and James Varnum spearheaded this effort. Due to the barrier the Merrimack had created, Dracut also did not receive protection from Chelmsford in times of need. The most notable of crises to strike Dracut's earliest settlers was King Philip's War. Samuel Varnum built a garrison house for Dracut during this time. After the Varnums and Coburns came numerous other families, including the Peabodys, Richardsons, Hildreths, and Clements.

As the town grew, the need for a meetinghouse became apparent, and on March 11, 1711, the town voted to construct its own. Rev. Thomas Parker was the first minister, serving from 1720 until 1765. He died in 1765 and was buried in the Claypit Cemetery; a century later, his remains were moved to the Woodbine Cemetery. By 1748, a second meetinghouse was needed, as the town's population was increasing on the western side of town. The second meetinghouse was built on Pleasant Street, and the town's third meetinghouse was built in what is now called the Dracut Center. Built in 1794, the Center Church, or the "Old Yellow Meetinghouse," has been the focal point of the Dracut Center ever since. Rev. Larry Zimmerman served as the pastor of the Old Yellow Meetinghouse for 33 years, retiring in 2008.

As the town expanded over the next century, the diversity of its population increased as well. When Michael Collins constructed his textile mills, Irish immigrants arrived in Dracut. Along the other end of Lakeview Avenue, a Greek community was established. Peter Laganas was the first Greek to settle in Dracut. He purchased a farm on Hampson Street in 1907. By the 1930s, Dracut's Greek community was becoming active in civic matters. In 1935, Arthur Skandalis became a member of the Dracut High School faculty, and in 1936, Arthur Cutrumbes ran for tree warden and Costas Caraganis for the school committee. George Neofotistos successfully ran for the school committee in 1938 and continued as a respected civic leader throughout his life. As the years continued on, many other names became synonymous with town government, such as Hector Berube and Dennis Piendak. Berube served as town assessor (1947–1949), tax collector (1947–1982), and town clerk (1949–1981). Piendak served as town manager (1986–2013) and oversaw many significant building projects—all without a Proposition 2½ override.

The individuals in this chapter are only a sampling of the many talented and industrious people who have worked to create the town of Dracut. Perhaps, in the future, one of my students will be inspired to write a second book on the many wonderful people of Dracut.

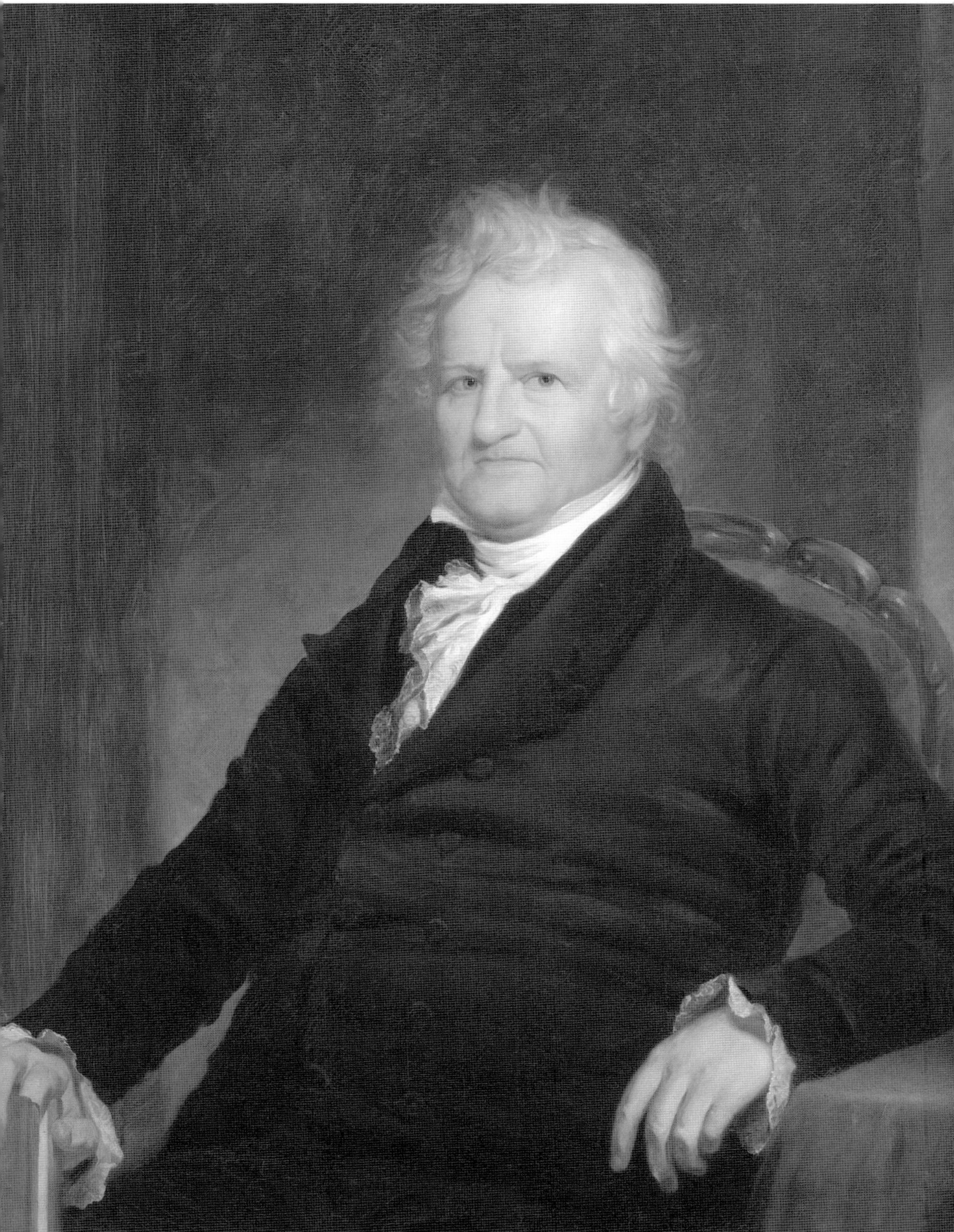

Joseph Bradley Varnum

No history of Dracut would be complete without mentioning Joseph Bradley Varnum. His home was located on the corner of Methuen Street and Parker Road, and like most homes of early Dracut settlers, it burned in 1930. Born in the family home on January 29, 1751, J.B. Varnum was a descendant of Samuel Varnum, Dracut's first permanent settler. With the outbreak of the Revolutionary War, J.B. Varnum served under Capt. Stephen Russell (whose home still stands on Pleasant Street) at the Battle of Lexington and Concord. Later, his company was at Saratoga when British general John Burgoyne surrendered. After the Revolution, the governor of Massachusetts called upon him to help put down Shay's Rebellion in 1786. After his military career, J.B. Varnum continued in public service and had an impressive political career. He held numerous positions in both state and national government, including state senator, US senator, US congressman, US speaker of the house, and justice of the court of common pleas. He also served as a delegate to the Massachusetts state convention during the debate over the ratification of the US Constitution in 1788. He served throughout his political career as a Democratic-Republican, which was the party of President Jefferson. Charles Elliott painted this oil-on-canvas portrait, which is part of the US House of Representatives collection. Varnum died on March 4, 1811, and is buried in the Varnum Cemetery, located near the intersection of Parker Road and Methuen Street. To celebrate and recognize one of the town's most storied citizens, the board of selectmen voted in January 2014 to recognize each January 29 as Varnum Day and nominate a citizen who exemplifies the civic virtue that Joseph Bradley Varnum demonstrated. (Opposite page, courtesy US House of Representatives Collection; below, courtesy Dracut Historical Society.)

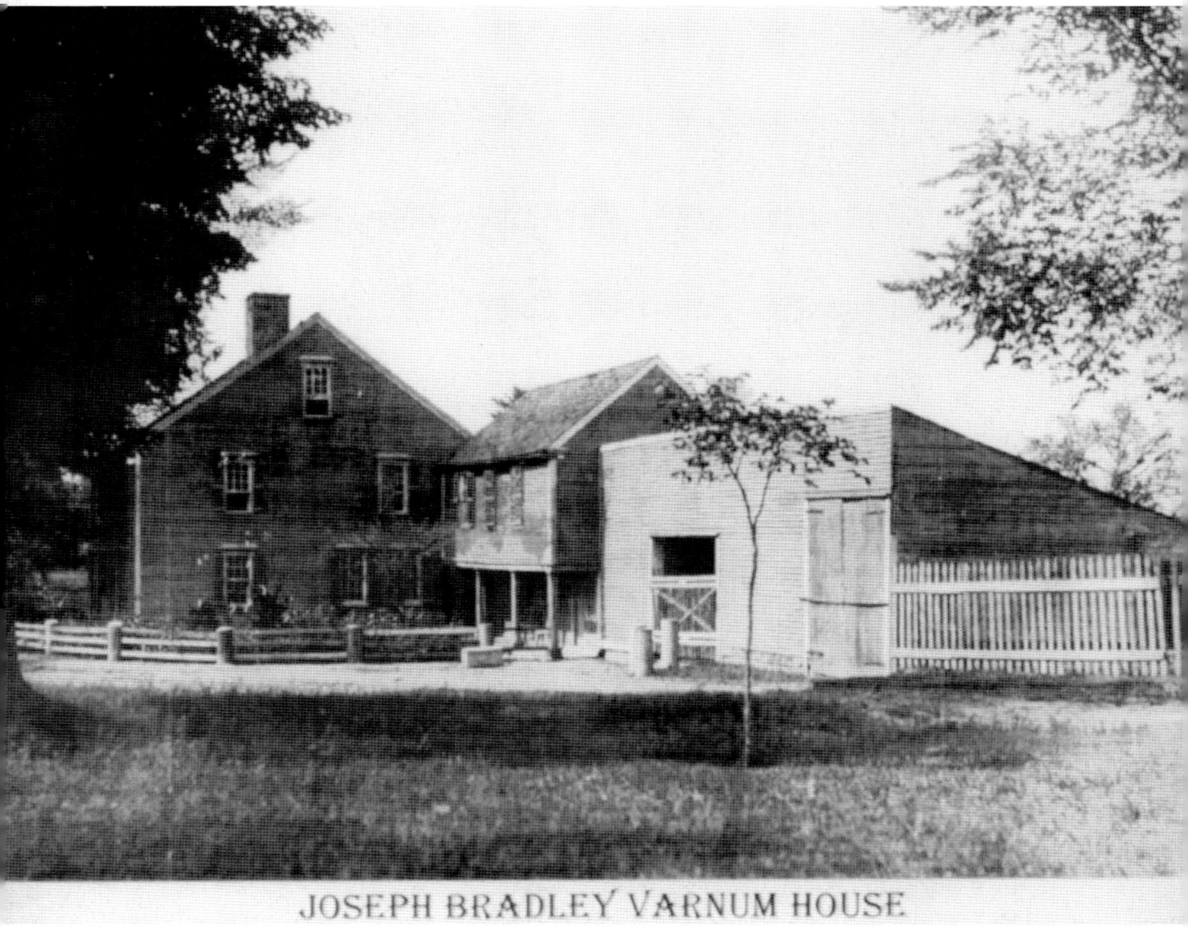

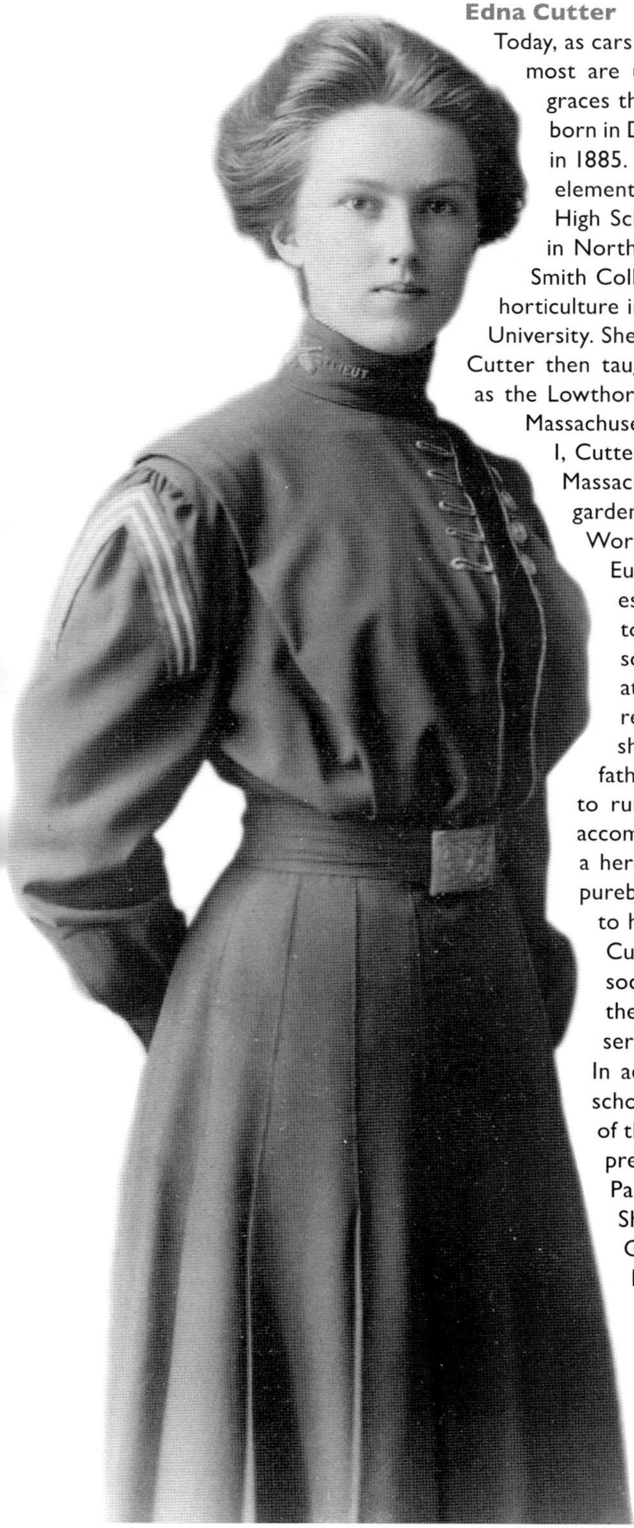

Edna Cutter

Today, as cars drive past the Cutter Farm on Mammoth Road, most are unaware of the remarkable lady whose name graces the sign at the farm's entrance. Edna Cutter was born in Dracut to Charles and Annie (Macomber) Cutter in 1885. A lifelong resident of the town, Cutter attended elementary school in Dracut, then graduated from Lowell High School in 1904, when she entered Smith College in Northampton, Massachusetts. Upon graduating from Smith College with a bachelor's in history and a minor in horticulture in 1908, she continued her education at Cornell University. She earned a master of arts in horticulture in 1912. Cutter then taught at her alma mater, Smith College, as well as the Lowthorpe School of Landscape Gardening in Groton, Massachusetts. When the United States entered World War I, Cutter went to work at the Crane estate in Ipswich, Massachusetts, teaching "farmerettes" how to farm and garden. A farmerette was the Rosie the Riveter of the World War I generation. When men were sent off to Europe, the Women's Land Army of America was established, and over 20,000 women were sent to work on America's farms. Cutter helped train some of the Massachusetts Land Army's women at the Crane estate. After World War I, Cutter returned to her hometown of Dracut, where she managed the family farm to help her aging father. When her father died in 1921, she continued to run the farm, and among her more remarkable accomplishments was the successful establishment of a herd of purebred Guernsey cows. She also raised purebred cocker and springer spaniels. In addition to her amazing work on the Mammoth Road farm, Cutter volunteered and served on numerous clubs, societies, and committees. She was a member of the Dracut and Pelham Historical Societies and served as a Dracut Library trustee for 30 years. In addition, she served on the school board (now school committee) for 19 years. While a member of the school board, Cutter fought against religious prejudice when hiring teachers, according to Donat Paquet in his *The Photographic History of Dracut.* She was also an active member of the Lowell Garden Club, which first met at the Whistler house in Lowell on May 16, 1927. Members of the Middlesex Women's Club wanted to improve local gardens and public awareness of horticulture, thus forming the garden club. Cutter served as the Lowell Garden Club's fourth president. At age 82, Edna passed away at her home. (Courtesy Craig Mahoney.)

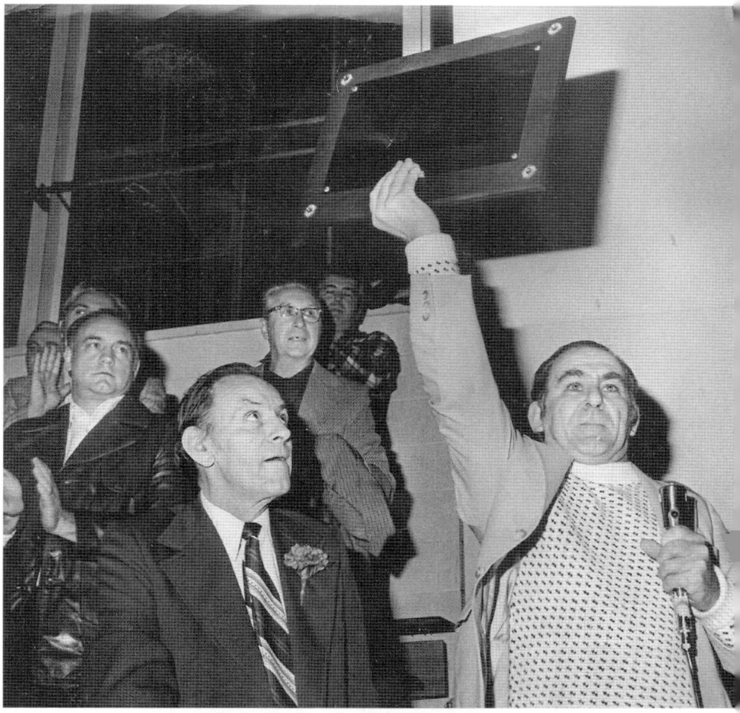

Lawrence "Bud" Peltier
Pictured here in the Dracut High School gymnasium is longtime school committee member Lawrence "Bud" Peltier (right), alongside his good friend Paul A. Merrill. This photograph was taken at the dedication of the gymnasium in honor of Merrill on January 6, 1980. Peltier served on the school committee for 17 years; at the time of this dedication, he was serving as the school committee chairman. In recognition of Peltier's service to the schools and children of Dracut, the school committee dedicated the softball fields next to the Richardson Middle School (formerly Lakeview Junior High School) in his honor. The dedication took place in 2004. (Courtesy Pat Merrill.)

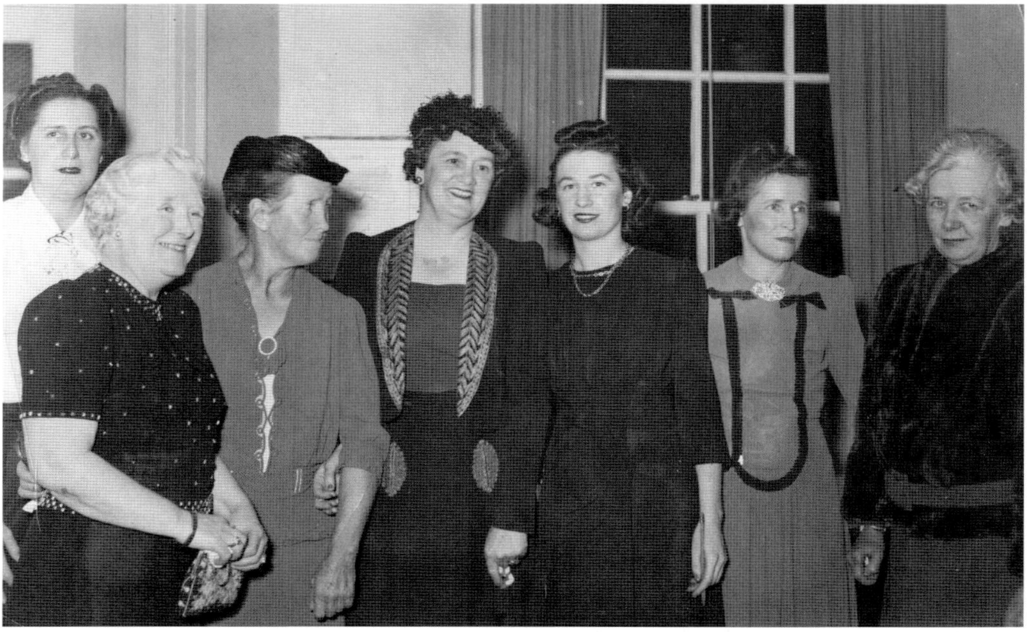

Library Trustees
Taken in the late 1930s, this photograph shows, from left to right, Nellie Morris, Mrs. Thomas Duffy, Kay Monahan, Mrs. Lewis A. Putnam (reviewer), Edna Cutter (library trustee), Mrs. F.A. Cotter (librarian), and Linda Darby. Edna Cutter served as a trustee of the Moses Greeley Parker Memorial Library for 30 years. In addition to setting policy, the board of trustees oversees the management and finances of the town's library. (Courtesy Anne Kennedy.)

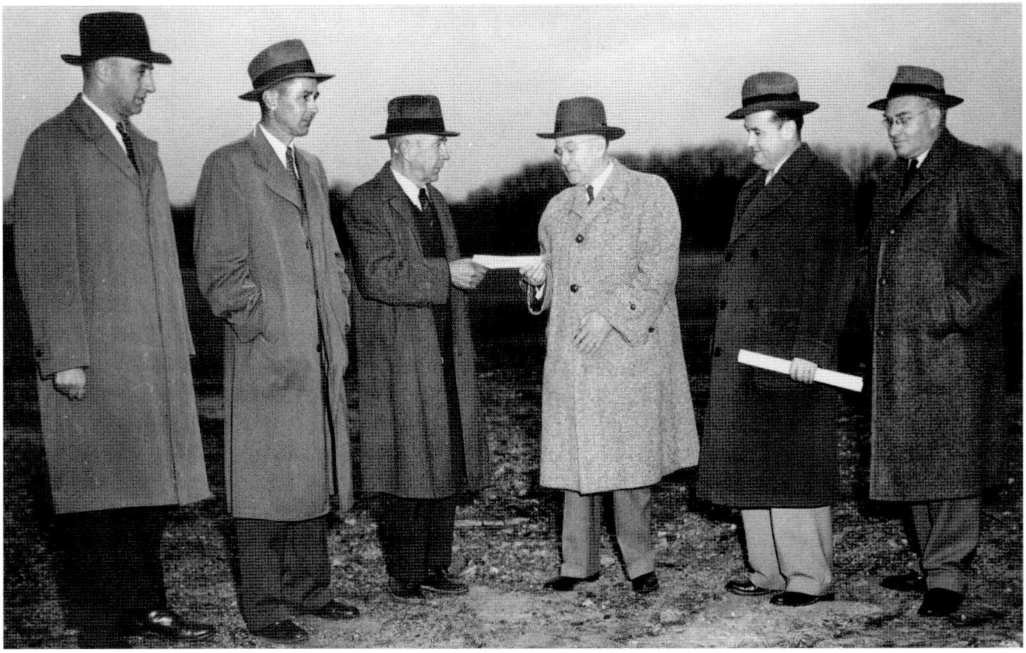

Justus C. Richardson and Francis Lappin
On December 30, 1953, Justus C. Richardson handed over the deed for the land for the new Dracut High School. Richardson donated 21.14 acres of his Beaver Brook Farm located along Lakeview Avenue to the town so a new high school could be built. From left to right are Paul Phaneuf (superintendent of schools), George B. Richardson, Justus C. Richardson, William Bromley (vice chairman of the school building committee), Francis Lappin (town counsel), and George H. Englesby (assistant superintendent). A graduate of Northeastern University Law School, Lappin maintained a private law practice from 1938 to 1962. In 1962, Gov. John Volpe appointed Lappin to the state superior court, where he served until his retirement in 1985. He passed away at age 78 in April 1993. (Courtesy Peter Richardson.)

Justus C. Richardson
In March 1958, Justus C. Richardson placed the final touches on the display case in the new Dracut High School, featuring photographs and the golden shovel of the ground-breaking ceremony. Richardson was born in Dracut on September 18, 1880, and died on December 21, 1968. He graduated from Lowell High School in 1899. Dracut did not have its own high school until the Greenmont Avenue Elementary School was converted in 1934. From left to right are Richardson, Paul Phaneuf, William Bromley, George Richardson, and Edward Moran (principal). (Courtesy Peter Richardson.)

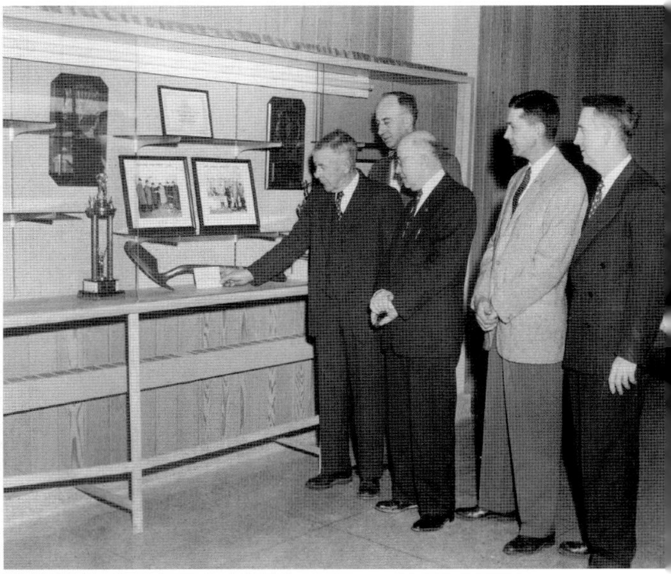

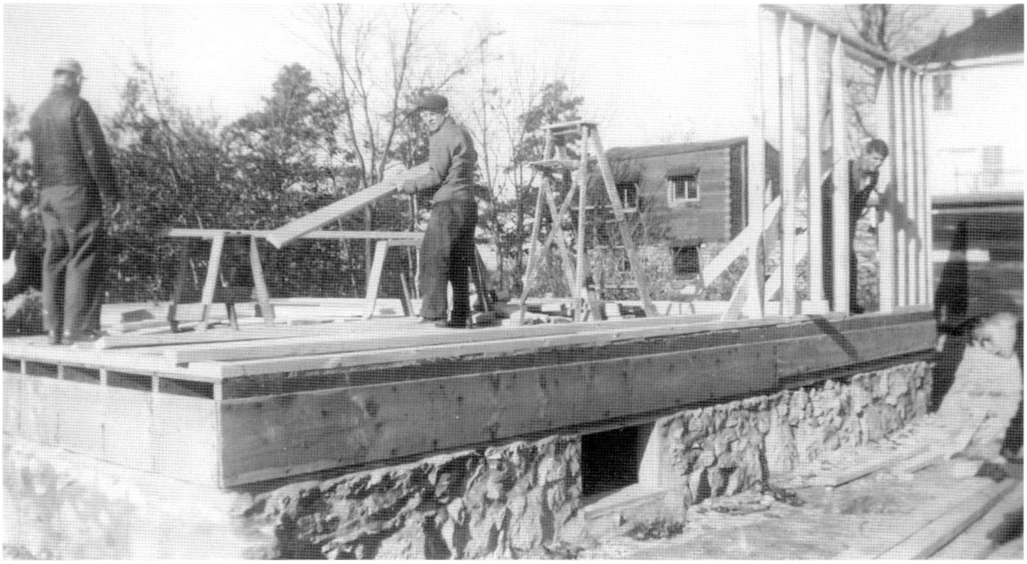

Henry Lafortune

Born in Lowell's "Little Canada" neighborhood in 1913, Henry Lafortune was the son of Joseph and Marie-Ann Lafortune. In 1937, he married his girlfriend, Lydia, and in 1947, the family moved to Gilmore Street in Dracut. In 1947, Gilmore Street was nothing more than an unpaved road with no telephone poles or water lines. For $125, Lafortune purchased a lot to build his family a home, which he constructed without the use of any power tools. It was the first home built on the Dracut section of Gilmore Street. Because World War II had just ended, nails were still difficult to come by due to the steel shortage, and Lafortune could only purchase five pounds at a time. The "Pioneer of Gilmore Street" and his family moved into their new home on January 1, 1948. The above photograph shows family and friends helping with the construction of the house. Henry and Lydia Lafortune are pictured below in 1951 at a family celebration held at the Jean Baptist Skating Rink on Pawtucket Street in Lowell. In the first row, third from right, is Lydia Lafortune, and next to her is Henry Lafortune. (Both, courtesy Normand Lafortune.)

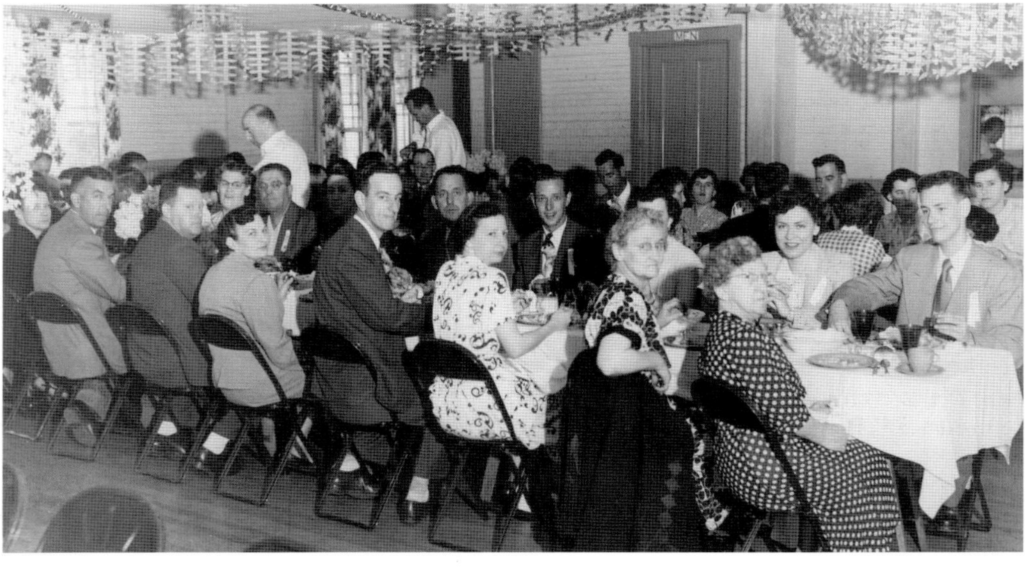

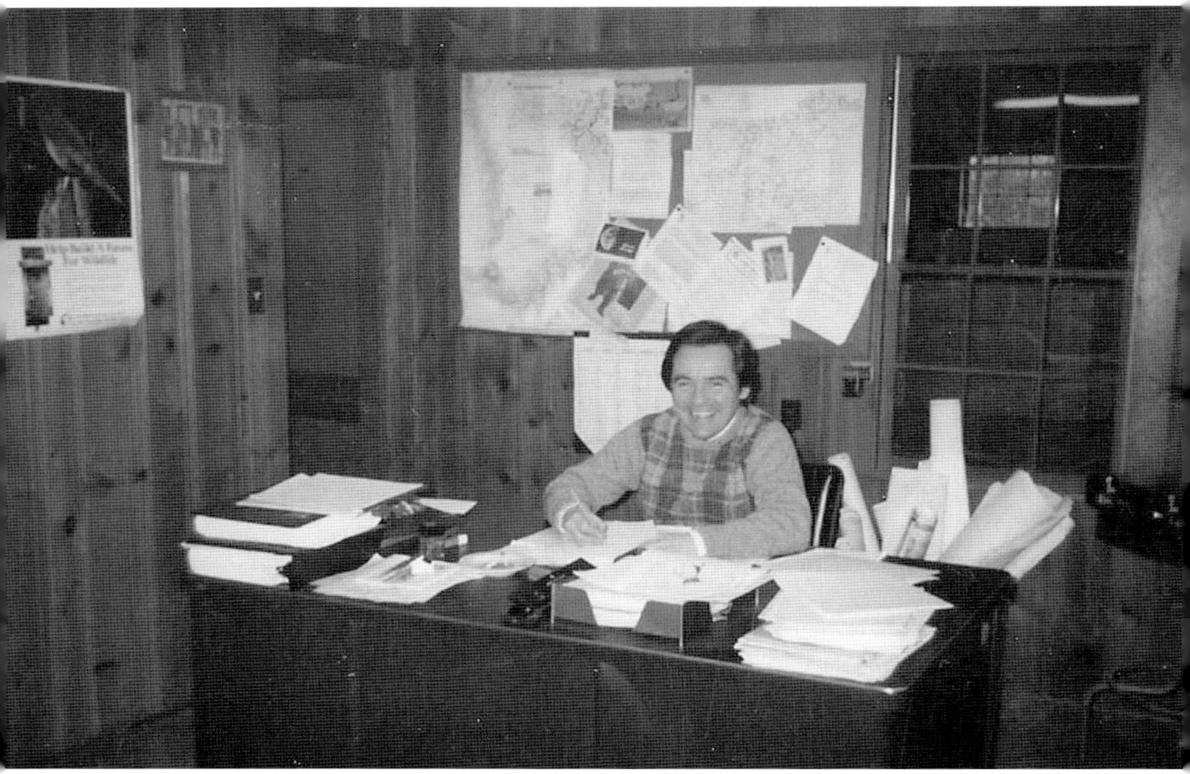

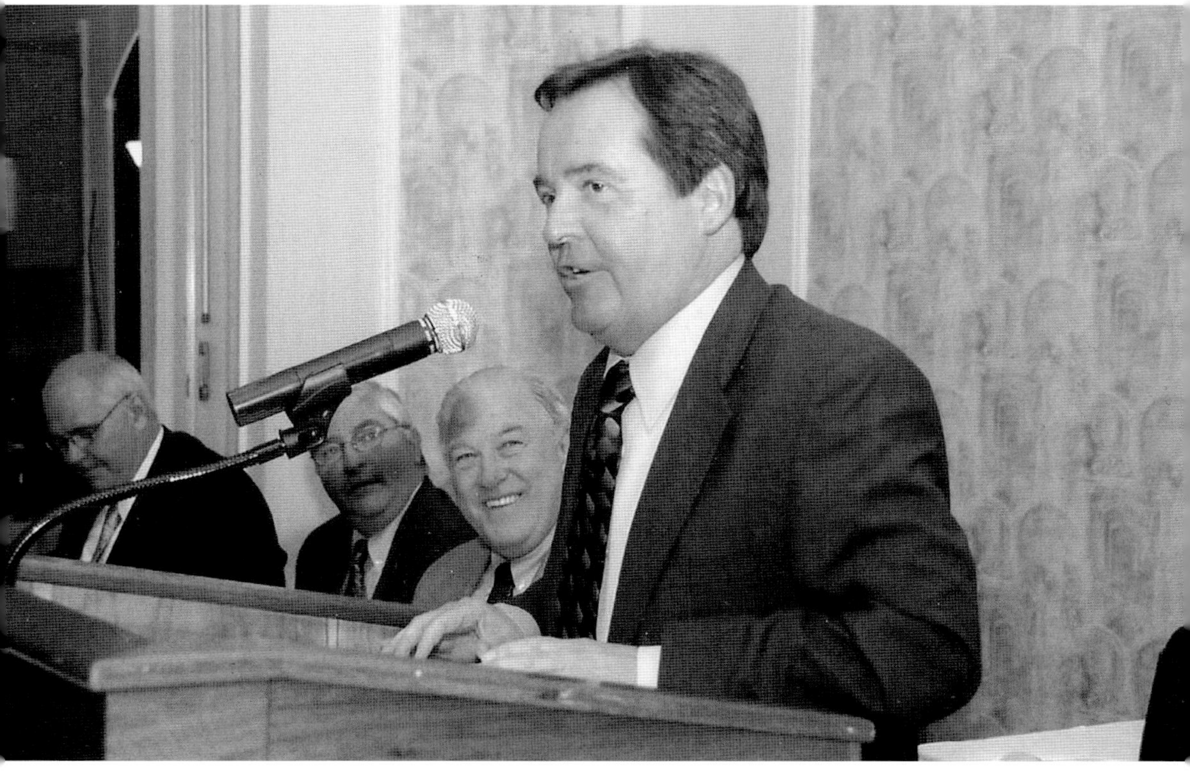

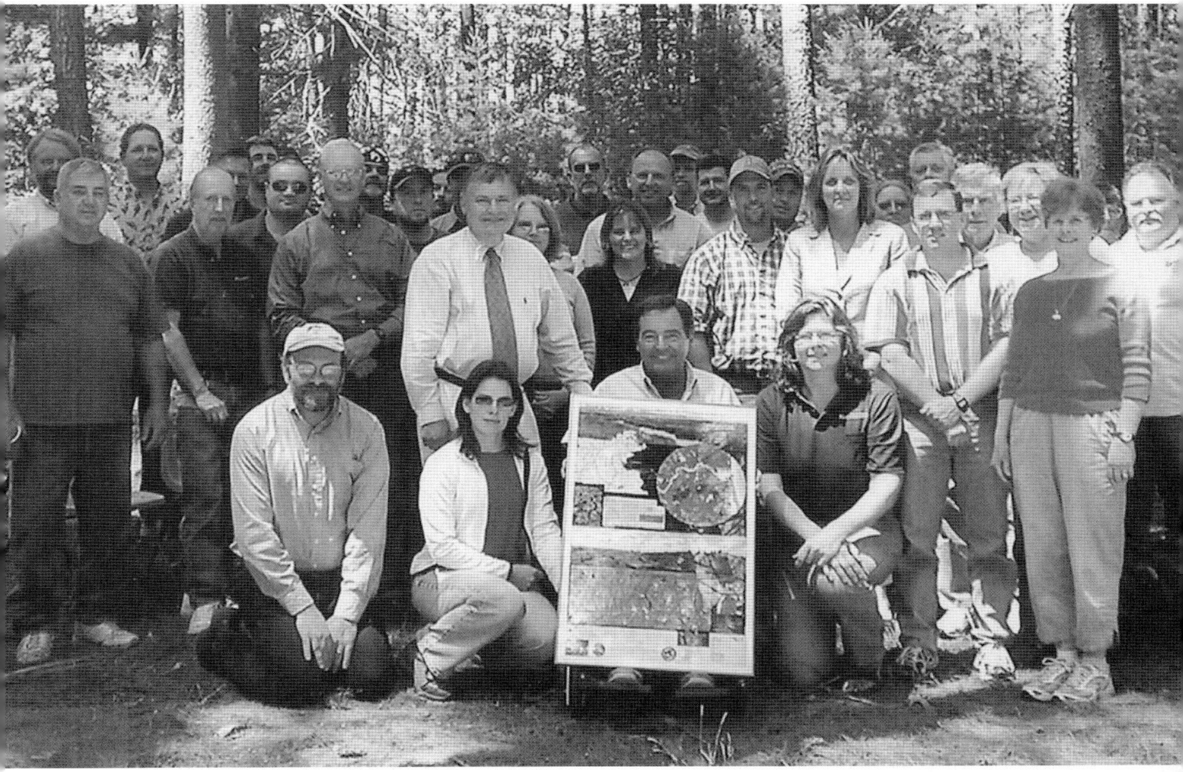

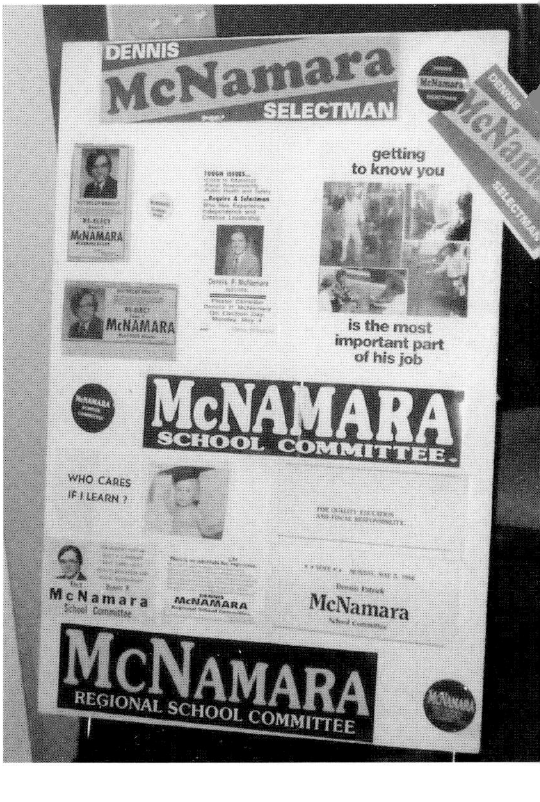

Dennis P. McNamara

Dennis P. McNamara, born in Lowell on July 6, 1953, was a well-known and beloved member of the Dracut community. A lifelong resident of Dracut, McNamara grew up in the Kenwood neighborhood and graduated from Dracut High School in 1971. As an active member of town politics, he served on the planning board and was elected to the school committee. In the early 1980s, McNamara was the executive secretary to the board of selectmen. During his employment as a land protection specialist with the commonwealth's Division of Fisheries and Wildlife, McNamara helped save over 5,000 acres of wildlife habitat and conservation land in Essex and Middlesex Counties. He was recognized with the establishment of a permanent town memorial, a wooded handicap-accessible trail named in his honor in the Kenwood neighborhood. (All, courtesy Michael F. McNamara.)

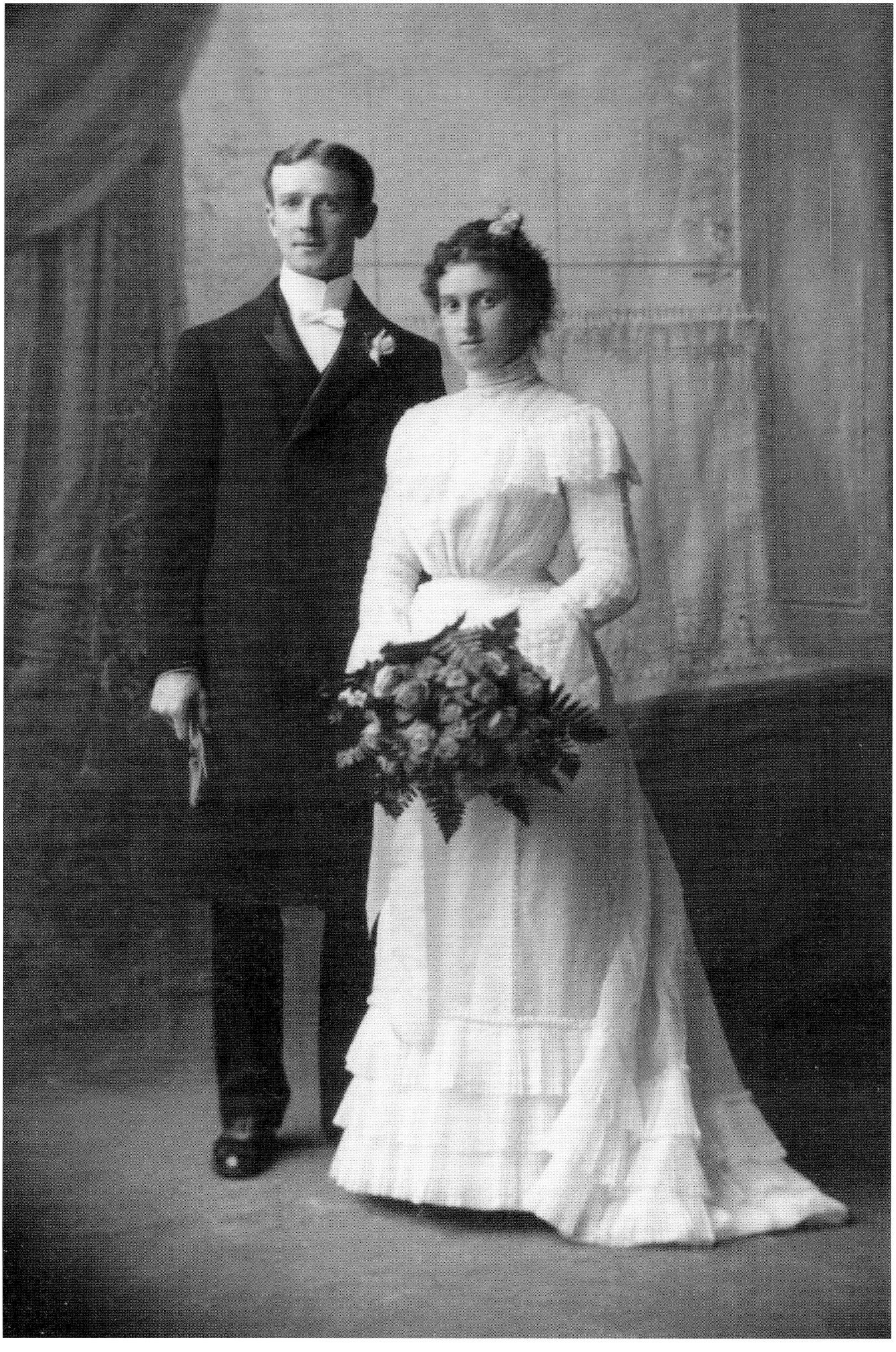

H. Francis Kiernan

April 30, 1950, marked the end of an era in Dracut, specifically in the Collinsville section of town. On that day, H. Francis Kiernan retired after 45 years as postmaster in Collinsville. Known as "Frank" by all who were acquainted with him, he was the son of John J. and Margaret Kiernan. He was born in Chelmsford, and in 1884 his father moved the family to Collinsville, where the elder Kiernan opened John J. Kiernan & Sons, Groceries and Provisions. Collinsville was a fast-growing area of town due to Michael Collins's mills, and the neighborhood had requested that the federal government establish a post office. The request was granted, and the elder Kiernan was appointed postmaster. H. Francis served as a postal clerk under his father, and eventually, George B. Cortelyou, postmaster general, appointed him as postmaster on April 30, 1905 by. There are many anecdotes about Kiernan's time as Collinsville postmaster, perhaps the most interesting of which happened on May 19, 1938, during National Air Mail Week. The Dracut Historical Society sponsored the only airmail flight to take off from Dracut to celebrate the 20th anniversary of the first airmail flight. In addition to serving as postmaster, Kiernan continued to operate the family grocery store until he sold it in 1945. He was also a member of the Elks and the National Association of Postmasters. In 1902, he married Katherine Cullinan, and they made their home in the big white house he had built at 1835 Lakeview Avenue. H. Francis Kiernan passed away on January 16, 1956. (Both, courtesy Martha K. Wolfe.)

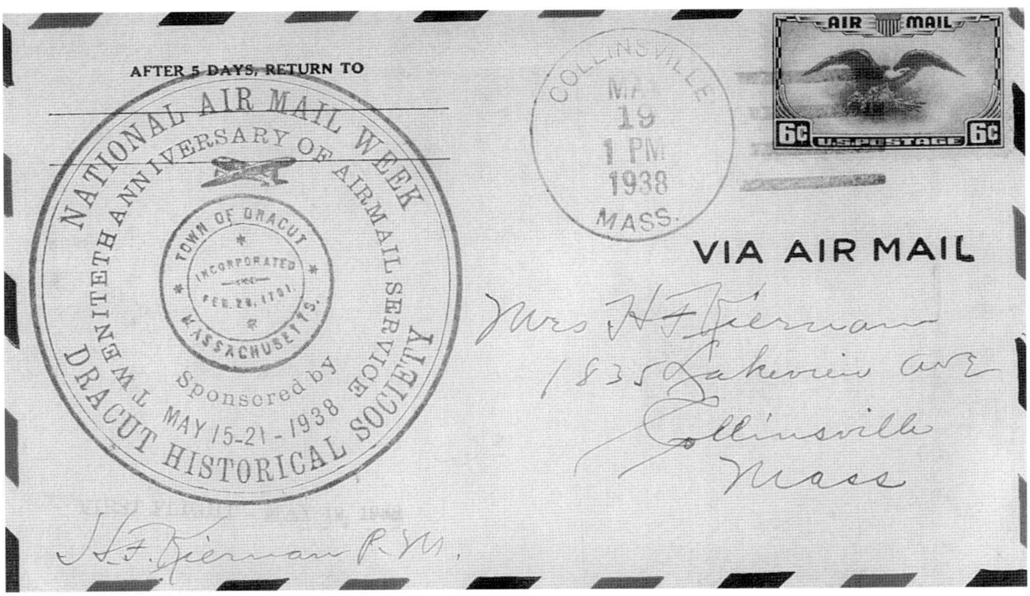

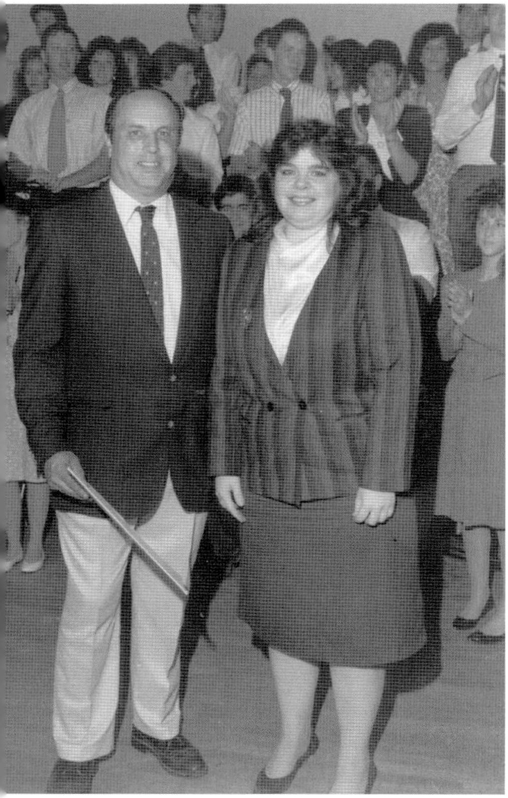

Colleen Garry

Colleen Garry was born to Martin P. and Mary Garry on July 21, 1962. A graduate of Dracut High School, she is pictured at left with longtime principal Bruce Hutchins. After graduating from Dracut High School, Garry earned a bachelor of science degree from the University of Massachusetts, Lowell, then went on to earn her law degree from Suffolk University, graduating in 1994. For eight years, she worked as a legislative aid to state representative John Cox. When a new district consisting of Dracut, Tyngsborough, and Dunstable was created in 1994, she decided to run and was elected. With 20 years of service, she is not only the town's longest-serving representative but also the first female state representative from Dracut. Currently, Garry serves on the Joint Committee on the Judiciary, the House Committee on Bonding, Capital Expenditures and State Assets, and the House Committee on Personnel and Administration. Below, Garry is shown with her parents, Mary and Martin, and Red Sox CEO Larry Lucchino at the statehouse in 2004, celebrating the Red Sox World Series victory. (Both, courtesy the Garry family.)

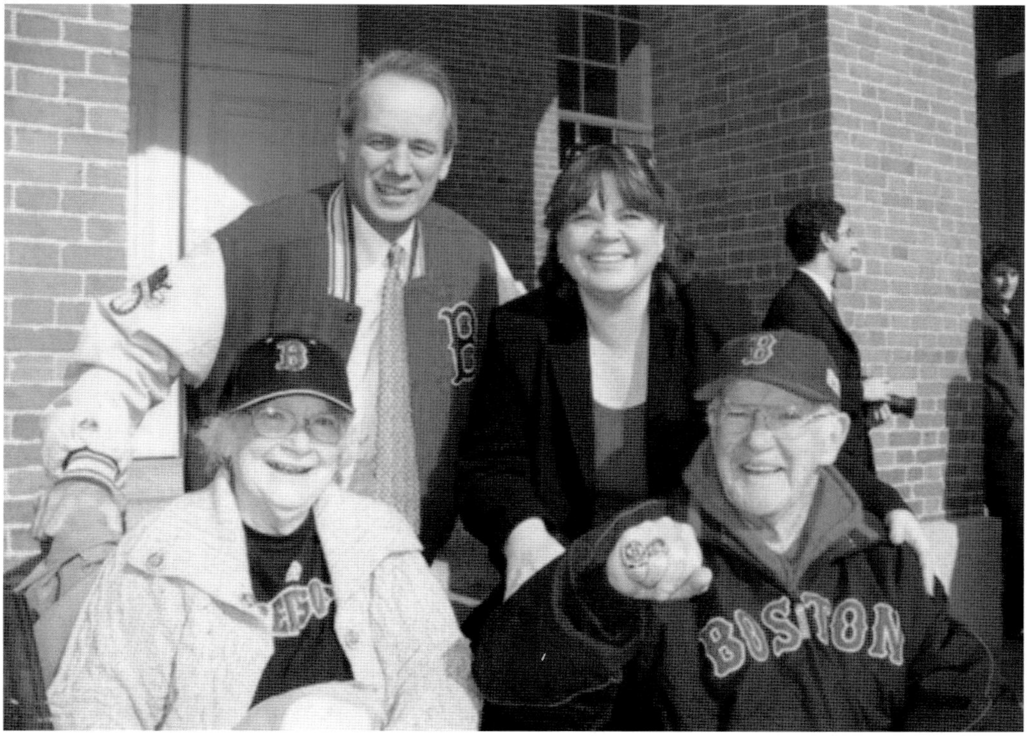

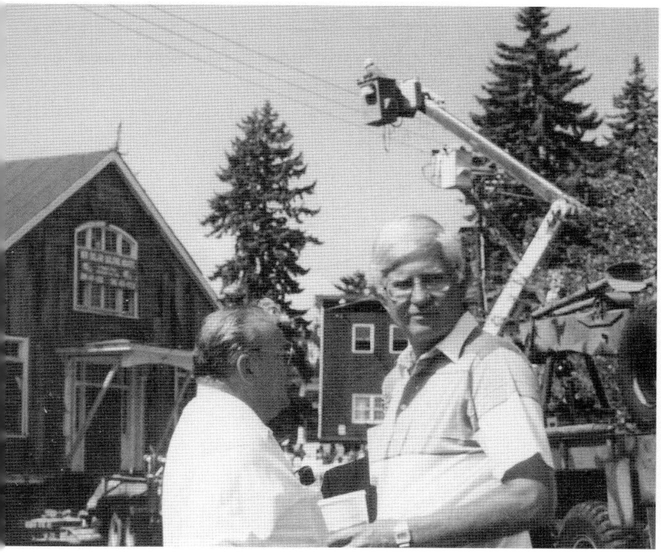

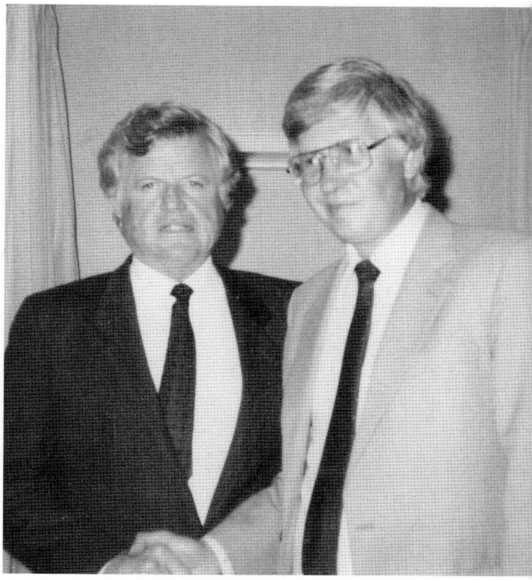

Dennis Piendak

In 1986, Dennis Piendak was hired as the second town manager, a position he held until his retirement in 2013. In total, Piendak has spent 42 years in public administration. He graduated from Bard College with a degree in government and from the University of Pittsburgh with a master of business degree. It was during college that he met his future wife, Sharon, and together, they have two children. During his tenure as Dracut's chief executive, he oversaw the construction of a new junior high school, a new police station, a new library, two high school renovations, a new town hall, two fire stations, and the preservation of Harmony Hall. When asked how all these projects were possible without a Proposition 2½ increase, Piendak cited the support of the board of selectmen he had throughout his tenure as well as the very giving nature of the community. In the above left image, Piendak is shown at the moving of Harmony Hall, and above right he is pictured with Sen. Edward Kennedy. Below is the old town hall Piendak worked in while town manager. It was demolished on Thursday, October 16, 2014. Dracut's new town hall opened in September 2014. (Above, courtesy Dennis Piendak; below, courtesy the Paul Dumont family.)

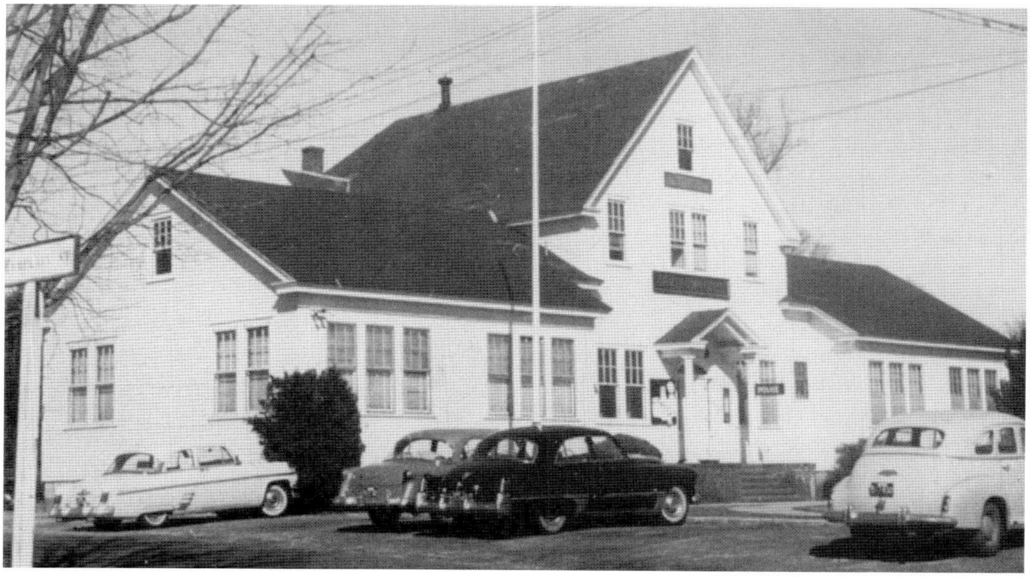

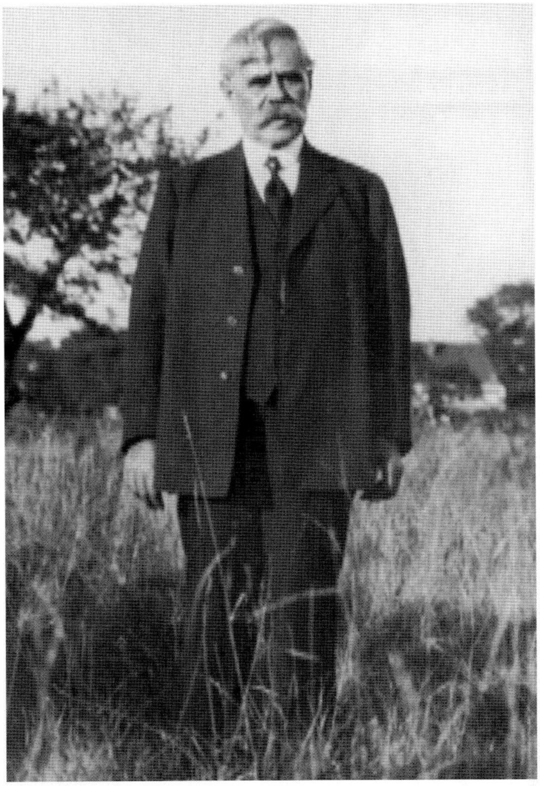

Peter Laganas
The first Greek to settle in Dracut was Peter Laganas. Born in 1863 in Sparta, Greece, he purchased a farm on Hampson Street in 1907 and moved his wife, Mary, and five children from Greece to Dracut. The store he established, Pete's Grains, is still in operation on Hampson Street. Laganas passed away in 1932. (Courtesy Ellis Neofotistos.)

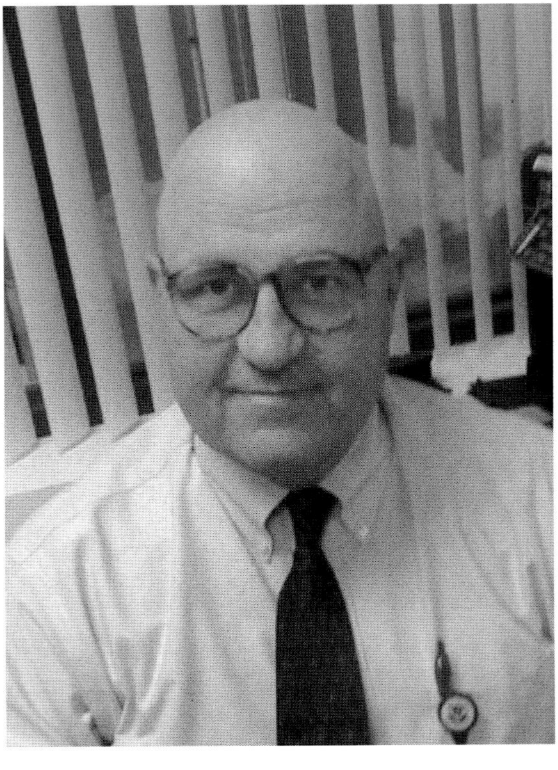

Dennis Williams
Though not a Dracut native, Dennis Williams served on both the board of selectmen and the school committee during the 1980s and 1990s. There are three things that Williams feels most proud about when he reflects on his time in Dracut town government: First, he was on the school committee that worked to get the Lakeview Junior High School built without a Proposition 2½ override. Secondly, as a selectman, he worked to stop the proliferation of small lots. Thirdly, working with Ken Cunha and other boards, as well as assistant town manager Glen Edwards, Williams worked to develop a 40B plan that stopped involuntary 40B projects. (Courtesy Dennis Williams.)

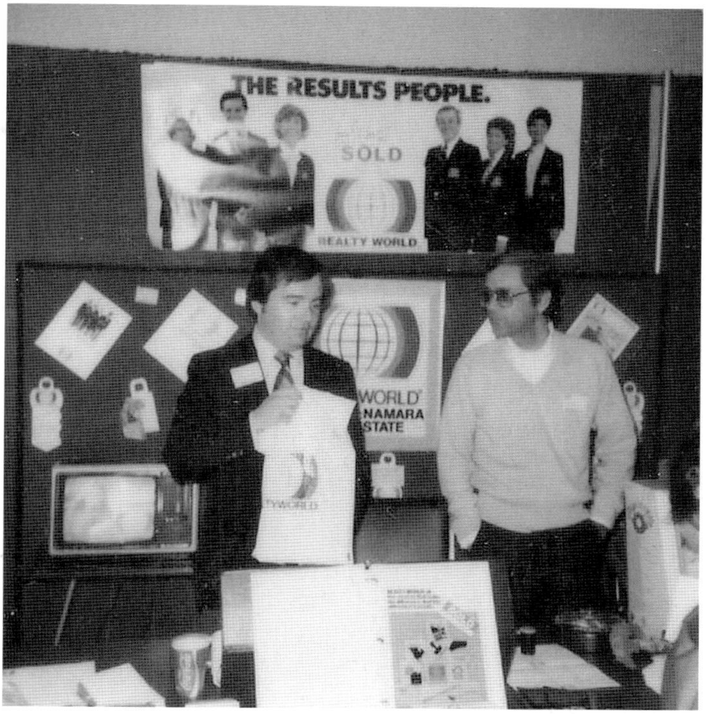

Ray Rowe
Pictured at McNamara's Realty World office in the mid-1980s are Dennis P. McNamara (left) and Ray Rowe. Rowe worked as a realtor with McNamara and sold town manager Dennis Piendak the home that he still lives in today with his wife, Sharon. Rowe helped write the town charter adopted in 1985 and served on the board of selectmen. He passed away in 1986. Made through volunteer efforts, the baseball fields behind Dracut High School are named in honor of Rowe. (Courtesy Michael F. McNamara.)

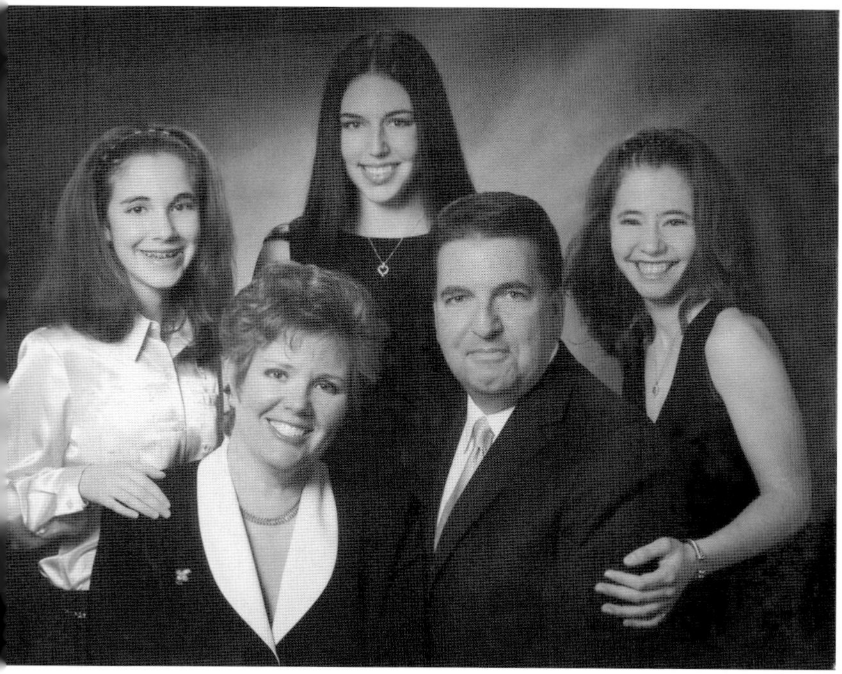

Jack DiTillio
Jack DiTillio was born in Los Angeles, California, on July 22, 1952. The DiTillio family moved to Buffalo, New York, when Jack was 14. He met his future wife, Kathleen Jonas, through a mutual friend. They were married for 32 years and had three daughters—Angela, Laura, and Julia. The DiTillios moved to Dracut in 1984 and bought a home on Surrey Lane. At the urging of town manager Dennis Piendak, DiTillio joined the Capital Planning Committee, then ran for the board of selectmen in 1992. He lost his first election but won on his second attempt in 1993. He served on the board of selectmen for 10 years. He died at age 53 on August 5, 2005. A memorial in his name was established with the Dracut Scholarship Foundation. (Courtesy Kathleen DiTillio.)

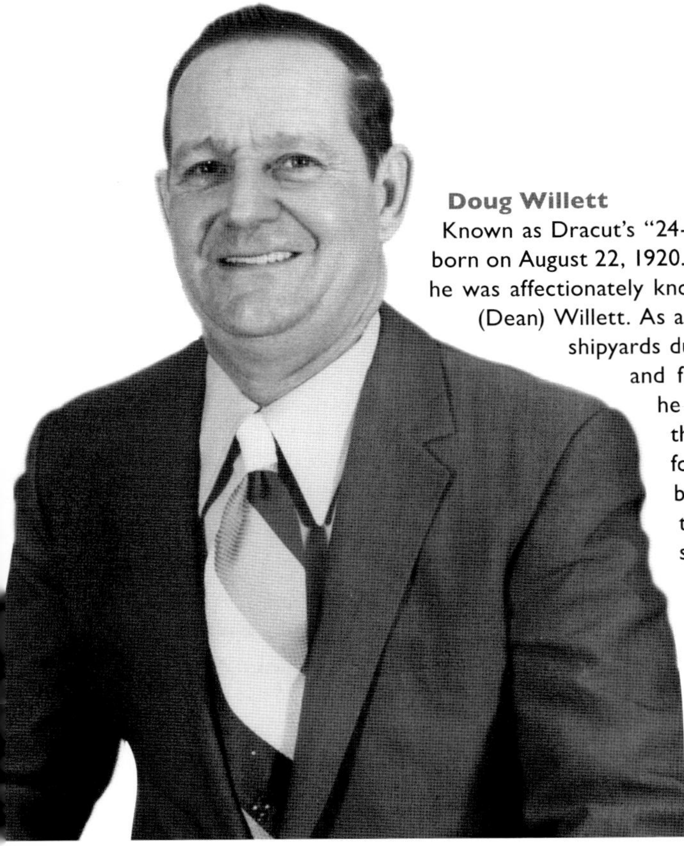

Doug Willett

Known as Dracut's "24-Hour Selectman," Douglas G. Willett was born on August 22, 1920. A lifelong resident of Dracut, "Dougie," as he was affectionately known, was married for 68 years to Barbara (Dean) Willett. As a young man, Willett worked in the Boston shipyards during World War II, then the Dracut mills, and finally, H.P. Hood for 30 years. However, he was best known from his time working at the Greater Lowell Technical High School for 27 years. Willett first won a seat on the board of selectmen in 1975, when he topped the ticket with 3,096 votes. In addition to serving as a 10-term selectmen, Willett loved working in his garden. (Both, courtesy Sandy Chaput.)

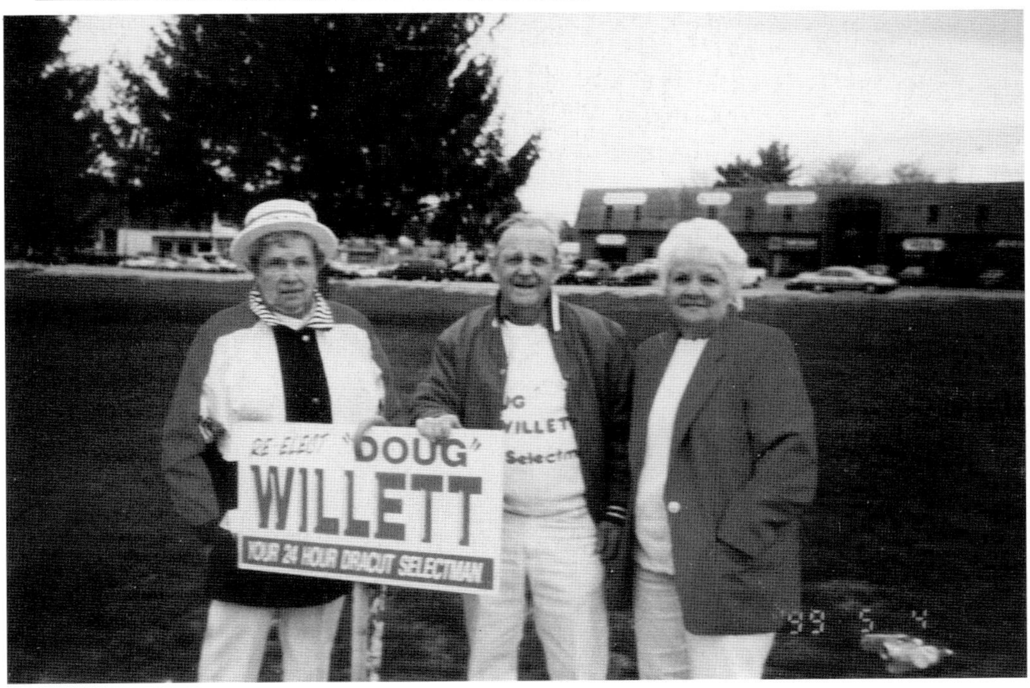

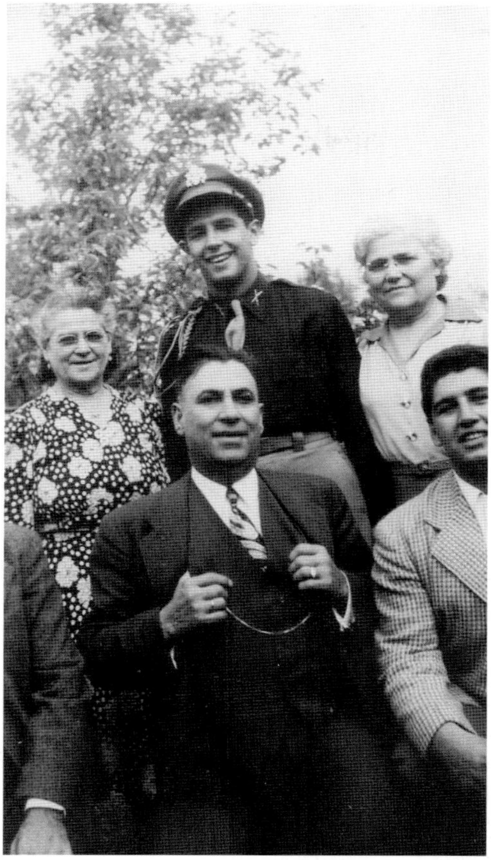

George Malliaros
Pictured at left is well-known businessman George Malliaros, who arrived in the United States at age 12. His family was from a small mountaintop village in the Sparta region of Greece. In the photograph, Malliaros is surrounded by, from left to right, Angleica Contopoulos, son John Malliaros, Katina Brumedes, and son Aristomenis Malliaros. As a young man, he worked in the A.J. Pollard Store. Saving his earnings, Malliaros opened the Malliaros Clothing Company in 1923. The store was located at 504 Merrimack Street in Lowell. In 1936, Malliaros was appointed to the Dracut Planning Board. (Left, courtesy Gail Malliaros Golec; below, courtesy George Malliaros.)

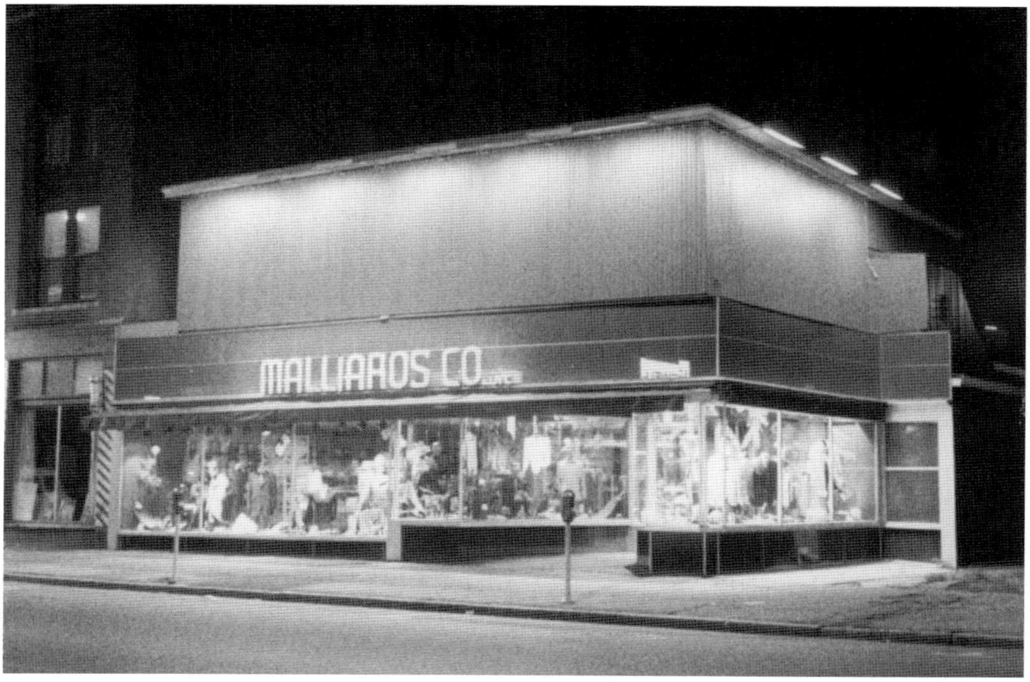

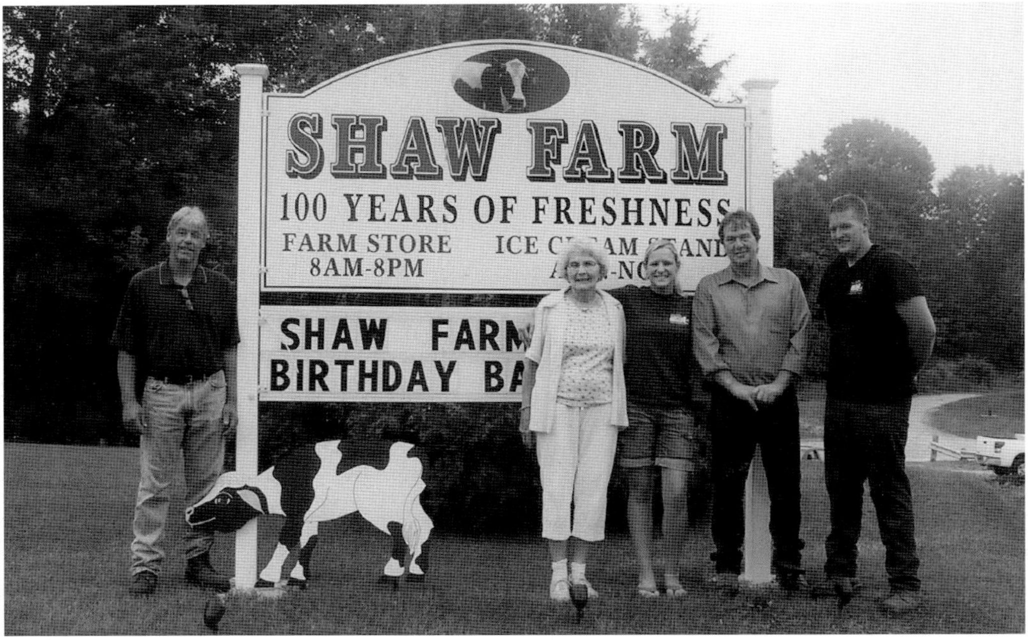

Warren Shaw

In addition to being the proprietor of Shaw Farm established in 1908 on New Boston Road, Warren Shaw has been active in town government, serving on the planning board and then as a selectman for 24 years. Shaw often cites the hiring of Dennis Piendak as town manager as the most important decision he was a part of while on the board of selectmen. Pictured from left to right are Wally Biedron, Nancy Shaw, Sarah Shaw, Warren Shaw, and Mark Shaw in 2008—the centennial of Shaw Farm. (Courtesy Warren Shaw.)

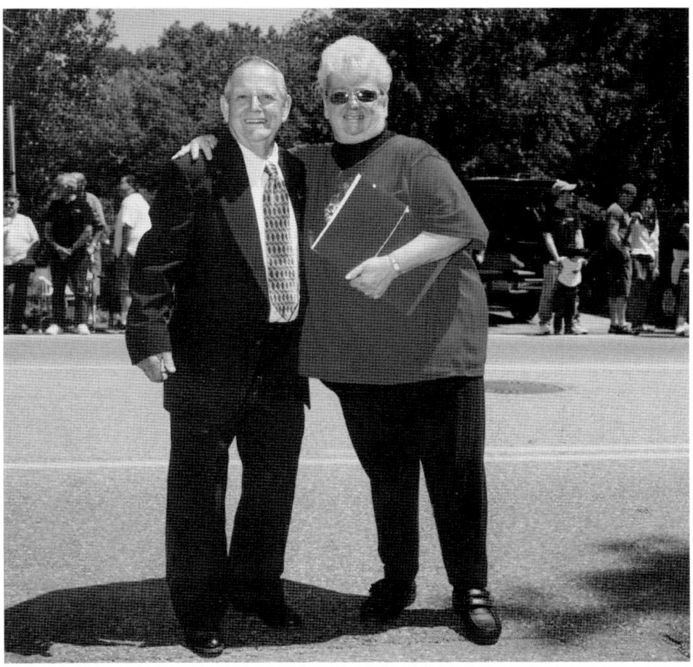

Barbara Souza

Raised on Parker Avenue, Barbara Souza is a lifelong Dracut resident who served as secretary to the board of selectmen for almost 30 years. She kept the business of the board running on a daily basis, preparing meeting agendas and taking phone calls, all from the second floor of town hall. When she first started, the board of selectmen consisted of Jack Lyons, Nick Lambros, Ray Rowe, Warren Shaw, and Doug Willett. Souza is pictured here with Selectman Doug Willett. (Courtesy Sandy Chaput.)

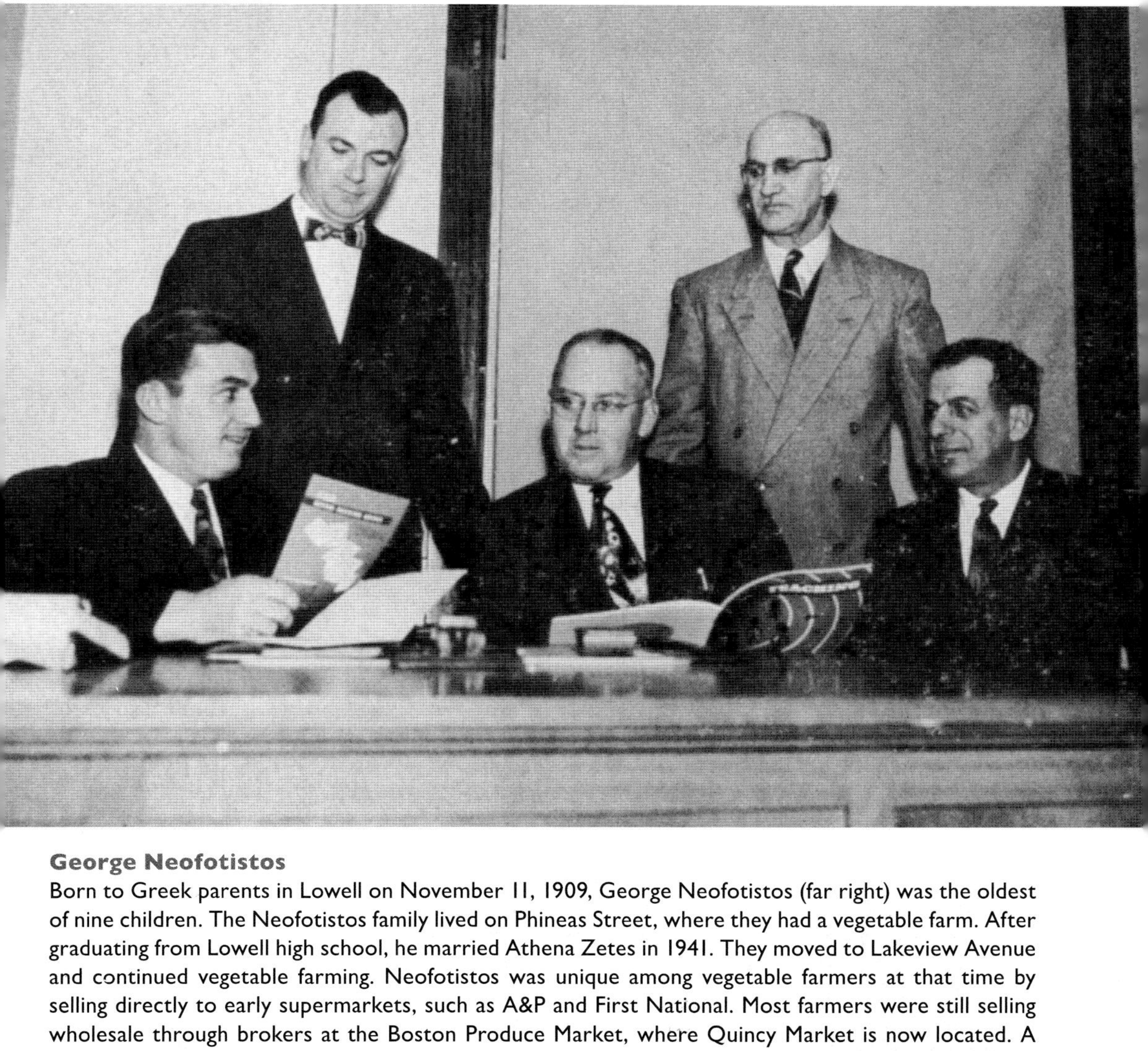

George Neofotistos

Born to Greek parents in Lowell on November 11, 1909, George Neofotistos (far right) was the oldest of nine children. The Neofotistos family lived on Phineas Street, where they had a vegetable farm. After graduating from Lowell high school, he married Athena Zetes in 1941. They moved to Lakeview Avenue and continued vegetable farming. Neofotistos was unique among vegetable farmers at that time by selling directly to early supermarkets, such as A&P and First National. Most farmers were still selling wholesale through brokers at the Boston Produce Market, where Quincy Market is now located. A successful farmer, Neofotistos was proud of his Greek heritage, and as such, he was a member of the Pan Laconian Society, the Leonidas Society in Lowell, which represents Sparta (from where his family had emigrated). He was the first Greek elected to public office in Dracut when he joined the school committee in 1938, serving until 1947; then he served again from 1953 to 1956. In addition, he served on the zoning board of appeals and the town bylaw committee. Above, he is pictured with, from left to right, (seated) Alexander Szymanski, George Englesby, and George Neofotistos; (standing) Robert T. Fox and Alfred J. Dufour. George Neofotistos passed away on April 26, 1993. (Above, courtesy Dracut Historical Society.)

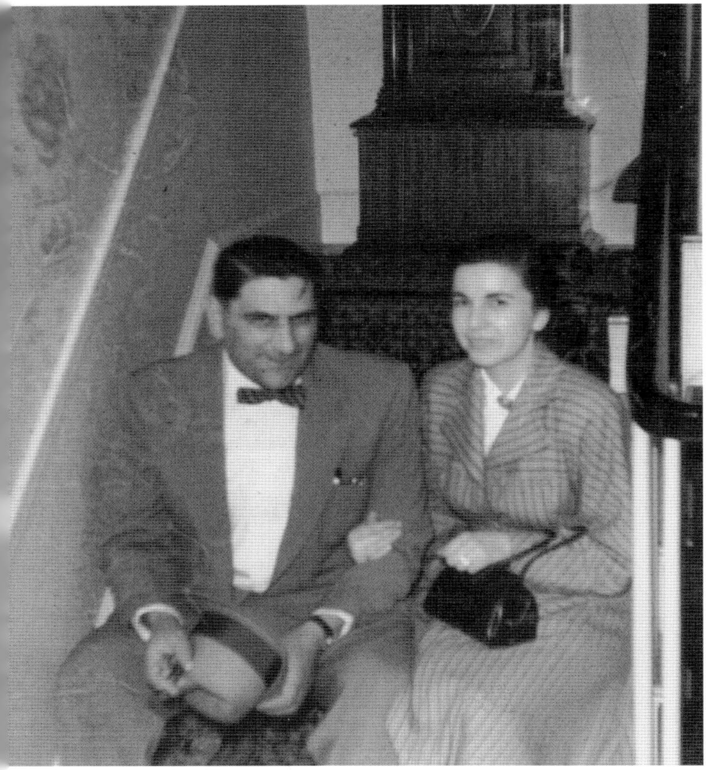

John Brox

John Brox is pictured at left with his wife, Antoinette (Rossi) Brox, whom he married in 1952. Born in 1910, Brox was a lifelong resident of Dracut. He was the son of Lebanese immigrant, Kalil Brox, and his wife, Margaret. The Brox family established their farm in Dracut in 1902, and John Brox continued farming until his death at age 85. In addition to maintaining the family farm, Brox served as Dracut's state representative for 16 years. During this time, Brox fought to have Interstate 93 constructed on the Dracut-Methuen line rather than its original plan for the Lawrence-Haverhill line, believing it would help connect Dracut to the new interstate system and thereby attract further industry to the town. Below, Brox is at center looking at Governor Volpe as legislation is passed in the governor's office. Brox passed away in 1995 at the age of 85. (Both, courtesy John Brox.)

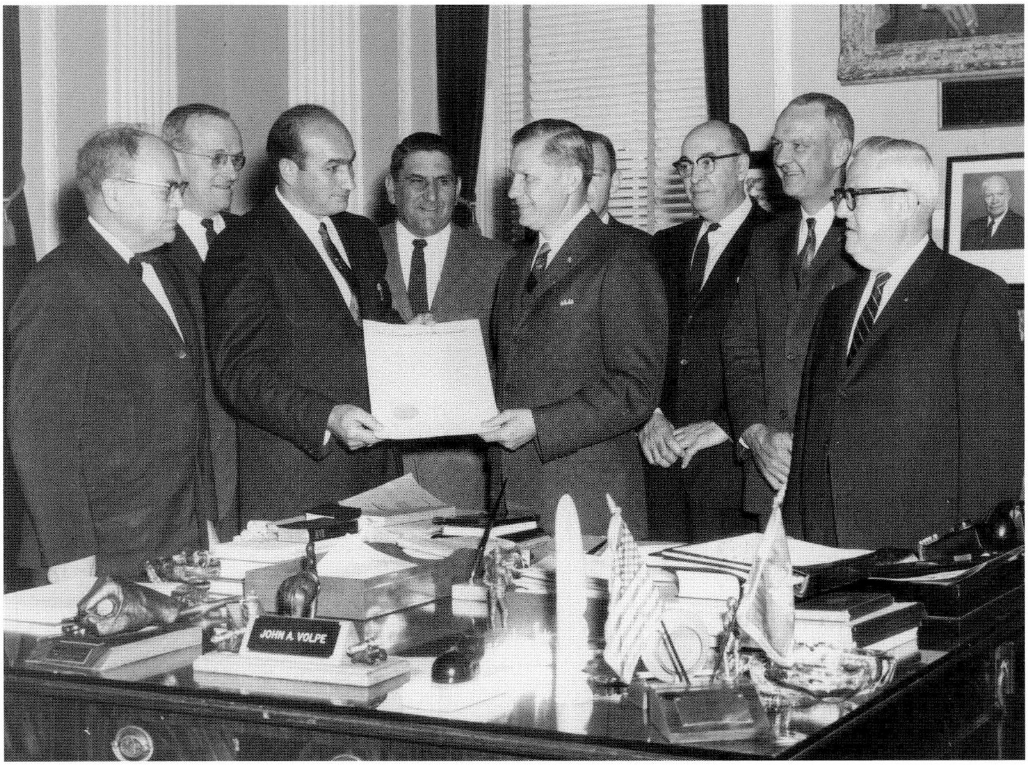

Larry Zimmerman

The Old Yellow Meeting House in the Dracut Center has been a fixture in town since 1794, when it was built at the corner of Arlington and Bridge Streets. The second-longest-serving minister of the Dracut Center Church, Rev. Larry Zimmerman arrived in Dracut in 1975 to serve as pastor and retired in 2008. He graduated from the University of Maine at Orono and the Bangor Theological Seminary. A Wisconsin native, Zimmerman was ordained at his home church in Shawano on June 22, 1975, and began serving as pastor in Dracut in September of that same year. During his time in Dracut, Zimmerman celebrated the 275th anniversary of the Old Yellow Meeting House in 1989, observed the renovations of the steeple and five of the church's large stained-glass windows, and became the fire department's chaplain, a position he still holds. Zimmerman married Alice Field in August 1975, and they have one daughter, Gretchen. (Both, courtesy Larry Zimmerman.)

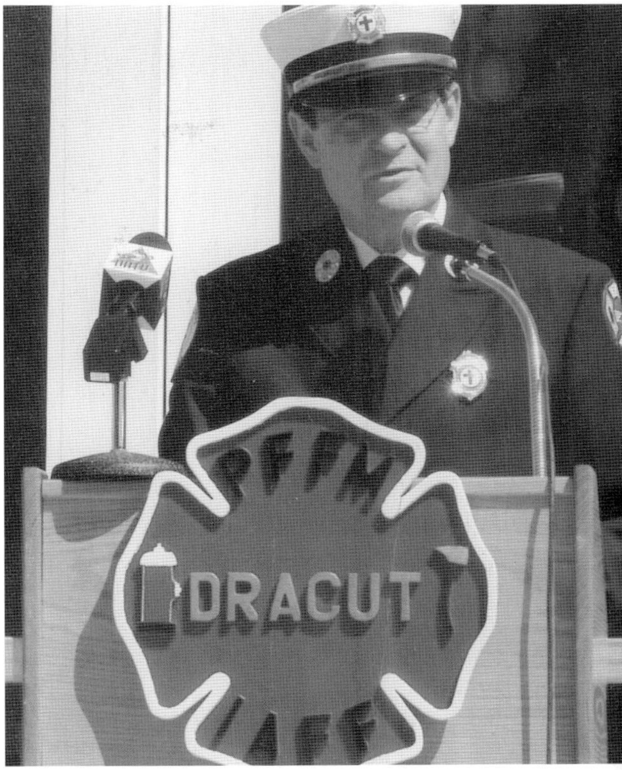

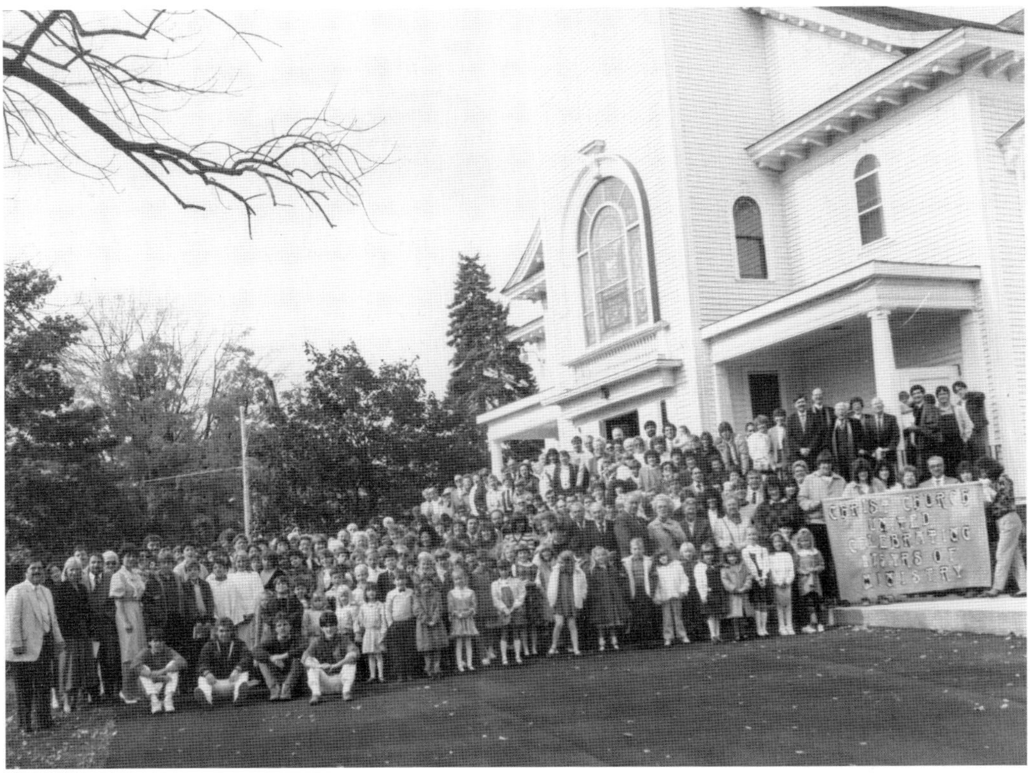

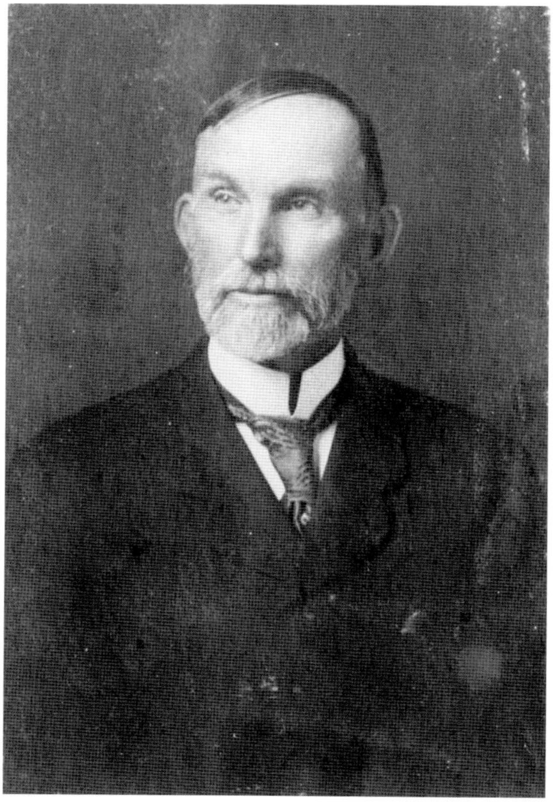

George Brown

George B. Brown donated land for the Collinsville Union Mission in 1896. Brown lived at the corner of Lakeview Avenue and Mammoth Road. Today, there is a gas station on that corner, which is referred to as Brown's Lane. The first church service was held on November 15, 1896. Those who worshipped there were predominantly Methodist, but all denominations were welcome. Now known as the Collinsville Bible Church, the church still holds services at 2075 Lakeview Avenue. (Both, courtesy Dracut Historical Society.)

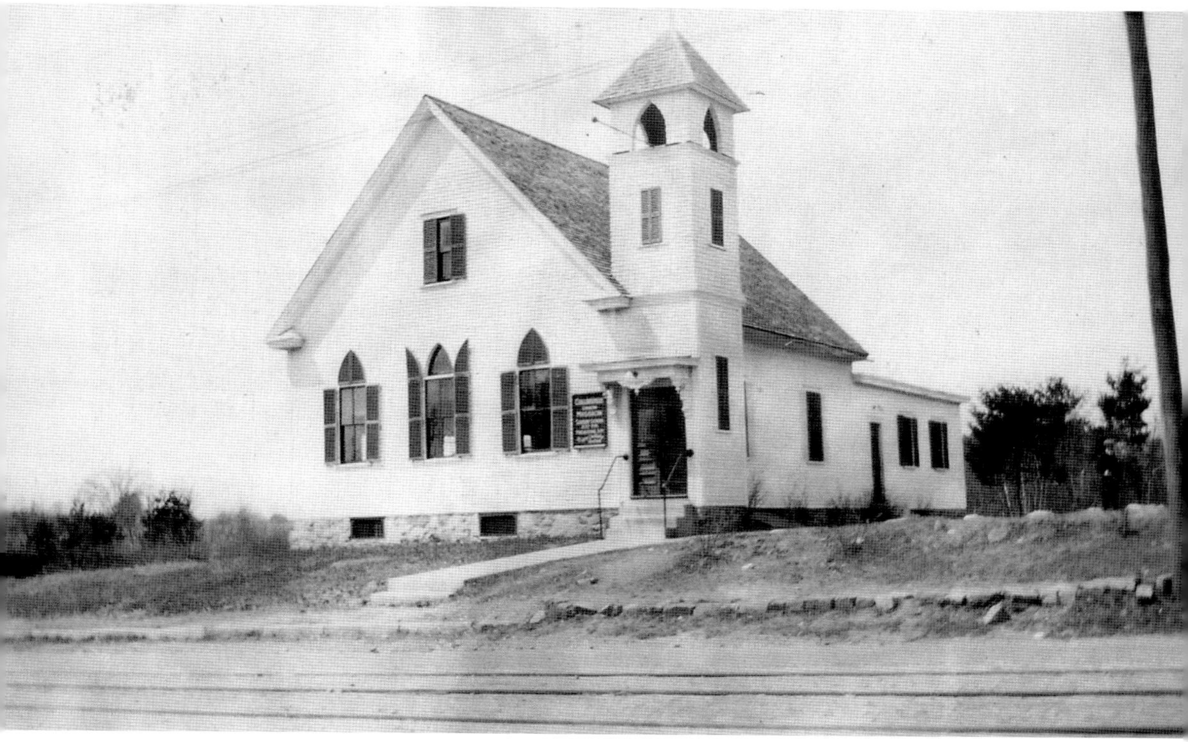

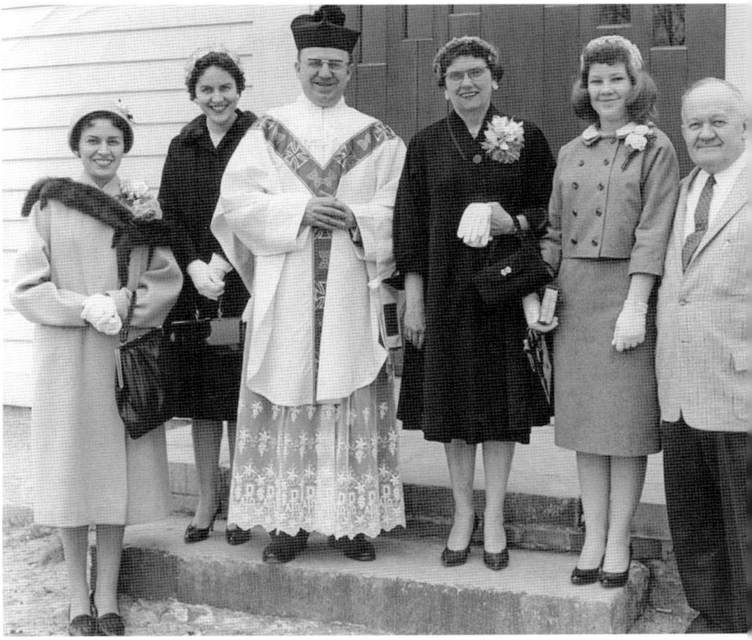

Armand Morissette
Established in 1939, St. Francis Church has grown tremendously over the years. Originally, priests from St. Michael's in Lowell were sent to hold services at the Kenwood School for Catholic residents in that part of town. Among these priests was Fr. Armand Morissette. Known as "Father Spike," he was born in Lowell in 1910. Father Morisette is shown here at St. Francis in the 1950s with the choir: (from left to right) Gertrude (Beaulieu) Hamel, Annette (Beaulieu) Koutrobis, Father Morissette, Cecilia Hamel, Nancy Green, and Victor Hamel. (Courtesy St. Francis Church.)

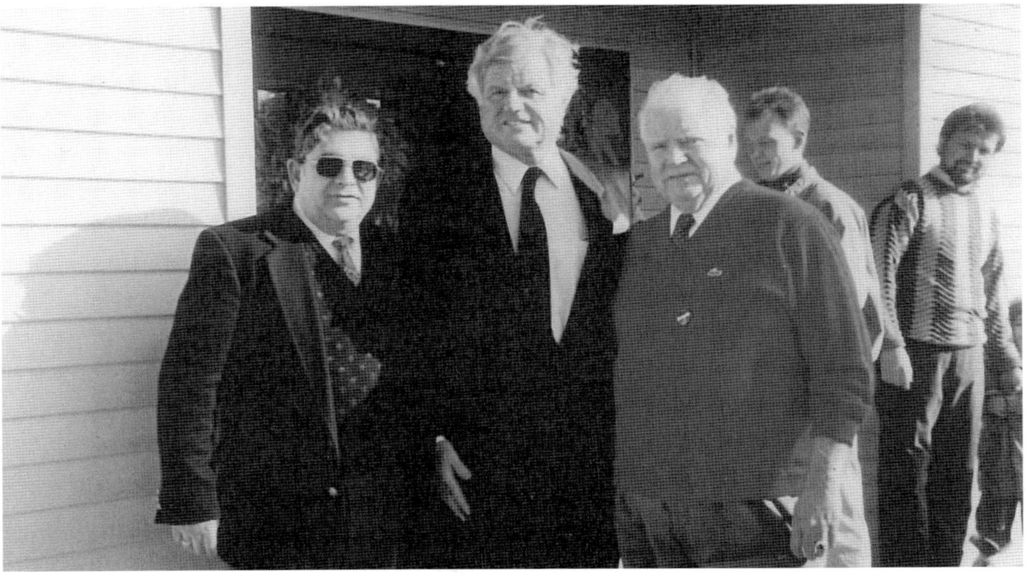

Michael Blatus
Mike Blatus was born on September 14, 1931, and graduated from Dracut High School in 1952. Having the opportunity to attend Boston University, Blatus instead decided to serve in the US Air Force until 1956. Upon returning to Dracut, Blatus married Antoinette Pasterczyk in 1959. Since then, he has been very active in town politics. He was first elected as a district clerk for the Dracut Water Supply District (DWSD) and held that position for 38 years. During that time, one of his accomplishments was extending the water main on Broadway 1,500 feet to Jones Avenue. In 1963, he was the first Greek American to serve as town assessor. He remained in that role for 30 years. Blatus credits Nicholas Lambros, Paul Merrill, Tom Duffy, and Christos Daoulas for encouraging him to enter town politics. Blatus, on the left, is pictured at the Dracut Council of Aging. (Courtesy Michael Blatus.)

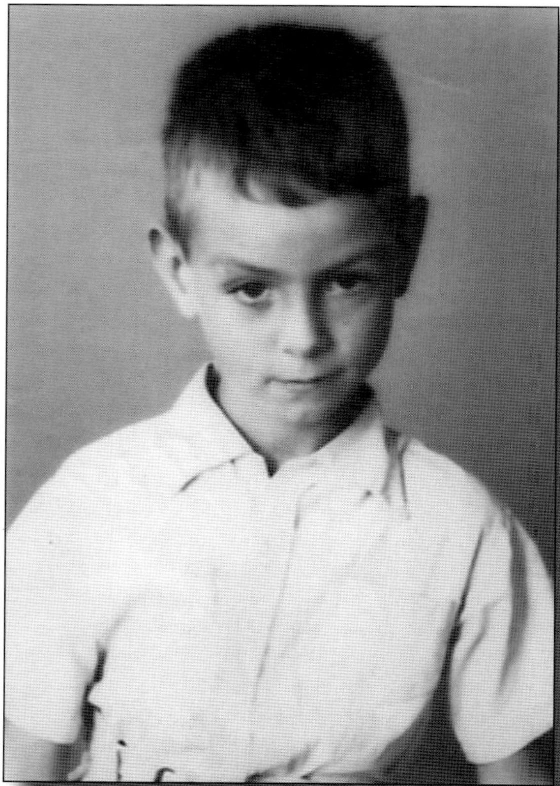

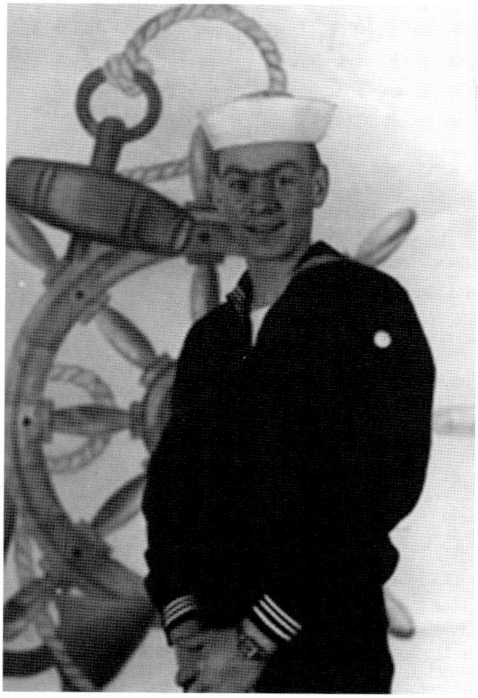

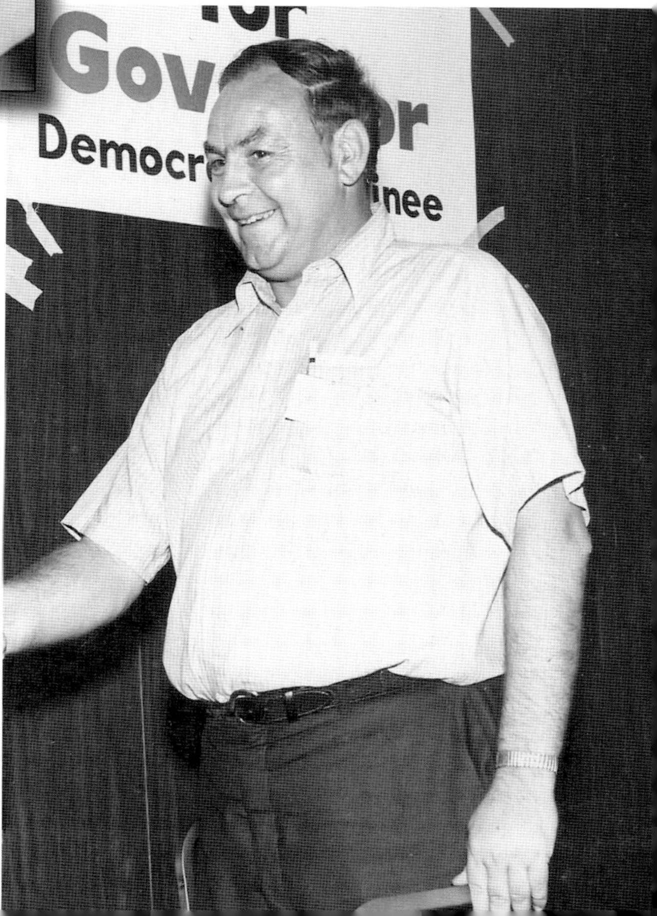

Paul A. Merrill
On January 6, 1980, the Dracut school committee dedicated the high school gymnasium in honor of Paul A. Merrill—a fitting tribute for a man who was active in youth athletics and served his hometown for 25 years. Merrill was born on September 3, 1932, and graduated from Dracut High School in 1949. During the late 1940s, "Goozy," as he was nicknamed, founded the town baseball league and later helped to establish the Dracut Recreation Commission. At age 19, Merrill was the youngest varsity basketball official in eastern Massachusetts. Merrill served as town moderator for 20 years and as town accountant for 8 years. Paul Albert Merrill died from cancer at age 48 on March 8, 1980. (All, courtesy Pat Merrill.)

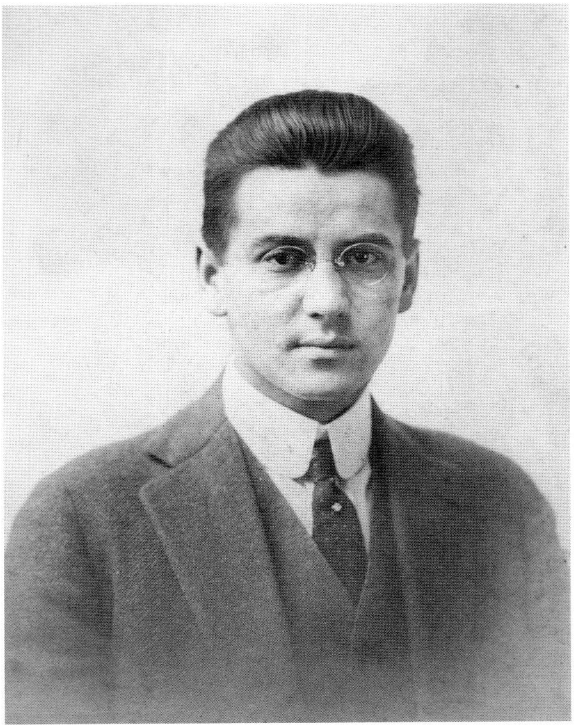

Edward Gaston Campbell
E. Gaston Campbell was born in Montreal, Canada, in 1891. His family moved to Lowell, and he graduated from Lowell High School. As a real estate and insurance agent, Campbell developed several areas in Dracut. His offices were located on Hildreth Street in Lowell. The photograph below shows the Long Pond Park development being constructed. In the foreground is Mammoth Road, with Passaconaway Drive going up the hill. Gaston proposed the development in 1926. The civil engineers for the project were Brooks, Jordan, and Graves of Lowell. The original proposal called for a tennis court, field house, and dance hall. For unknown reasons, these structures were not built. Gaston also developed the area around Peter's Pond, and the street names in that development are members of his family. (Both, courtesy Cynthia Campbell.)

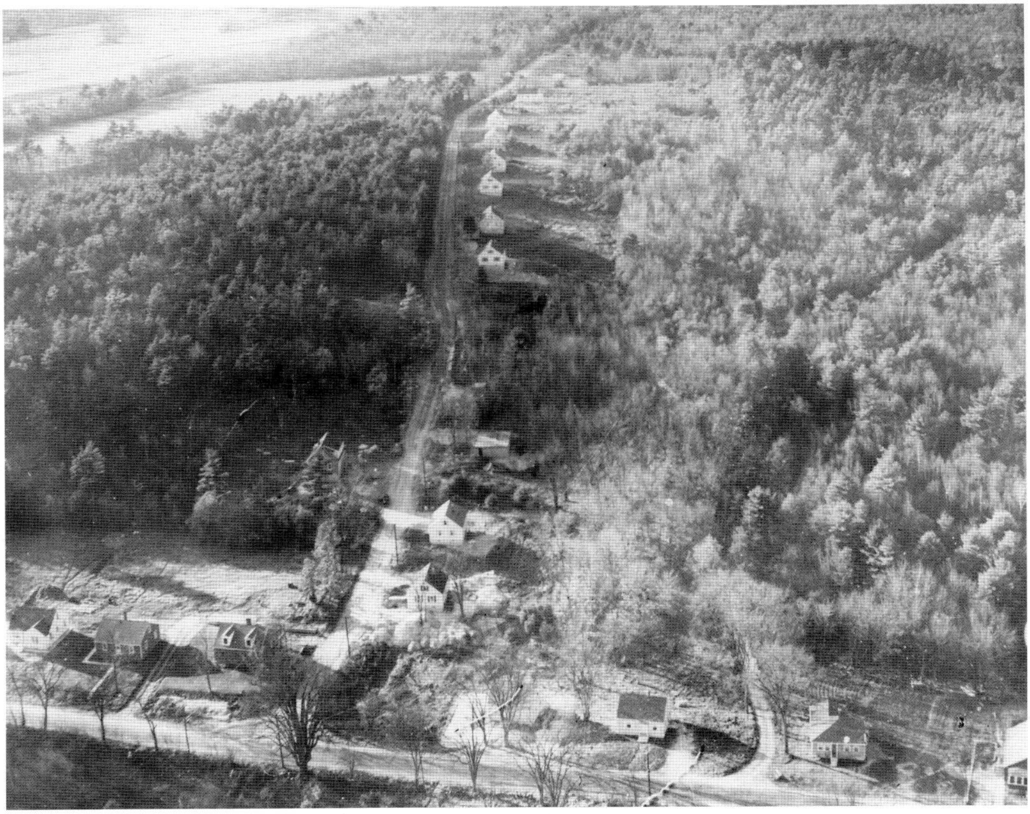

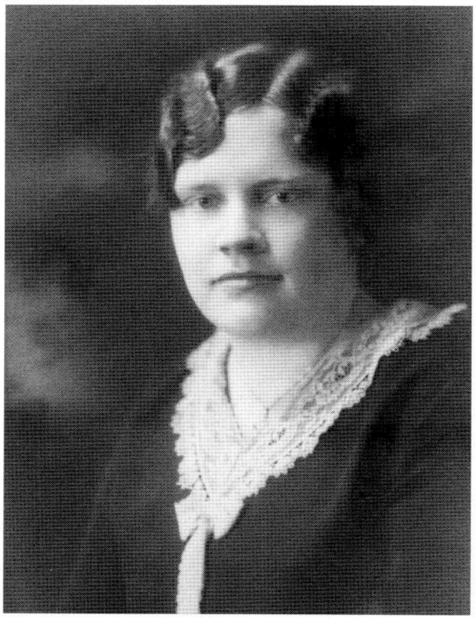

Pauline Varnum

Pauline Varnum was a direct descendant of Samuel Varnum, who was one of the town's first settlers. Daughter of Joseph and Jennie (Fox) Varnum, she was born on May 15, 1909. Varnum began her teaching career at Greensboro High School in Greensboro, Vermont, in 1932. After two years in Vermont, she returned to Dracut as a faculty member at Dracut High School. She also served as principal and vice principal of Dracut High School. Her retirement party in 1972 was held at the Coq D'Or Restaurant and celebrated her many years of service to the schools. She died on October 3, 1979. (Courtesy Dracut Historical Society.)

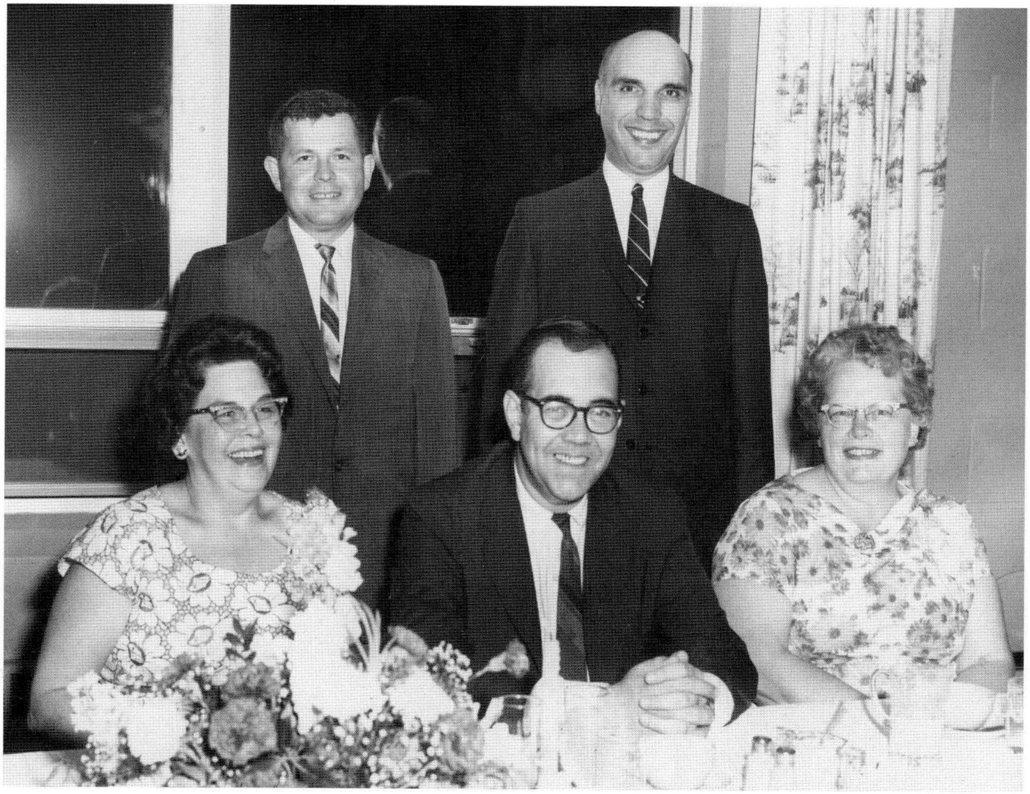

Bradford Morse

In June 1964, Dracut High School held an alumni dinner at the Harris Inn in Pelham, New Hampshire. Standing on the left is Harvey Gagnon and on the right Christos Daoulas, superintendent of schools. Seated from left to right are Myrtle Crowe, Bradford Morse, and Pauline Varnum. Bradford Morse (1921–1994) served as US representative from Lowell from 1960 to 1972. In 1972, he was appointed to the position of under-secretary-general for the United Nations. He is buried in Arlington National Cemetery. (Courtesy Dracut Historical Society.)

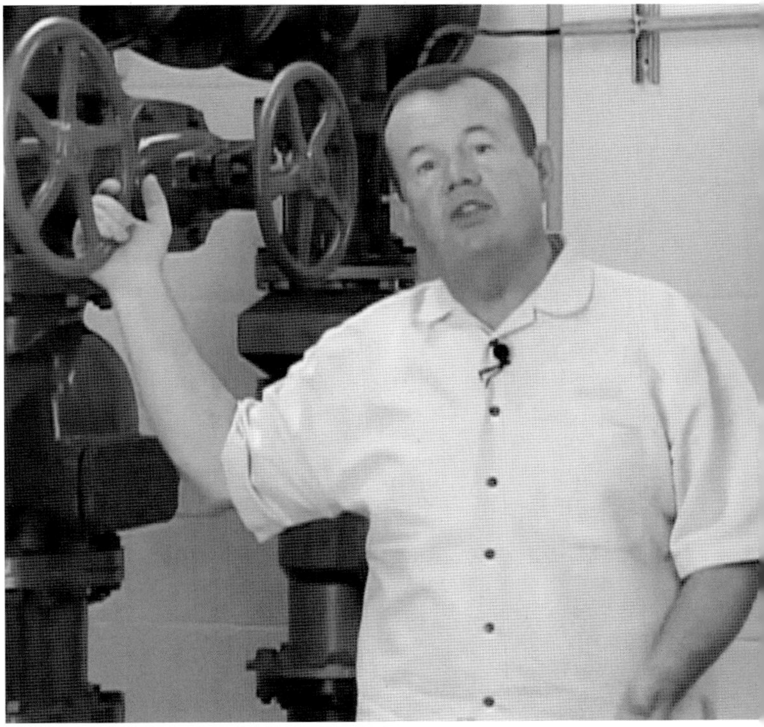

Gary McCarthy
When Gary McCarthy retired on August 20, 2010, the headline in the *Valley Dispatch* fittingly called him "Dracut's Mr. Everything," as he had held numerous positions in town government. After serving in the Air Force in the 1970s, McCarthy taught at the Dracut Middle School (today's Brookside Elementary) for 17 years. From 1981 to 2001, he simultaneously served as town clerk and assistant town manager. When he retired, he was serving in the Dracut Water Supply District. (Courtesy Town of Dracut.)

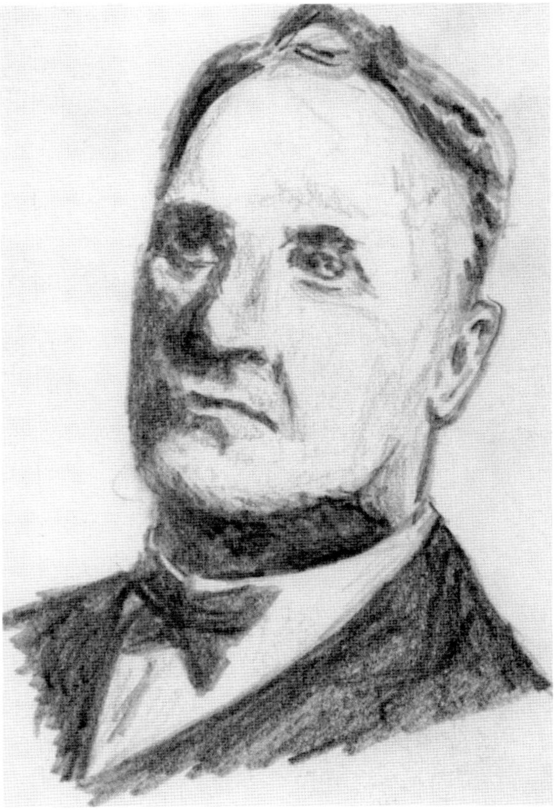

Thomas F. Carrick
Born in Amesbury to John and Mary Carrick, Thomas F. Carrick moved to Dracut with his family after graduating from grammar school. Though not a Dracut native, the beloved Carrick was a longtime resident of the town. He graduated from Lowell High School, and his first job was in the Dracut Mills. Then he worked for the Bower brothers at Lakeview, captaining the *Willow Oak* steamer on Lake Mascuppic. For the next 27 years, Carrick served as Dracut's tree warden and moth superintendent until he died in August 1935. He lived in Collinsville, and in 1938, Carrick Field was named in his honor. The field was constructed using Work Projects Administration (WPA) funds, which seems appropriate since Carrick was a staunch Democrat. (Courtesy Tyler Bettencourt.)

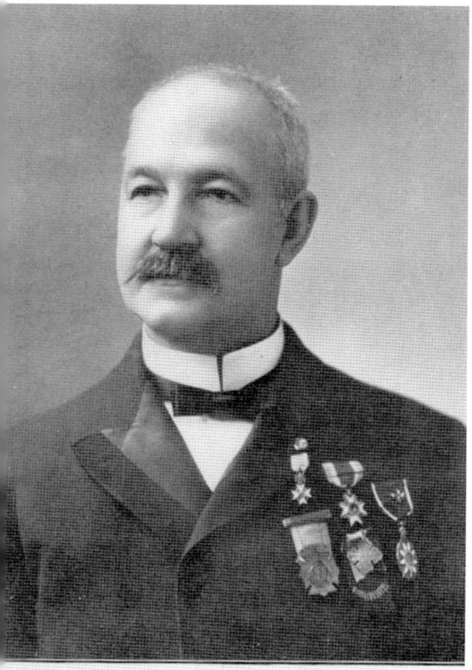

MOSES GREELEY PARKER, M.D.
President Massachusetts Society, S. A. R.

Moses Greeley Parker

Moses Greeley Parker is one of Dracut's most famous residents. He was a descendant of Deacon Thomas Parker, who arrived in America in 1635 and became Dracut's first minister. Born in 1842, M.G. Parker graduated from Phillips Academy in Andover, then Harvard Medical School in 1864. Upon graduation, he enlisted in the Army to fight for the Union during the Civil War and served as an assistant surgeon in the 2nd US Colored Cavalry. When was honorably discharged, Parker established his own medical practice in Lowell in 1866. During his career, he served as a trustee of Lowell General Hospital, as president of the Middlesex North District Medical Society, and even as a member of the executive committee of the New England Telephone and Telegraph Company. In 1892, Parker became an active member in the Sons of the American Revolution. Housed on the second floor of town hall, the library was first established by town meeting in 1900. With the $10,000 that Parker donated just prior to his death in 1917, a new permanent home was built for the town's library in 1923. He died in 1917 and is buried in Lowell Cemetery. (Left, courtesy Dracut Historical Society; below, courtesy the Paul Dumont family.)

Moses Greeley Parker Memorial Library, Dracut, M

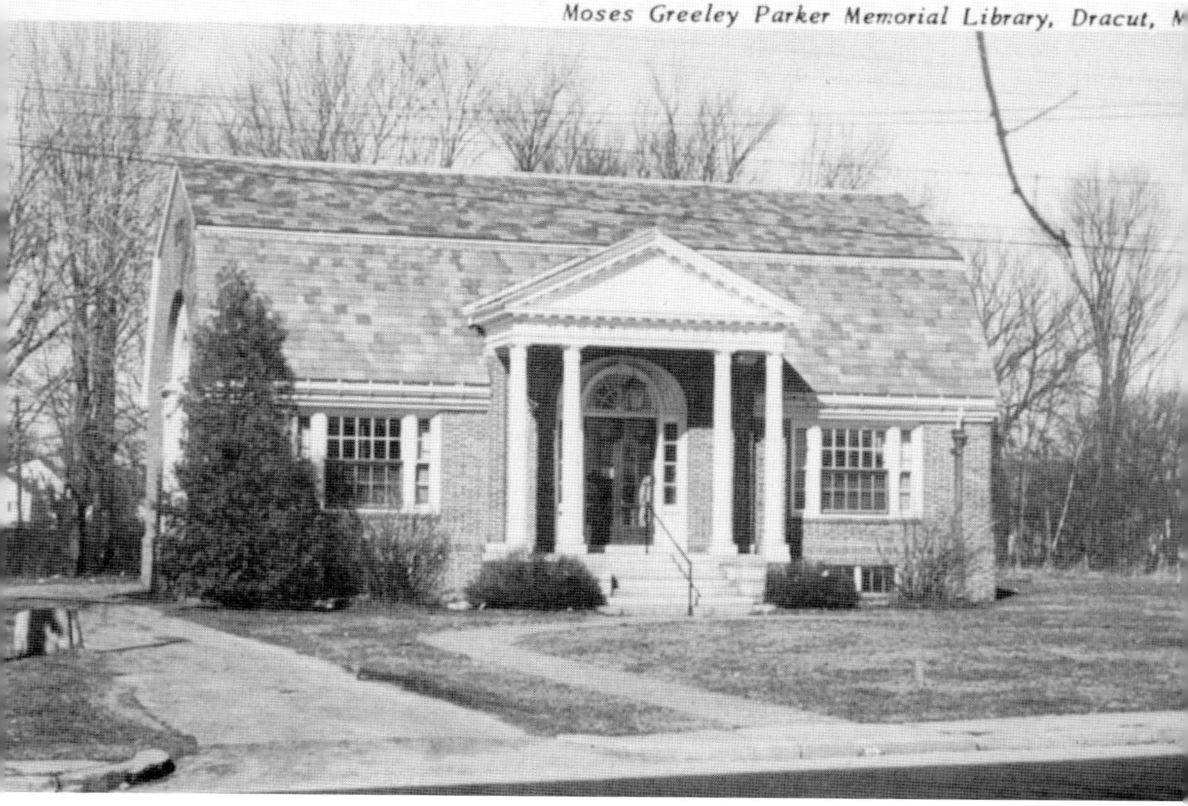

CHAPTER TWO

The Noblest Profession

The Teachers

This chapter's title is a bit misleading because any successful school department is not just comprised of teachers. Education is truly a community effort, and within the halls of our schools, working with Dracut students are teachers, administrators, coaches, volunteers, staff, and elected officials. From the beginning, Dracut was concerned with ensuring education for the town's children. On October 1, 1736, the selectmen voted to hire Phineas Stevens of Andover to establish a school in Dracut to teach reading and writing. In 1821, the first schoolhouse was erected on land from Ephraim Coburn. Known as the Coburn Mission, it was torn down in 1965. As the town grew in the 20th century, so did the need for an expanded school department. Built in 1891, the Collinsville Grammar School received honorable mention at the 1893 World's Fair as an "ideal country school and grounds." Students who continued with their secondary education were sent to Lowell High School until 1936, when Dracut High School was established. Today's Greenmont Elementary School was the home to Dracut's first high school.

The longest-serving superintendent in Massachusetts hails from Dracut; Dr. Christos Daoulas served as superintendent from 1962 until his retirement in 1998. Following him was Elaine A. Espindle, who begun her career in Peabody as an English teacher before entering administration. She served as the principal of the Higgins Middle School, then as assistant superintendent, and finally, as interim superintendent. After serving in Peabody, she became the Dracut superintendent in 1998.

The 2013–2014 school year saw another exciting era begin for the town's schools. Under the leadership of Supt. Steven Stone, the district underwent a major reorganization. The Brookside, Campbell, Englesby, and Greenmont Schools house kindergarten through fifth grade, Lakeview Junior High School houses grades six through eight, and Dracut High School continues to house grades nine through twelve. In addition, the Lakeview Junior High School was renamed the Justus C. Richardson Middle School, and Dracut High School reopened after a major renovation that included construction of a new academic wing, theater, cafeteria, and updated classrooms. As Superintendent Stone often says with pride, "Dracut High is the envy of the valley." In fact, the entire school system is the envy of the valley—from its leadership, teachers, staff, students, and coaches. Dracut Public Schools are building on the foundation of past legendary locals.

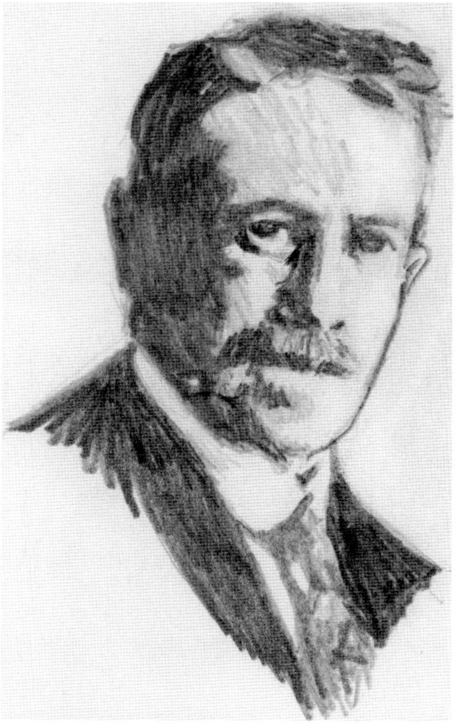

Charles Randall
In 1881, the town established a school committee and superintendent to administer the schools. Charles Randall served as superintendent from 1913 to 1943, when he was succeed by Dr. Garland B. Russell. Randall was a well-respected school leader and faced a serious challenge in 1928 when Irene Gourgeon, an eight-year-old student at the Collinsville school, died from a sore throat. Fear of an epidemic raced through the Collinsville neighborhood. Randall called in state health officials, and fears were allayed. Randall also oversaw the creation of the first Dracut High School. Ground breaking for the high school took place in October 1934. The auditorium at the high school (today's Greenmont) was dedicated to Charles Randall. (Courtesy Tyler Bettencourt.)

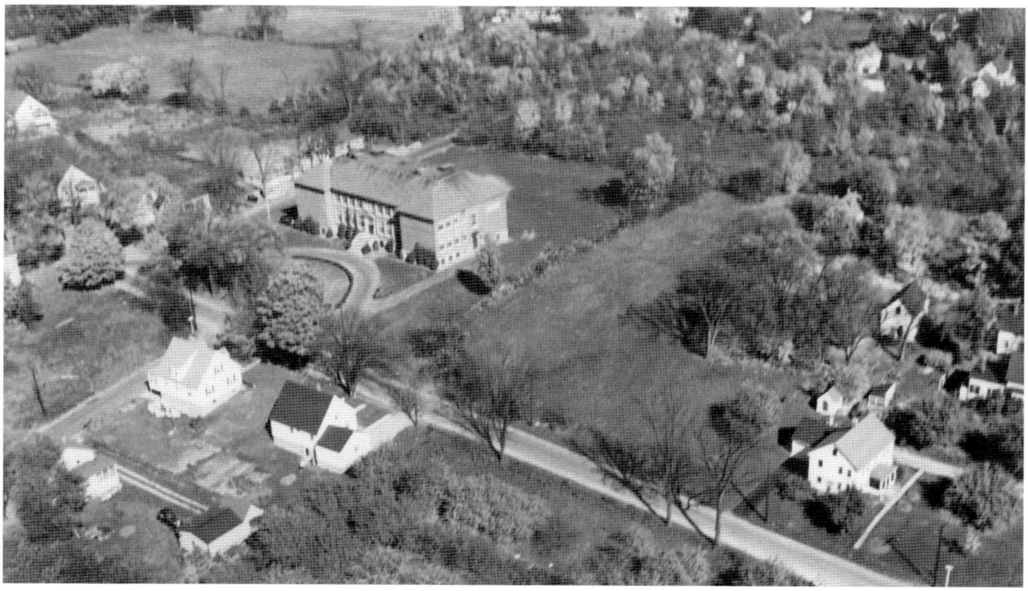

Dracut High School
In 1928, the Greenmont Elementary School was built under Supt. Charles Randall. It was used as an elementary school until 1933–1934, when it was converted to Dracut's first high school. It originally opened as a two-year high school, with the students finishing their junior and senior years at Lowell High School. It later became a four-year high school, and the first class graduated in 1936. The principal in 1936 was James C. Riley. Greenmont was used as the town's high school until 1957, when a new high school was built on Lakeview Avenue on land donated by Justus C. Richardson. (Courtesy William F. O'Neill.)

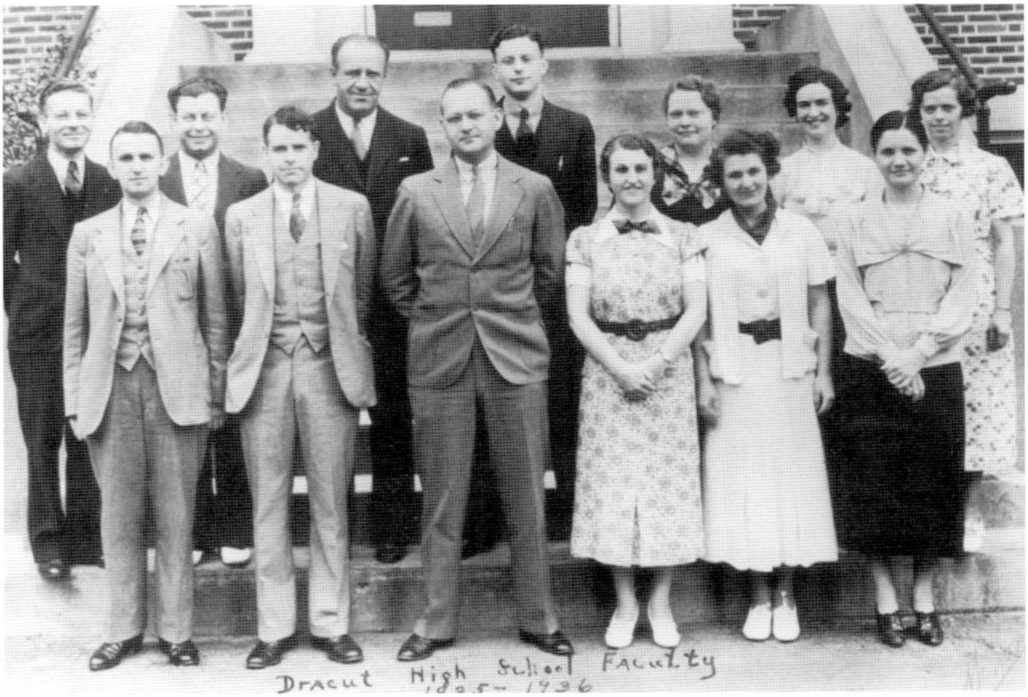

Faculty at Dracut High School, 1936

Pictured here is the faculty of Dracut's first high school. From left to right are (first row) Arthur Skandalis, Donald Shanahan, James Riley (principal), Marie McKenna, Ora Parks, and Katherine Prior; (second row) Henry Koneiczny, John Guenard, Spencer Sullivan (coach), Rene Bernadin, Pauline Varnum, Helen Shea, and Jeanne Dozios. Arthur Skandalis was the first Greek American hired to teach in the Dracut Public Schools, and Pauline Varnum later served as high school principal and vice principal. (Courtesy Dracut Historical Society.)

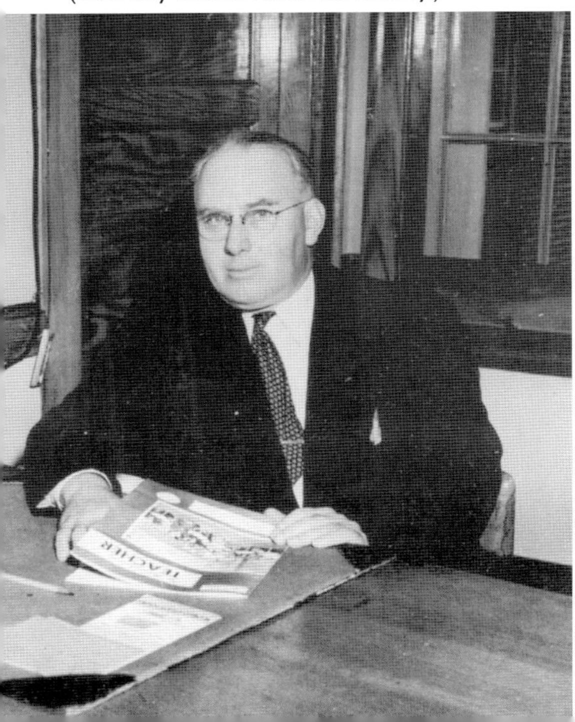

George H. Englesby Jr.

To honor assistant superintendent George H. Englesby Jr., 400 people gathered at his retirement party in June 1967. This turnout was a testament to how beloved he was after serving in the Dracut Public Schools for 40 years. Born to George and Rose (Lynch) Englesby on April 21, 1907, he was a lifelong Dracut resident who lived at 32 School Street in the Navy Yard district. He was a graduate of Boston University, a World War II veteran, and a communicant of St. Michael's. Englesby passed away unexpectedly on December 28, 1971. In June 1972, the Dracut Junior High School was renamed in his honor. (Courtesy Dracut Historical Society.)

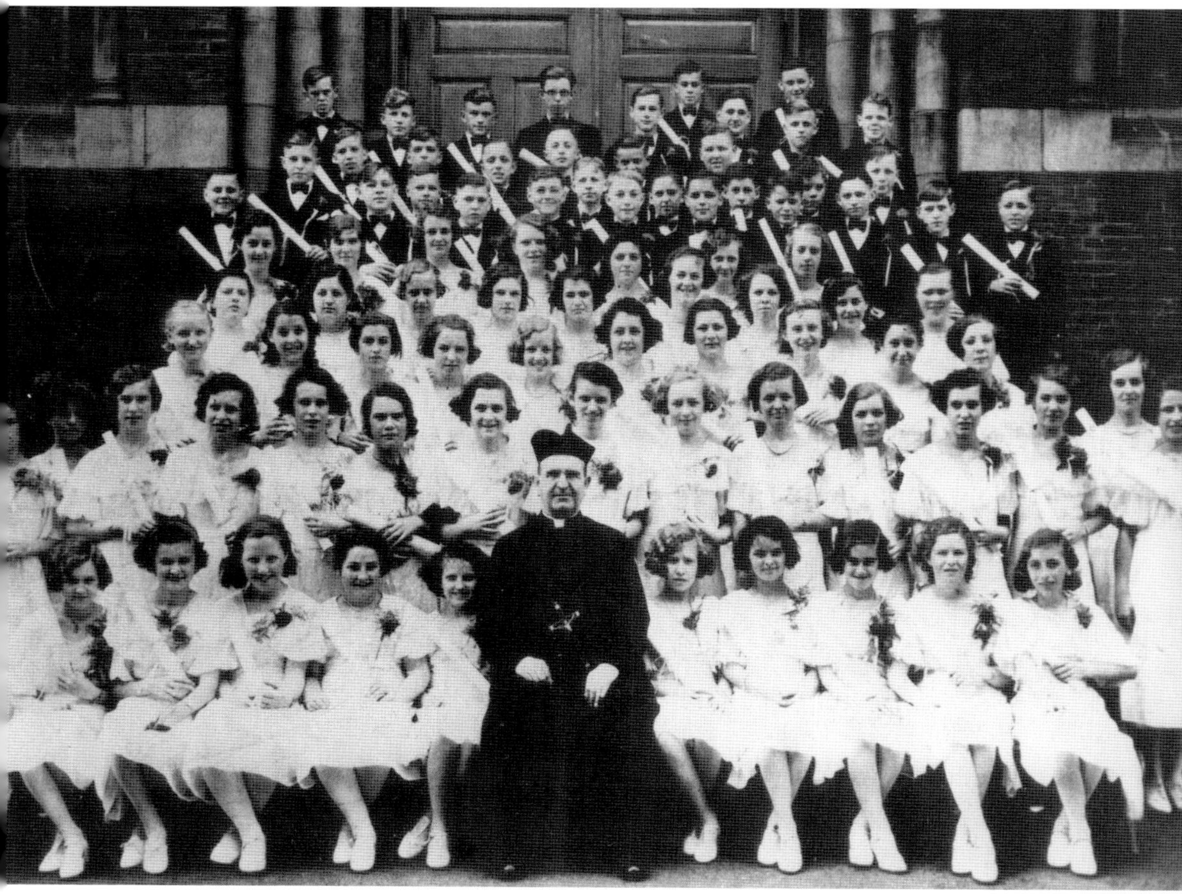

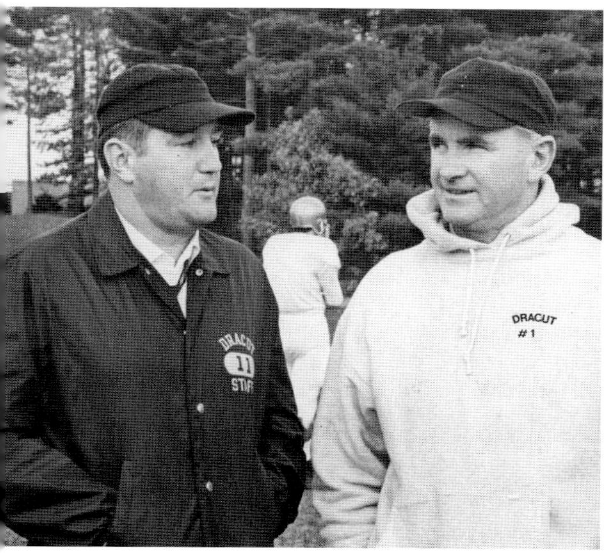
DRACUT
11
STAFF
DRACUT
#1

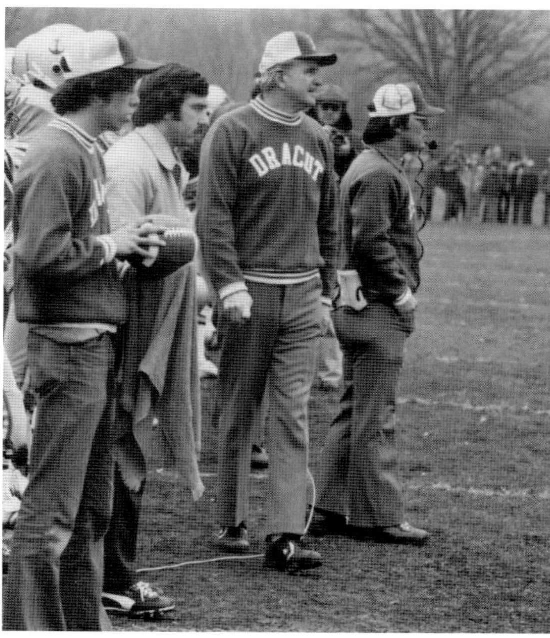
DRACUT

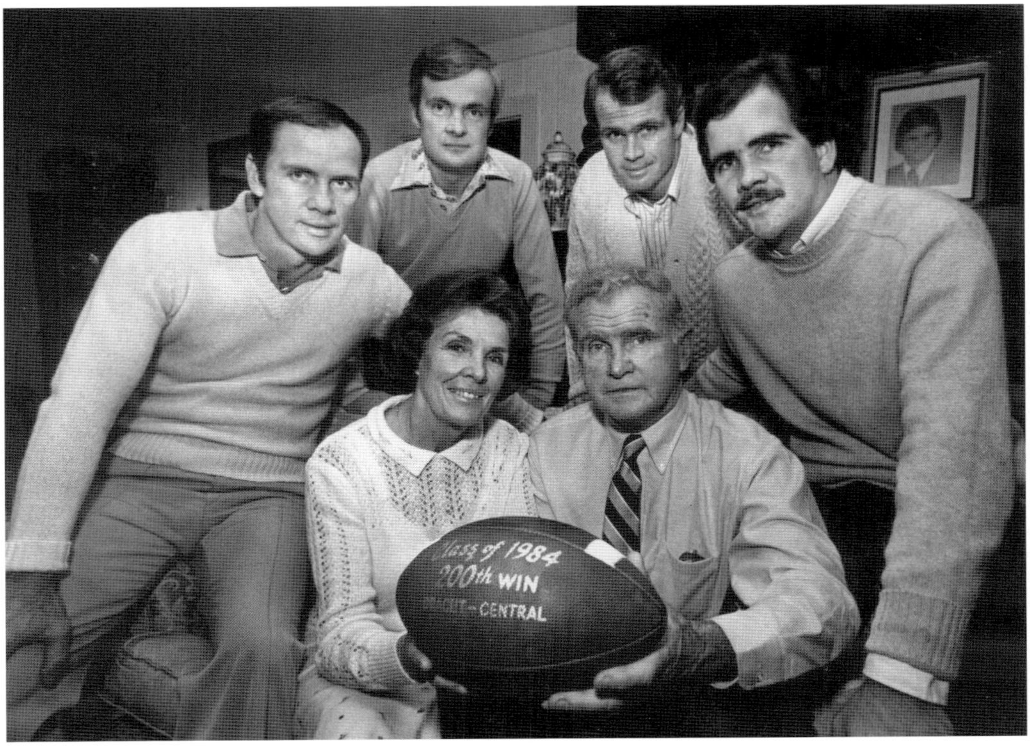

Edmund Murphy

Born in Lowell in 1919, Edmund Murphy attended Sacred Heart. On the opposite page, above, he is pictured in the top row, third from left, on his eighth grade graduation day. He then graduated from Lowell High School in 1937, Seton Hall Prep in 1939, and College of the Holy Cross in 1943. During World War II, Murphy served in the Marines and faced fierce fighting with the Japanese on the South Pacific island of Peleliu. After the war, he married Justine Powers, with whom he shared 65 years of marriage. Though drafted by the Pittsburgh Steelers, Murphy accepted the head coaching position at Dracut High School in 1946 and remained head coach until 1994. Known in the Merrimack Valley as the dean of high school football, Murphy led his undefeated 1988 team to win the Massachusetts Super Bowl. On the opposite page, bottom left, he is pictured with longtime assistant coach David Stecchi.

Pictured above holding the football are Murphy and his wife, Justine. From left to right are their four sons: Daniel, Brian, Dennis, and David. At right, Coach Murphy is at practice in the early 1960s with (from left to right) Dennis Quebec, Ron Close, Gus Fitzgerald, and Jerry Davidson. (All, courtesy Edmund Murphy.)

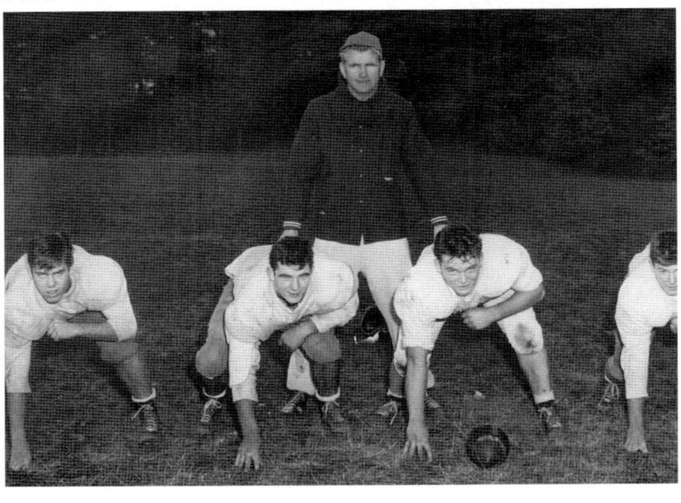

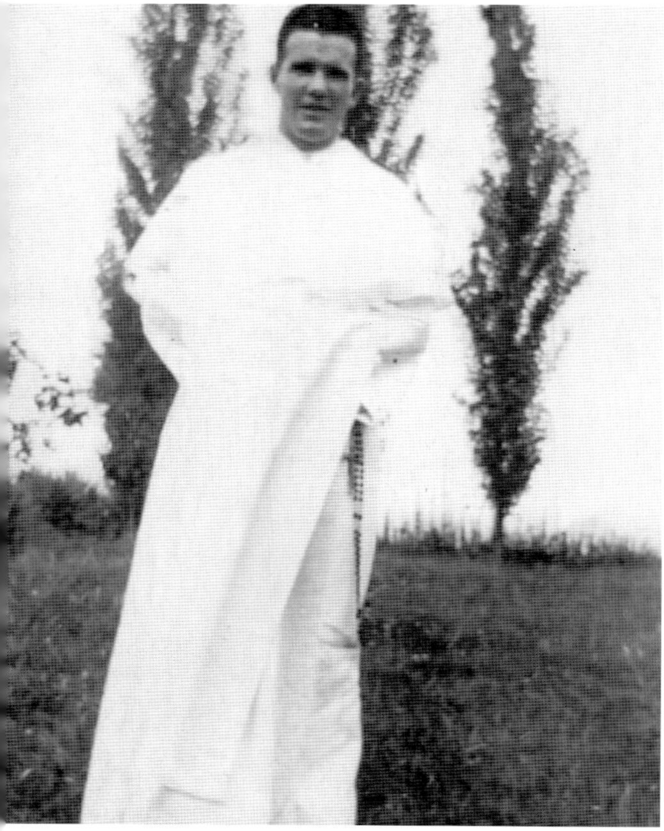

Martin P. Garry

Martin P. Garry was born in Brooklyn, New York, on June 21, 1928. His family moved to Massachusetts, where Garry graduated from St. John the Evangelist in Cambridge in 1946. After graduation, Garry entered the Dominican Seminary. He left the seminary and earned degrees from Providence College and Boston University. On August 22, 1959, he married Mary Burke, with whom he shared 50 years of marriage. Together, they had three children: Maureen, Colleen, and Cathleen. Garry spent 32 years with the Dracut Public Schools. Among the positions he held were high school principal, guidance counselor, director of secondary curriculum, and assistant superintendent. In 2006, the high school guidance suite was dedicated as the Martin P. Garry and William F. O'Neill Guidance Suite. (Both, courtesy the Garry family.)

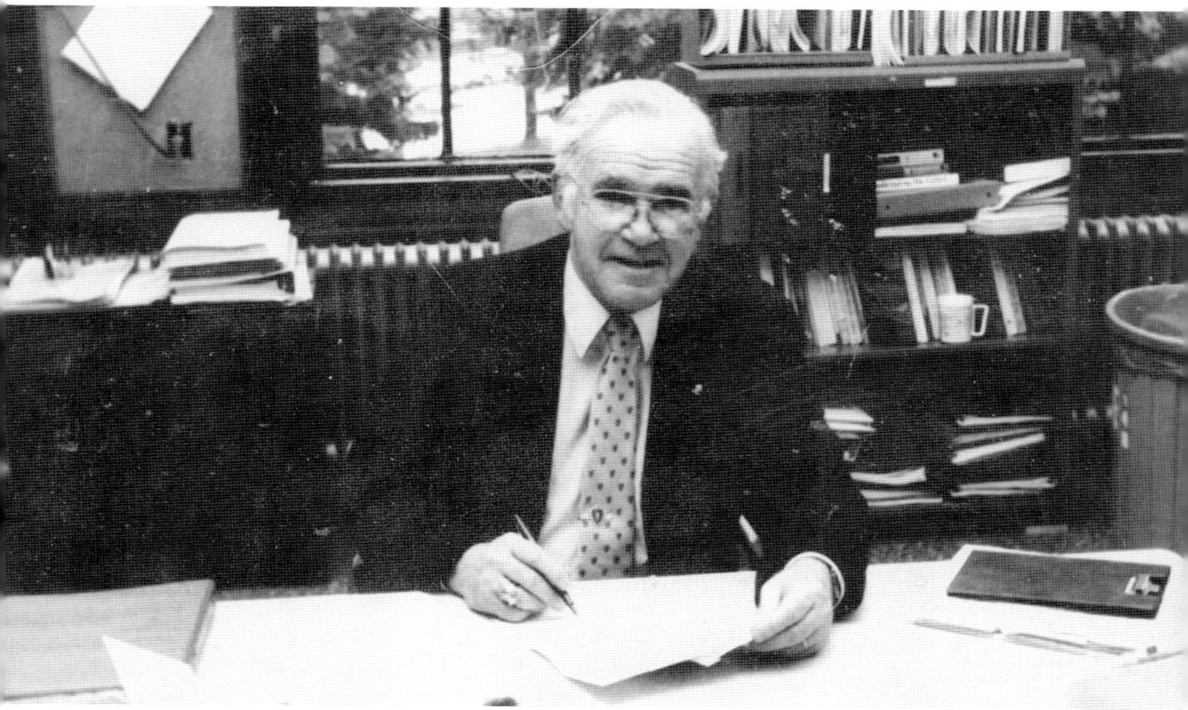

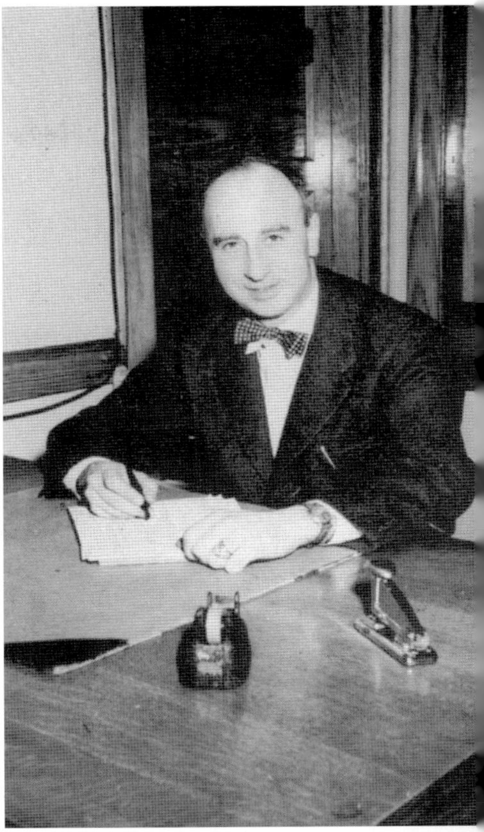

Paul Phaneuf

Paul Phaneuf served as Dracut's superintendent from 1943 to 1962. Though not as famous as the man who took over when he left in 1962, Phaneuf oversaw significant changes in the Dracut Public Schools during his tenure. Most notably, the new Dracut High School was built on Lakeview Avenue. He also hired many of the people who would later become icons in the school department: Christos Daoulas, William F. O'Neill, Martin Garry, and Maurice Pepin. George H. Englesby Jr. filled in as acting superintendent when Phaneuf took a leave of absence to serve in the Korean War. (Courtesy Dracut Historical Society.)

Daniel W. Smith Jr.

For 25 years, two names were synonymous with Dracut High School—Dan Smith and Bruce Hutchins (see page 50). Serving as vice principal of the high school, Smith was a respected administrator for the high standards he held for the students at the school. Smith was born on December 6, 1935, and married Gudron Rohland on July 14, 1956. He earned his bachelor's and master's degrees from Boston University and was appointed vice principal at Dracut High in 1972. He retired in 1997. He is pictured below at Dracut High School's annual Pride Night in 1985 with students, from left to right, Joe Gangi, Peter Witts, Mike Fauvel, Rich Leboeuf, George Lafortune, and Richard McElhinney. (Courtesy Dracut Historical Society.)

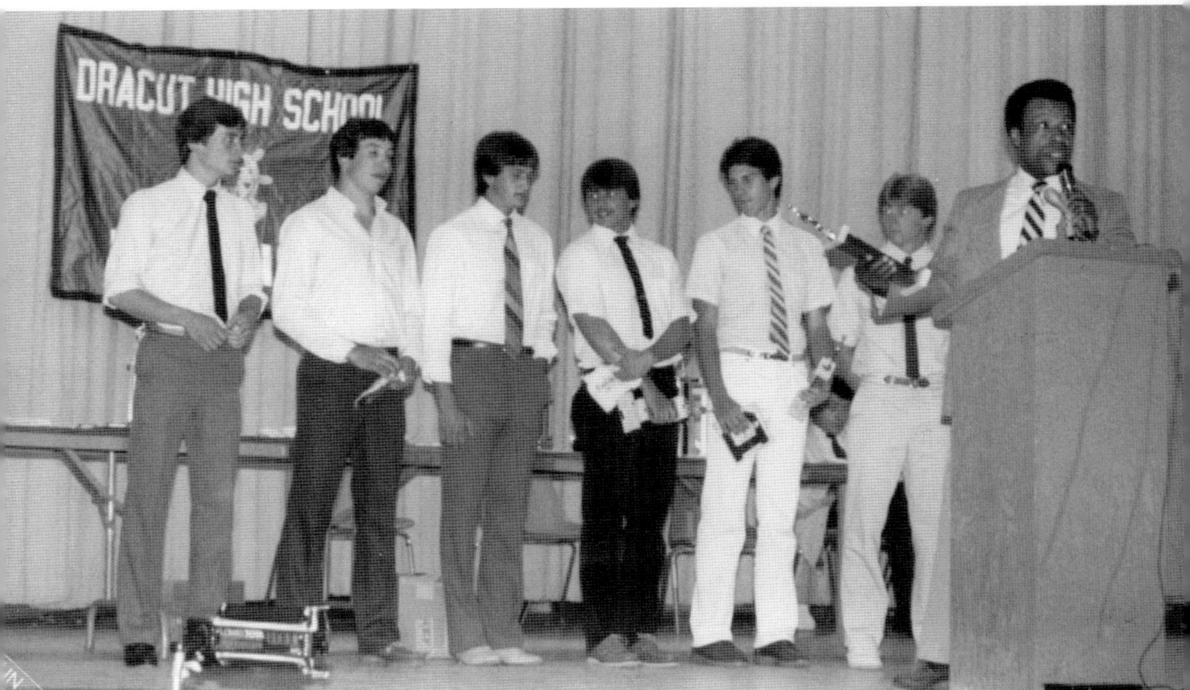

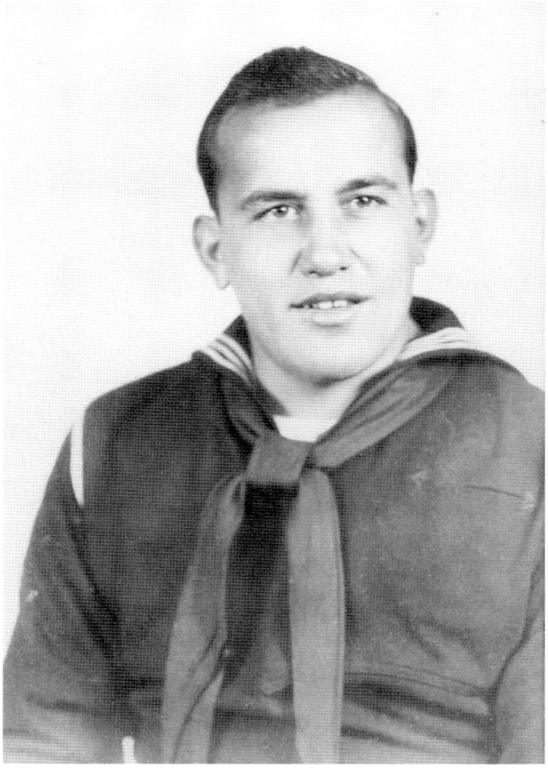

Arthur J. Beaudry

Since 1966, Dracut High School football games have been played on the Arthur J. Beaudry Memorial Field. Beaudry was born in Dracut on June 21, 1921. During World War II, he served in the US Coast Guard, then returned to his hometown, where he was extremely active in youth athletics and other civic organizations. Beaudry married Helen Piccirello and lived on Jacob Street in the Kenwood section of town. He was a very close friend to Coach Edmund Murphy and was his unofficial assistant coach for years. As president of the Dracut Boosters Club, he built the jumping pit at the track. Beaudry died at age 45 on August 1, 1966. (Courtesy Arthur J. Beaudry Jr.)

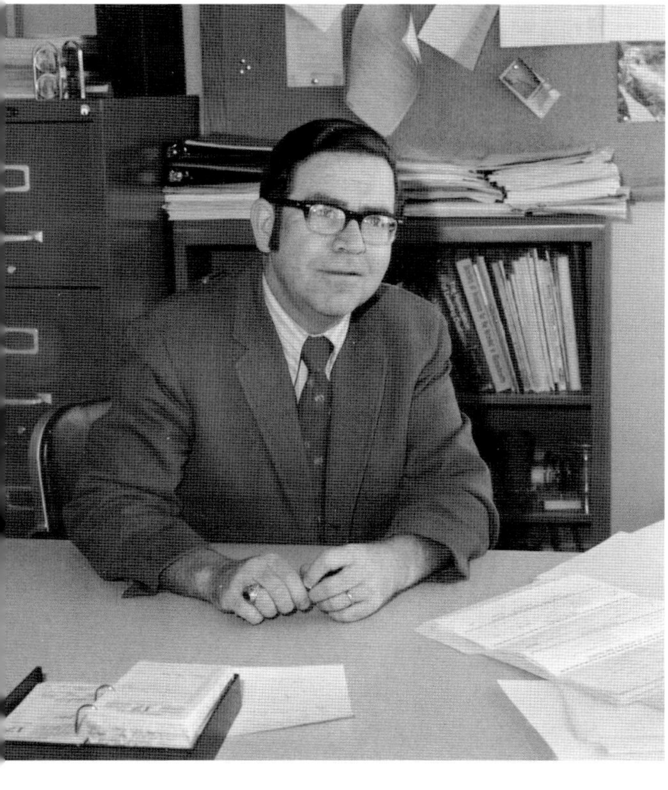

William F. O'Neill

In 1950, William F. O'Neill began his career in education as a permanent substitute in the Dracut Public Schools. The following year, he became a full-time teacher, and in 1954, he began working as a part-time guidance counselor in addition to teaching. By 1959, he was working full-time in the guidance department and eventually became the director of elementary curriculum. During the 1968–1969 school year, O'Neill served as acting superintendent while Superintendent Daoulas was on sabbatical earning his doctorate. During that time, he oversaw the construction of the Dracut Middle School (now Brookside). He retired in 1989. On May 21, 2014, the National Junior Honor Society was renamed the William F. O'Neill Chapter in recognition of his establishing the honor society in Dracut and serving as its first adviser. (Courtesy William F. O'Neill.)

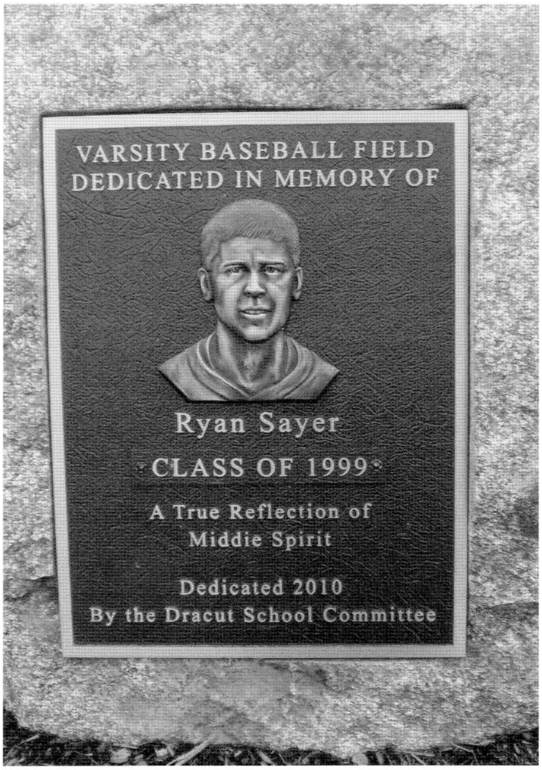

Ryan Sayer
Ryan Sayer was a standout baseball player for Dracut High School. In 1999, he died tragically in an automobile accident. To keep his memory alive and to recognize his outstanding sports career, the baseball field at Dracut High School was dedicated in his honor on April 15, 2010. (Author's collection.)

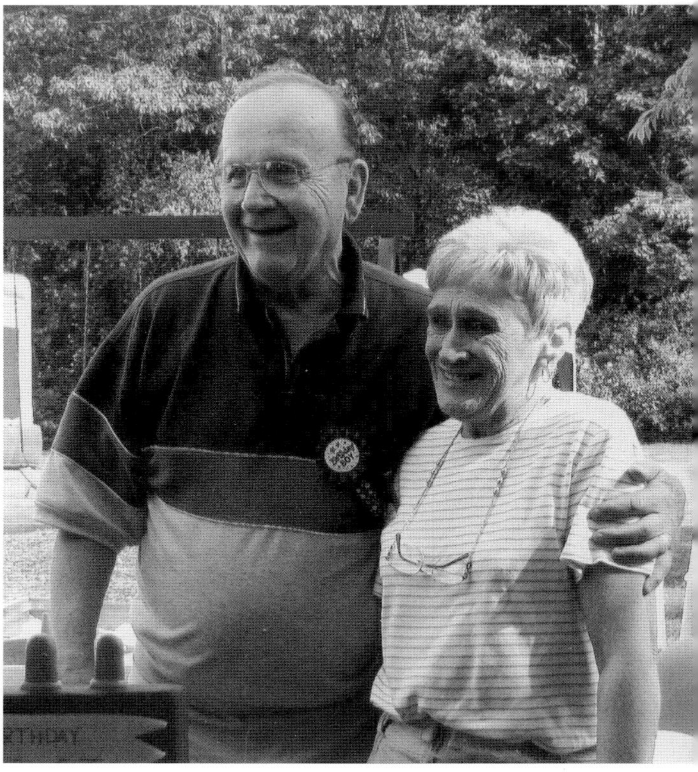

Joe and Maureen Wilkie
Joe and Maureen Wilkie were married in 1969 and moved to Dracut in 1984. The Wilkies and their children became involved in town sports and were active in the Dracut Boosters Club. In 1990, Superintendent Daoulas hired Maureen Wilkie to work in the school's Central Office. She fondly recalls Dr. Daoulas as "compassionate" and "a true gentleman." She worked in the Dracut Public Schools until 2001. (Courtesy Maureen Wilkie.)

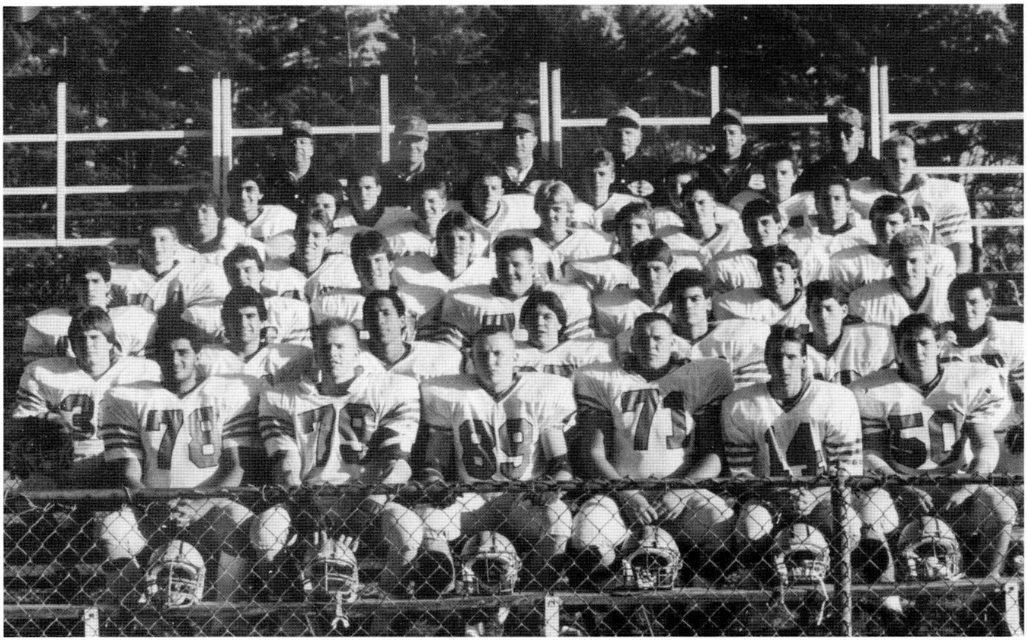

Dracut High School Super Bowl Champions, 1988
Under Coach Murphy, the 1988 Dracut High School football team won the Super Bowl, defeating the author's hometown high school of Beverly. From left to right are (first row) B. Alian, K. Farley, J. Wagner, J. Desmais (cocaptain), J. Halko (cocaptain), and J. Roy; (second row) J. Dahlinger, T. Rothe, D. Smith, S. Palermo, P. Skambas, R. Leahy, and A. Draper; (third row) T. Dehney, D. Couture, E. Zannoni, K. Baron, R. Cloutier, W. Hutchins, and W. Gibson; (fourth row) D. Hebert, M. Paquette, J. Kinnal, D. Brouillette, J. Daigle, and T. Walsh; (fifth row) J. Angluin, B. Casey, J. Honan, R. Lacoss, A. Monteiro, and C. Boumil; (sixth row) A. Alian, E. Kara, T. Lacourse, M. Williams, D. Perrin, C. Bourassa, and C. Coughlin; (seventh row) coaches H. Golec, D. Murphy, D. Stecchi, E. Murphy, P. Krafton, and R. Rudolph. Missing from the photograph are T. Kara, M. Difonso, D. Hood, and D. Ayotte. (Courtesy Janice Stecchi.)

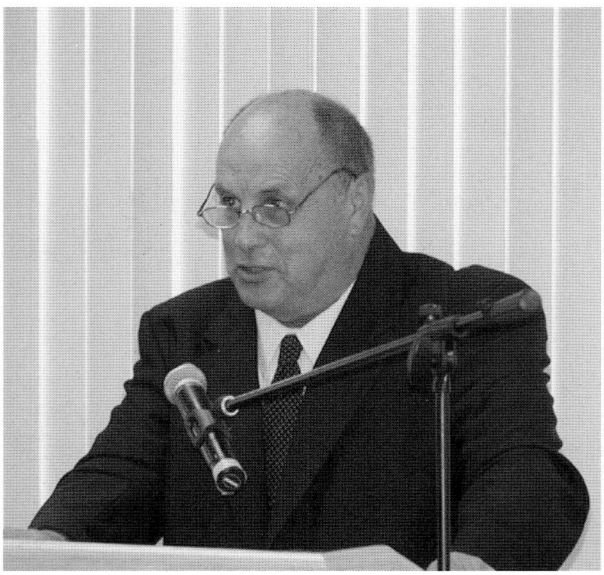

Bruce Hutchins
For 30 years, Bruce Hutchins was the principal of Dracut High School. When he was hired in 1972 at age 31, he was the youngest principal in Massachusetts, and at his retirement in 2002, he was the longest-tenured principal in Massachusetts. Hutchins was born in New York and graduated from Colgate University. During his time at Dracut High School, Hutchins oversaw the beginning of three cherished traditions: the bagpipes leading the graduation processional, the annual telethon, and the pre-prom event. (Courtesy O'Connor Studios.)

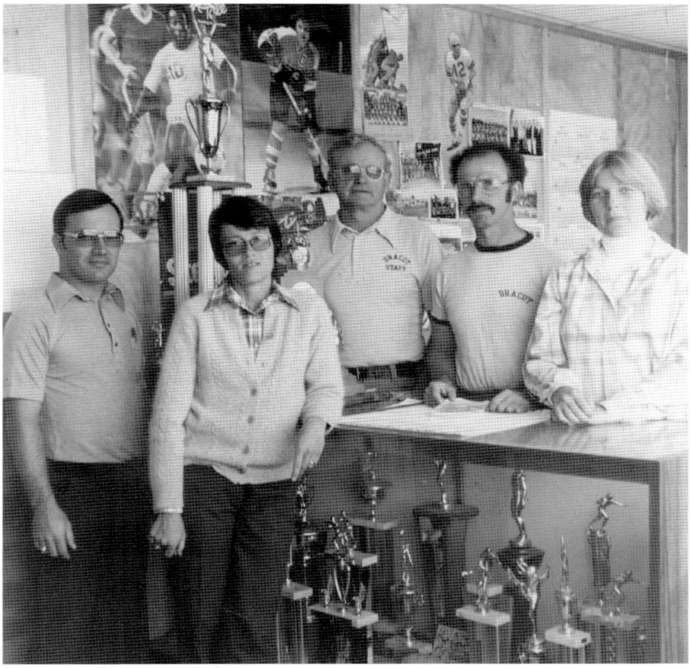

Robert Rudolph

When Bob Rudolph retired in 2006, the *Lowell Sun* stated, "A generation of Dracut High School athletic fans have never known life without Bob Rudolph." That statement could not be more true. Rudolph graduated from the University of New Hampshire, where he met his future wife, Denise Cappi, and in 1972, he started teaching and coaching at Dracut High School. Rudolph was a health and physical education teacher and a three-sport coach—wrestling coach, assistant football coach, and junior varsity baseball coach. Rudolph is pictured above during his teaching years in the late 1970s. From left to right are Rudolph, Jean Lemieux, Ed Murphy, Bill Miller, and Anne Marie Anderson. The highlight of his coaching career was winning the 2004 Division 2 state title for wrestling. That winning team is pictured below. (Above, courtesy Edmund Murphy; below, courtesy Robert Rudolph.)

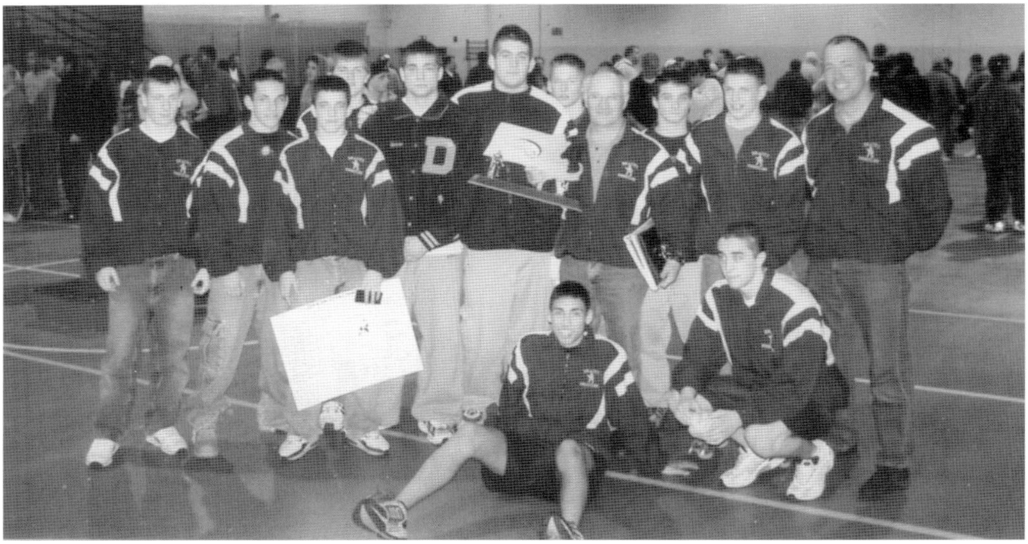

Elaine A. Espindle

Born in Cambridge, Elaine A. Espindle served as superintendent of the Dracut Public Schools from 1998 to 2008 and returned as interim superintendent in 2010. During her tenure as superintendent, the town's new junior high school was built. It was the first major construction project in the school department since the Joseph Campbell Elementary School was built in 1973. With 138,000 square feet, the new junior high school was considerably larger than the previous one. Building the junior high school was a major accomplishment for which former superintendent Espindle was proud. She described the building of the junior high school and creation of the intermediate schools as "a dynamic era for all, and [it] drew excitement from all aspects of the school system." Espindle was the driving force behind the renovated Dracut High School. She attended numerous meetings and spent countless hours preparing the necessary paperwork for the Massachusetts School Building Authority. The renovated Dracut High School opened in September 2014. On November 24, 2013, the school's library was renamed the Elaine A. Espindle Library for her years of dedication and service. Espindle passed away at age 65 on December 30, 2013. (Right, courtesy O'Connor Studios; below left, courtesy Shawn Ashe; below right, author's collection.)

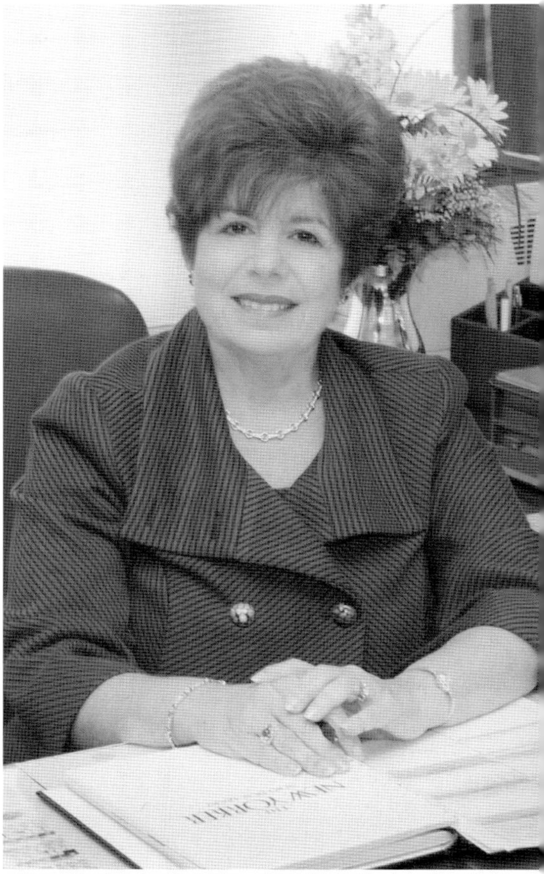

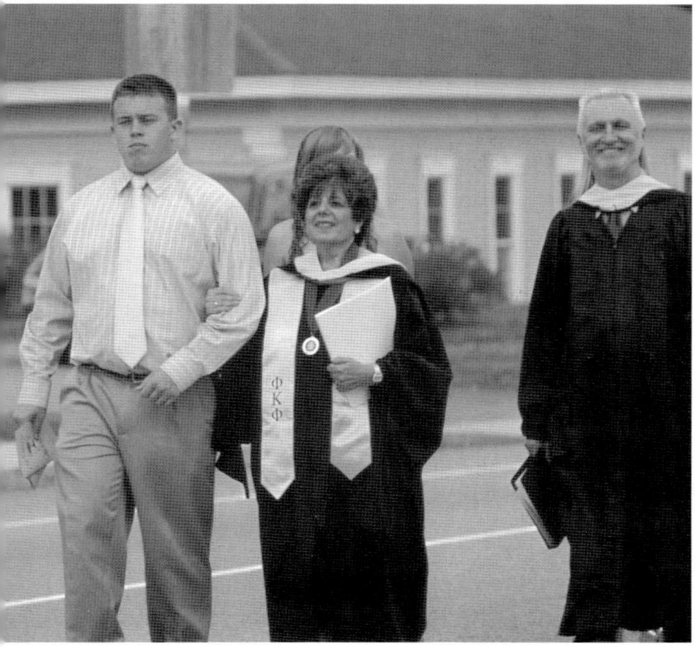

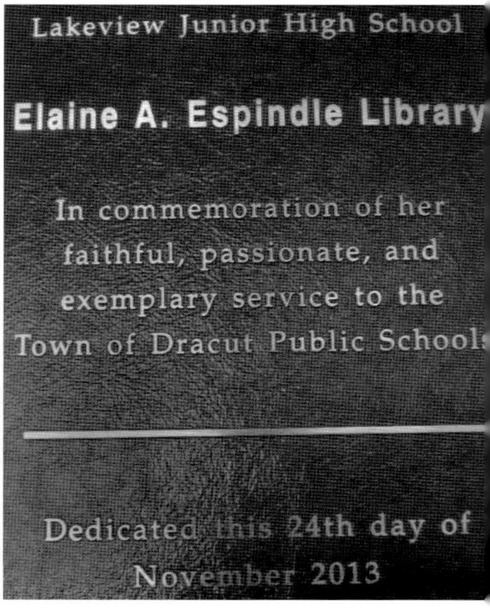

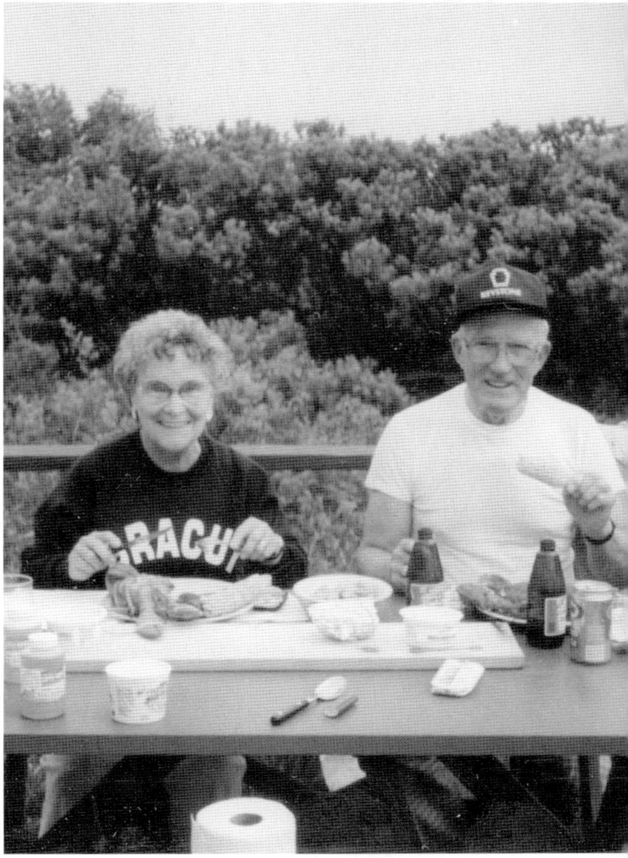

Arthur C. Eldridge

Though often referred to as simply "Central Office," the building that houses the school district's administration department is actually the Eldridge Administration Building, named in honor of Arthur C. Eldridge, a World War II veteran who served nine years on the school committee. Eldridge served as the chair of the building committee for the Dracut Junior High School (now the Englesby Elementary). When he retired in 1971, the committee voted to name the building after him, but he never told his family, who discovered the recognition in his personal papers. His family asked then superintendent Espindle and the school committee to honor the vote from 28 years earlier. They did and the dedication took place after Eldridge had passed in 1999. Pictured below are Supt. Elaine Espindle and committee member Tim Woods unveiling the plaque in Eldridge's honor. Eldridge was married to Camilla Travierso for 56 years, and together, they enjoyed summering on Cape Cod, as seen at right. (Both, courtesy Robert P. Eldridge.)

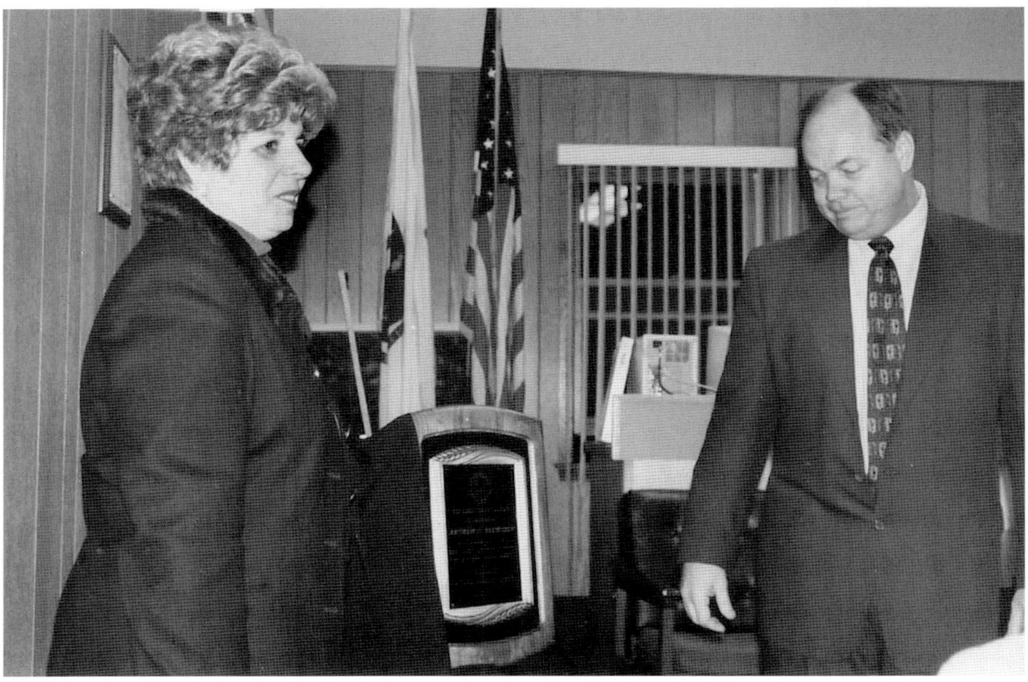

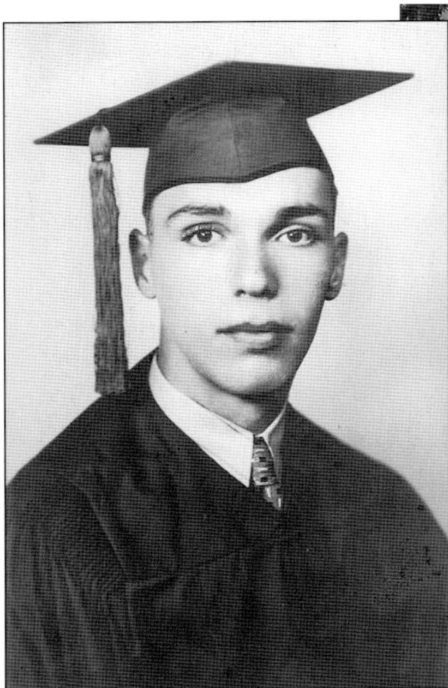

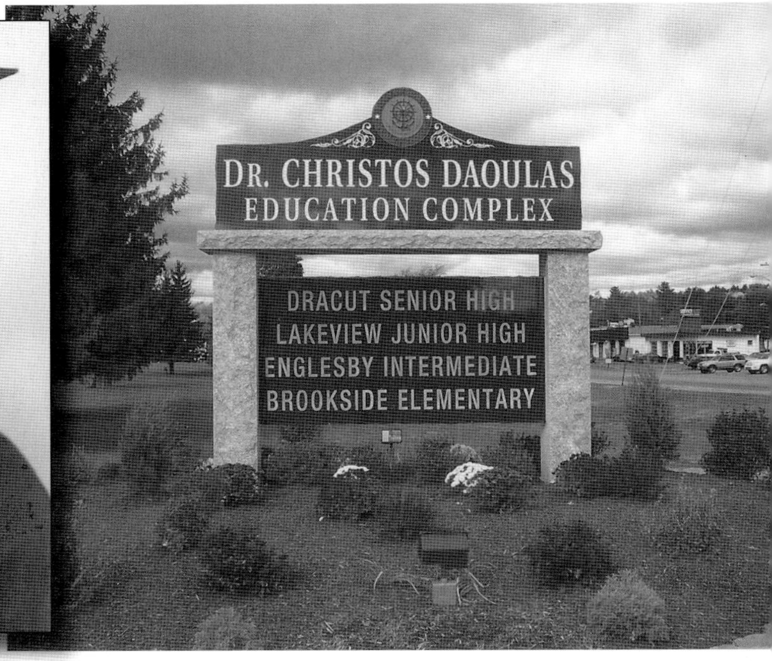

Dr. Christos Daoulas
After graduating from Dracut High School as the class of 1936 valedictorian, Christos Daoulas embarked on a life of service to his country and town. He entered the Army in 1942 and was honorably discharged in 1945. After the war, he attended Boston University on the GI Bill and earned his bachelor's, master's, and doctoral degrees. He began teaching science in 1949, in addition to coaching and serving as athletic director. By 1960, Daoulas had been appointed principal of the high school, and only two years later, he was appointed as superintendent, a position he held for an unmatched 38 years. He also served on numerous community organizations and groups, such as the Greater Lowell Council of the Boy Scouts, the Dracut Scholarship Foundation, and the board of trustees at the Transfiguration church. His brother Arthur proudly describes his late brother as "a model citizen who set the example for thousands of children and young adults." (All, courtesy Arthur Daoulas.)

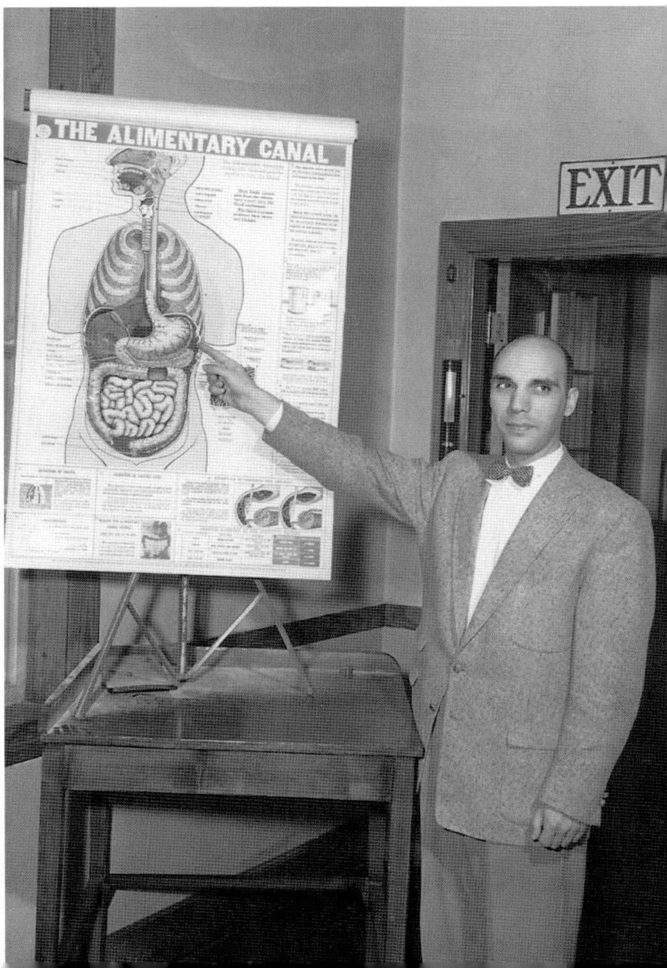

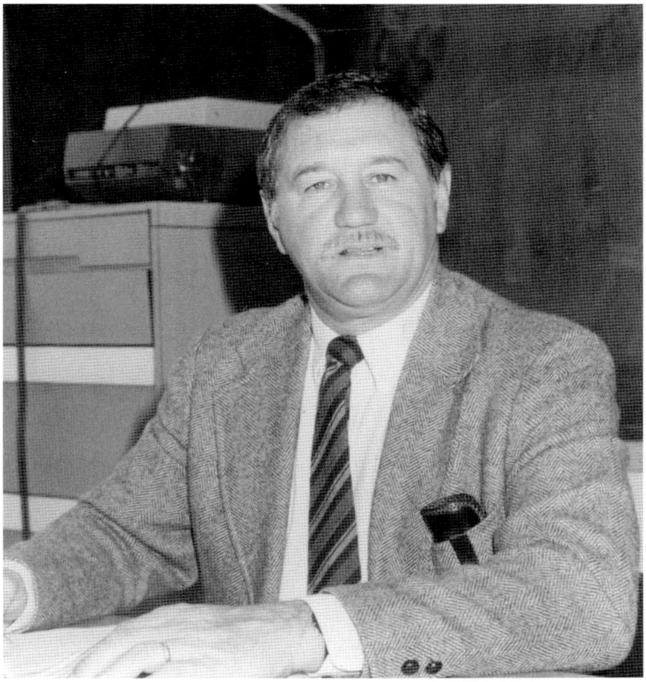

David Stecchi
In addition to teaching at Dracut High School for 35 years, David Stecchi was the assistant football coach, head football coach, and head spring track coach. Though he is best known for his coaching positions, the students who played under him realized that Stecchi was far more than just a long-serving coach. As Chris Tierney wrote in the *Lowell Sun* about his former coach, "He was truly a mentor and friend." A lieutenant in the US Marine Corps in the 1950s, Stecchi married Janice M. Horman, and they had four sons. David Stecchi passed away at age 76 on January 7, 2012. (Both, courtesy Janice Stecchi.)

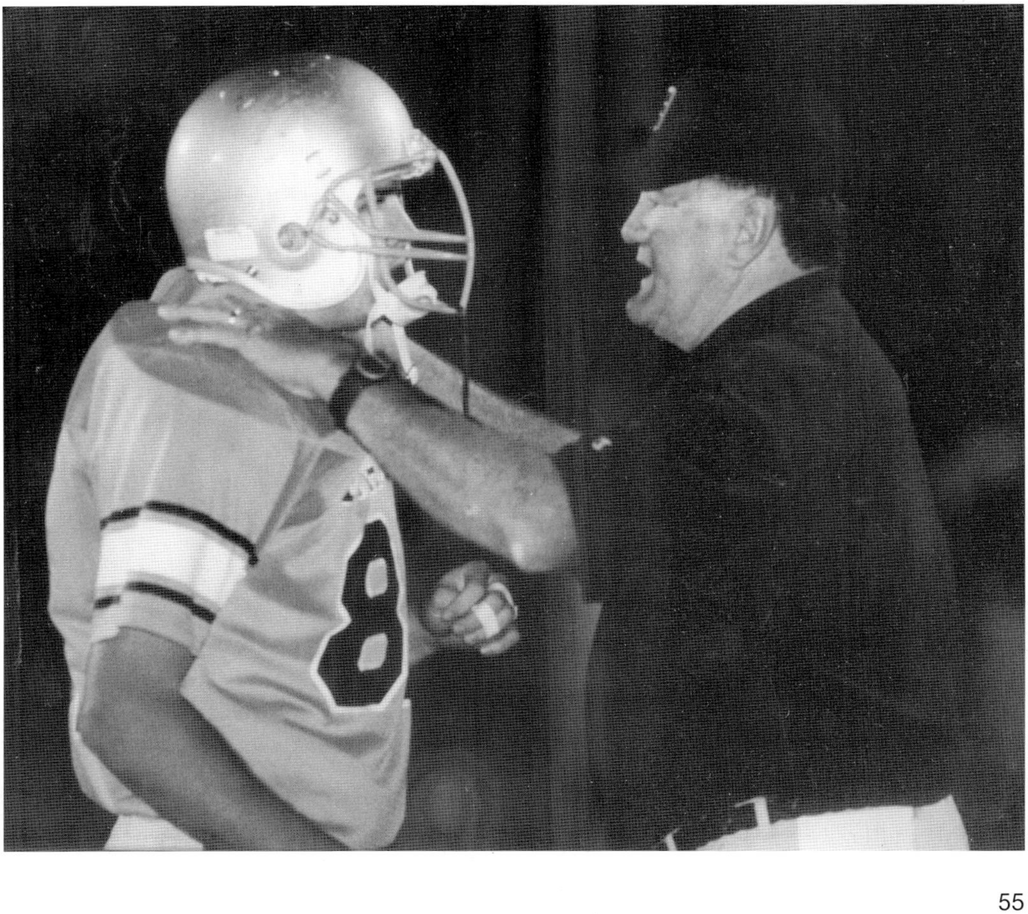

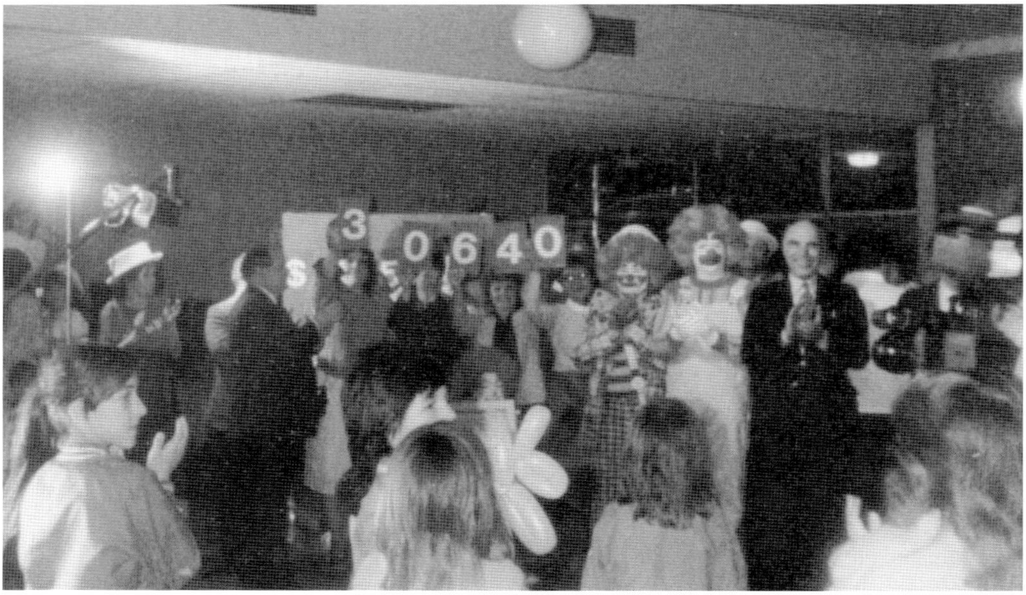

Dracut Scholarship Foundation
Since 1957, when the first scholarships were awarded by the Dracut Scholarship Foundation (DSF), the foundation has awarded over $2 million to Dracut High School seniors heading off to college. The DSF was founded as a partnership between the schools and local businesses to help college-bound graduates. The board consists of 29 volunteers, and only two people have been voted the title emeritus board director: Harvey Gagnon and Bruce Hutchins. Gagnon served on the board for 40 years, and Hutchins was principal of Dracut High school for 30 years and established the annual DSF Telethon. The telethon airs on local access television each March and features local talent, school groups, and business sponsors. Shown above is the 1985 telethon in the high school lobby. Below is a more recent telethon with performers in the high school's auditorium. (Above courtesy Dracut Historical Society; below courtesy Lenny Proposki.)

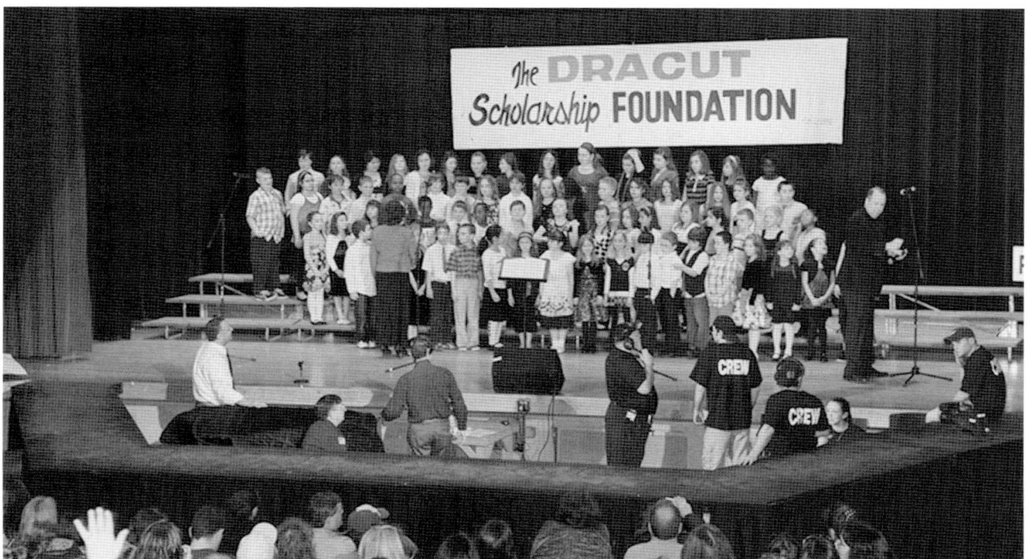

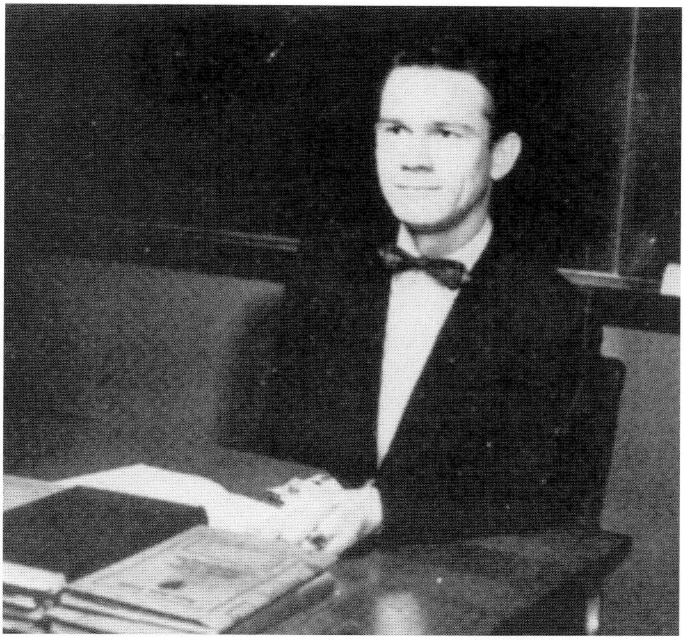

Francis K. Neilon
The Francis K. Neilon Chapter of the National Honor Society was named after the long-serving English teacher of Dracut High School. Active in school activities, he helped to incorporate the Dracut Scholarship Foundation in 1959. Neilon graduated from St. Anslem's and Fitchburg State College, and on August 26, 1967, he married Madeline McLaughlin. When Neilon passed away unexpectedly, the students at Dracut High School wanted to honor their beloved teacher by naming their honor society chapter after him. (Courtesy Dracut Historical Society.)

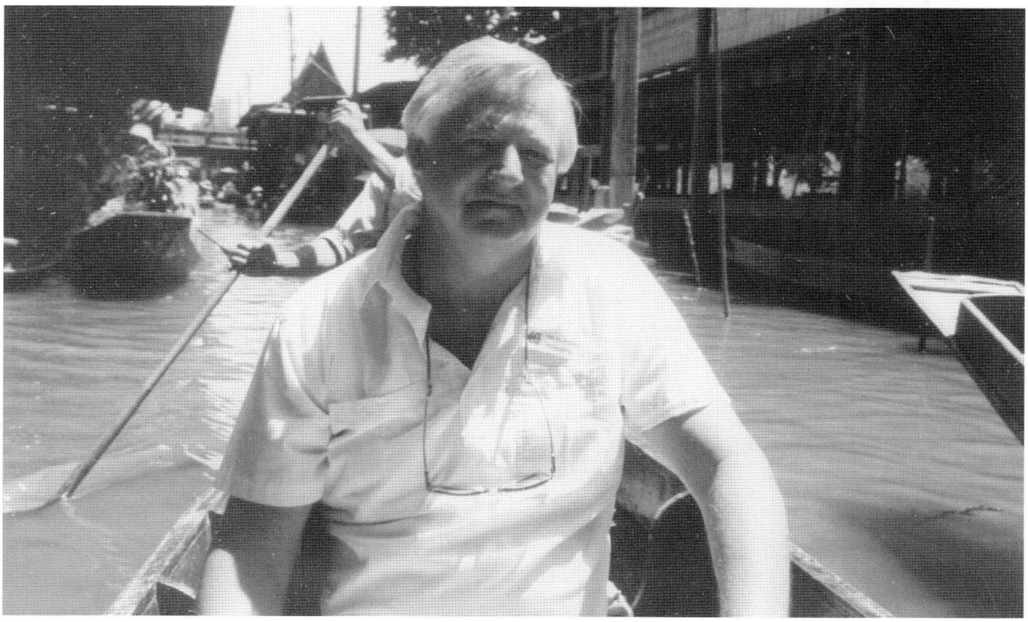

Leonard K. Smith
As Dracut's first director of special education, Leonard K. Smith worked tirelessly to successfully implement Chapter 766, which is the Massachusetts act that guarantees the creation and implementation of a custom educational plan for students with special needs. In 1997, Smith received the Community Guardian Angel Award from Community Teamwork, Inc., for his work with special needs students as well as his partnership with CTI to establish the Foster Grandparent Program in the Dracut Public Schools, which was the first program of its type in the nation. The newly renovated Dracut High School includes an area with adaptive equipment that has been named the Leonard K. Smith Adaptive Gymnasium in his memory. (Courtesy Ann Smith.)

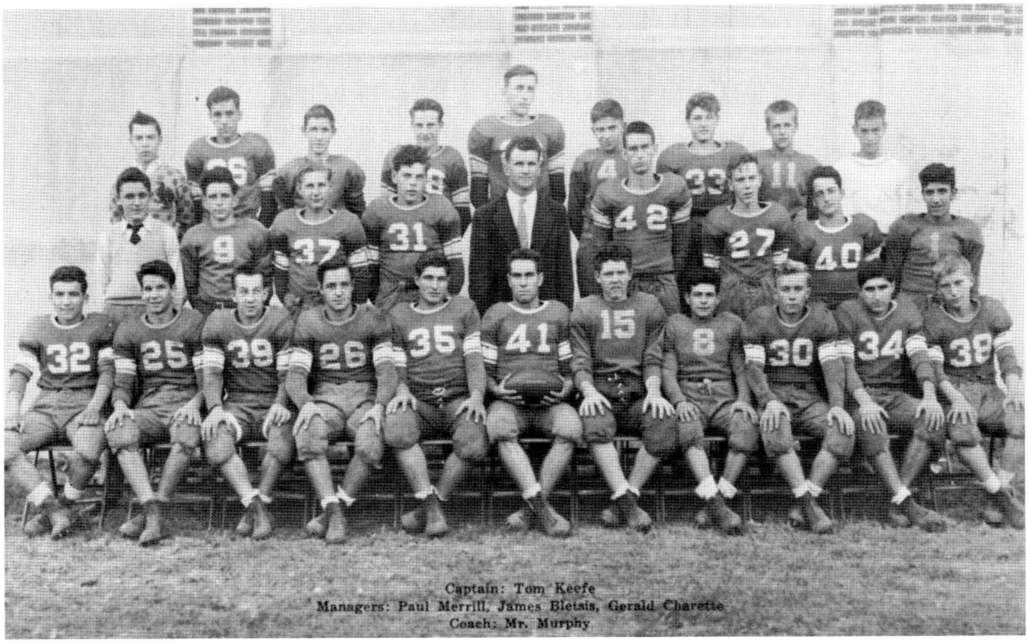

Dracut High School Football Team, 1946
Pictured above is the Dracut High School football team in 1946. Ed Murphy was appointed head football coach in 1946. When Dracut High School moved to its present location on Lakeview Avenue, the team began practicing and playing on the field there. Prior to 1958, the team used the Pleasant Street (now Monahan) Park. In 1960, the school committee transferred the Pleasant Street field back to the town for local activities and events. (Courtesy Dracut Historical Society.)

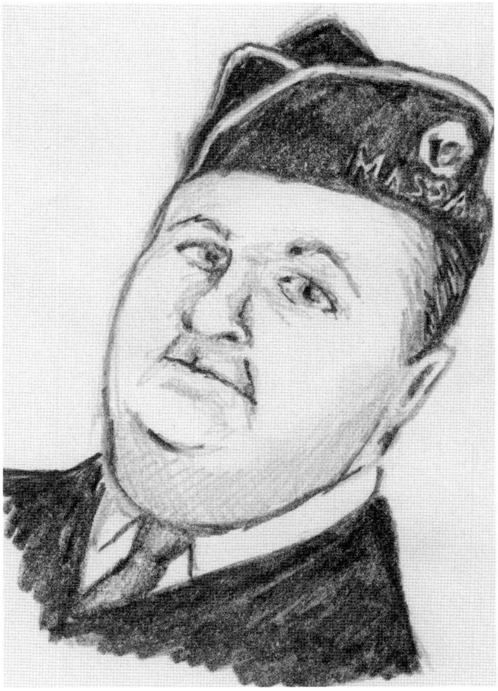

Joseph A. Campbell Jr.
A popular and respected member of the Kenwood neighborhood, Joseph A. Campbell Jr. was a World War II veteran, member of St. Francis Parish, and Dracut police officer. He died unexpectedly on April 27, 1971, and that October, the Kenwood School was renamed the Joseph A. Campbell Jr. School in his honor, the ceremony for which drew 300 people. In her remarks about Campbell, school committee chair Bernard Bettencourt said, "Their [the students] school experience teaches them it is very important to care about others and that people should be ready to make big personal sacrifices in order that their community may be a better place in which to live. These are the particular qualities which will always be remembered fondly about the late Joseph A. Campbell Jr." When the Kenwood School was rebuilt in 1973, the name was transferred to the new building. (Courtesy Tyler Bettencourt.)

CHAPTER THREE

Artistic Endeavors

Musicians, Actors, Authors, and Entertainers

Though probably best known for its farms and its mills along Beaver Brook, Dracut has also been a place where creativity and a passion for the arts have flourished. Dracut was fortunate to have Lakeview Park, one of the most popular lakeside resort areas on the shores of Lake Mascuppic. Dracut artist Betty Baroni donated a beautiful painting of the Lakeview Carousel to the Dracut Historical Society, and Dracut photographer Lenny Proposki has been to Forest Park, New York, to photograph it numerous times. Dracut has also been the hometown of actors who have found fame in Hollywood, including Wendell Corey and, more recently, Scott Grimes. Even successful authors have hailed from Dracut, in some cases using their hometown as inspiration.

The Dracut Public Schools have one of the best fine and performing arts departments in the Merrimack Valley. The names Maurice Pepin and Leon Grande bring back many fond memories to the students who participated their classes and drama productions. More important, perhaps, is the love of the arts that they instilled in their students, who have gone on to become musicians, actors and actresses, and teachers themselves.

For the past 30 years, students and local residents have volunteered to showcase their talent and creativity on Dracut Access Television during the annual telethon. Choral groups, bands, and singers have all appeared on the annual telethon to share their talent while helping to support the Dracut Scholarship Foundation. March would not be the same in Dracut if James Buxton were not the opening act when the telethon aired. For a small town, Dracut has had a history rich in culture and arts.

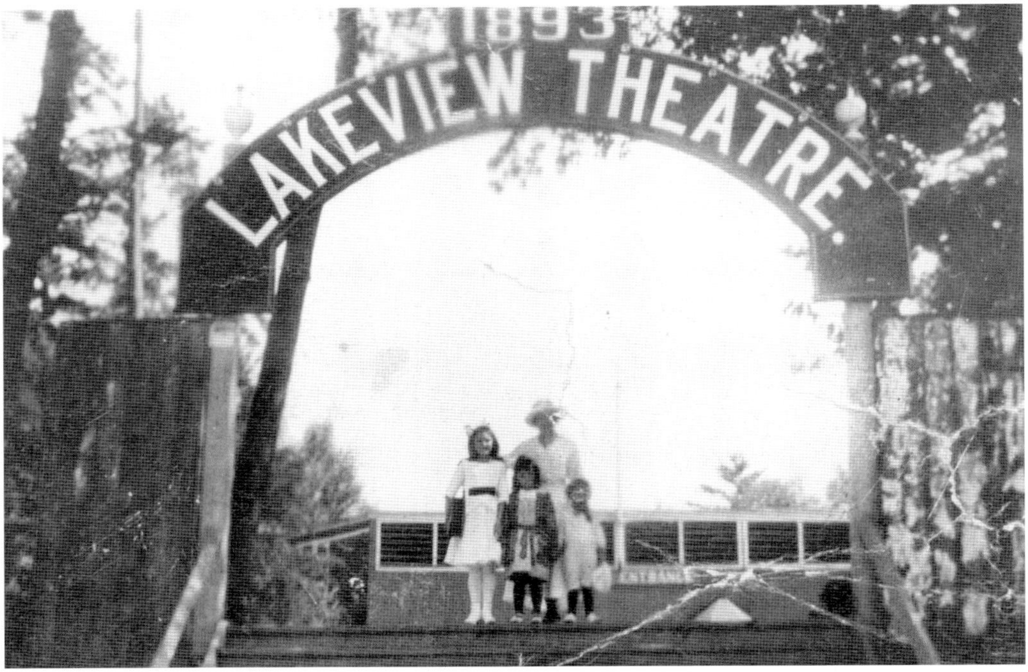

Lakeview Theatre

One of the attractions at Lakeview was a summer theater. The Lakeview Theatre opened on July 1, 1893, and closed on August 24, 1912. Beginning in 1918, the building was used for Sunday mass so visitors need not travel to St. Mary's in Collinsville. In 1931, it was decided that a church should be built near the lake, abating the need for the old theater, which was razed in 1938. Initially, the new church was called St. Mary's by the Lake; today, it is known as St. Mary Magdalen. Pictured above in July 1919 is Cecilia Gamache and her three children: (from left to right) Loretta, Edna, and Arthur. (Both, courtesy Dracut Historical Society.)

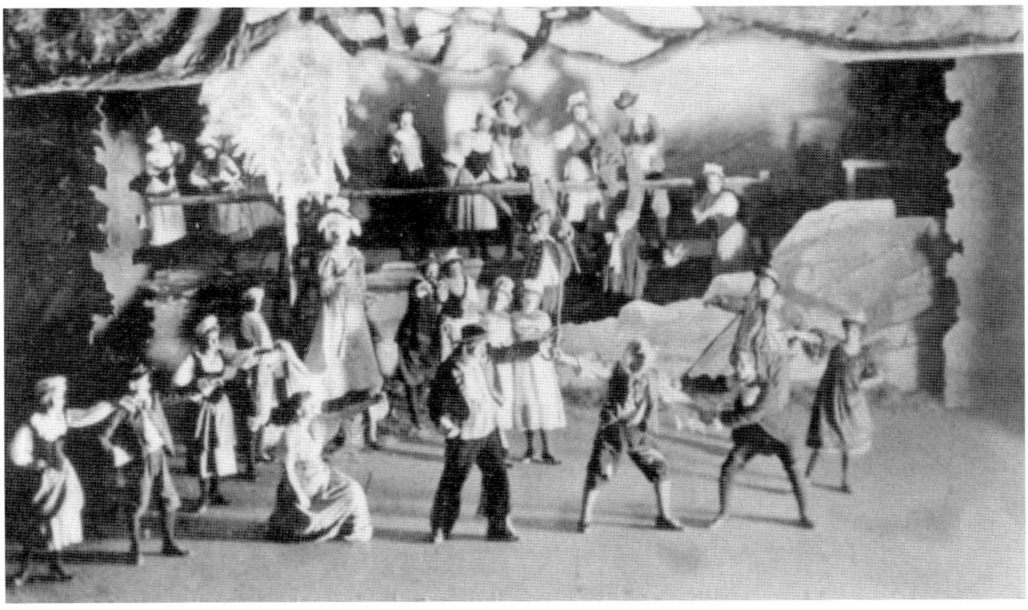

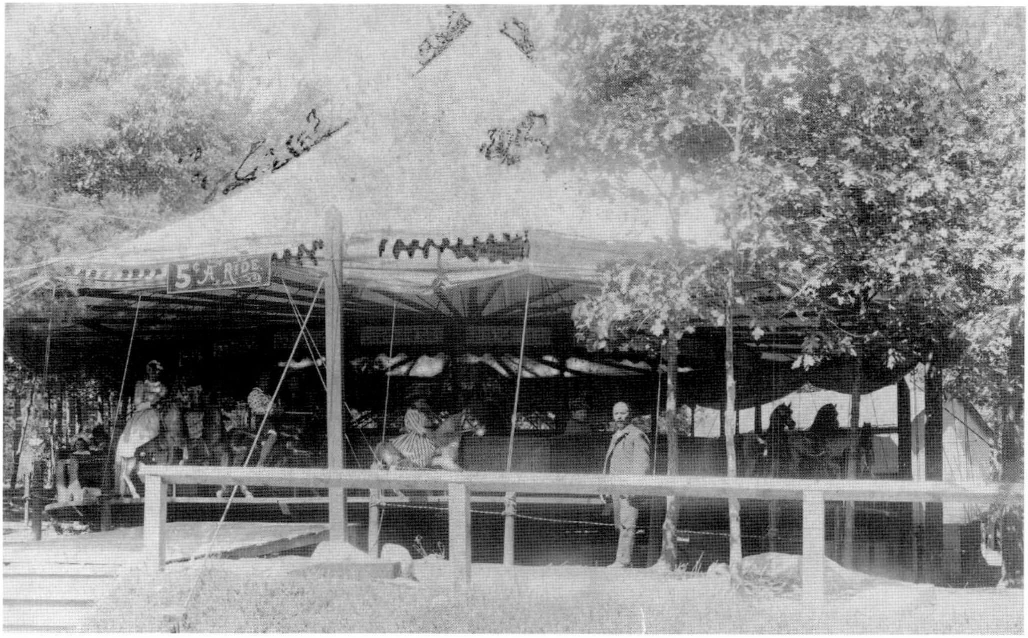

Lakeview Carousel
While not working on their farms or in the mills, Dracut residents had the opportunity to spend their weekends and other free time at Lakeview Park on Lake Mascuppic. The Lowell and Suburban Trolley Company established the recreational spot in 1889. One of the main attractions at Lakeview was the merry-go-round, pictured above in 1889. Operated by Louis Bopp, the "Flying Horses" were brought in from Germany for the park's opening. (Both, courtesy Dracut Historical Society.)

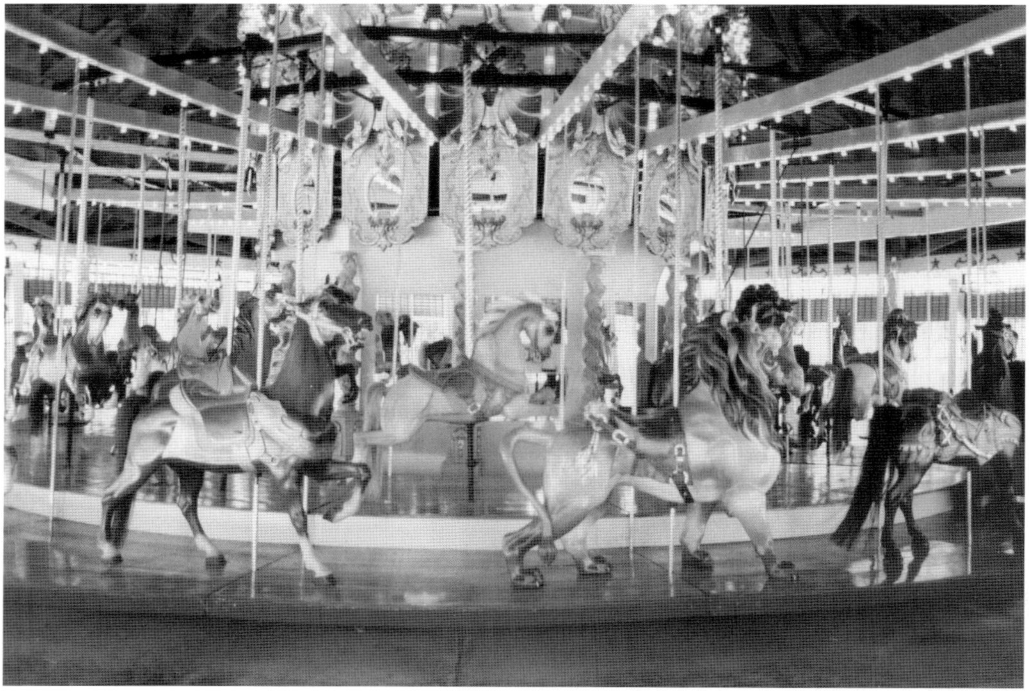

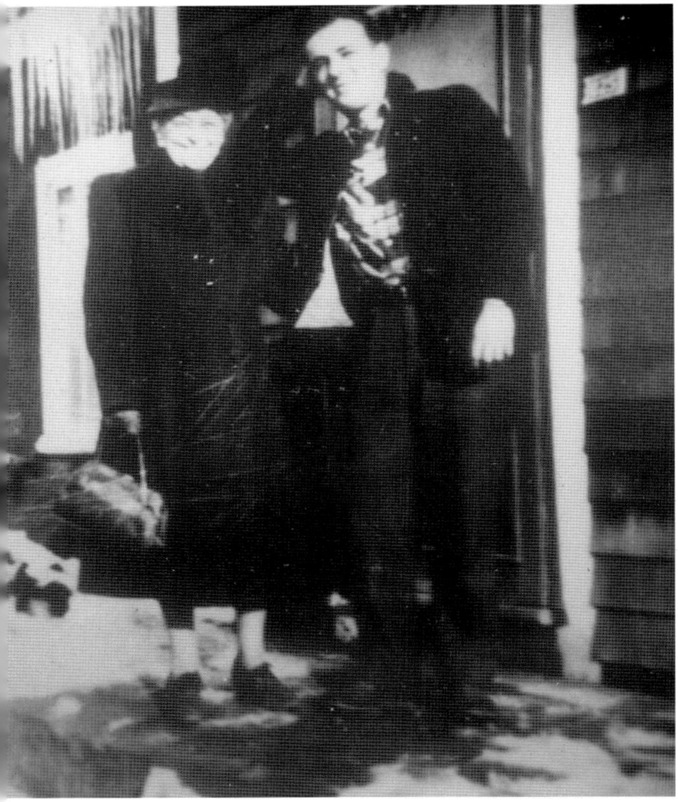

Alice "Belle" Varnum-Isherwood

Alice "Belle" Varnum-Isherwood, who lived on the Varnum estate along Methuen Street (Route 110) in the Kenwood district, created a recreational area known as Belle Grove along the Merrimack River (between Jackson Street and Mount Pleasant Avenue). In addition to the cabins, campgrounds, and picnic areas, the site also had an inn, making it a popular destination between World War I and World War II. The inn had to be razed after a devastating fire in 1934, which fire chief Ernest Gunther investigated and determined had begun in the kitchen. Constructed before the boulevard was built along the river, the inn was only about 40 years old at the time of the fire. After the 1935 flood ruined Belle Grove, it did not reopen. (Left, courtesy Dracut Historical Society; below, courtesy the Paul Dumont family.)

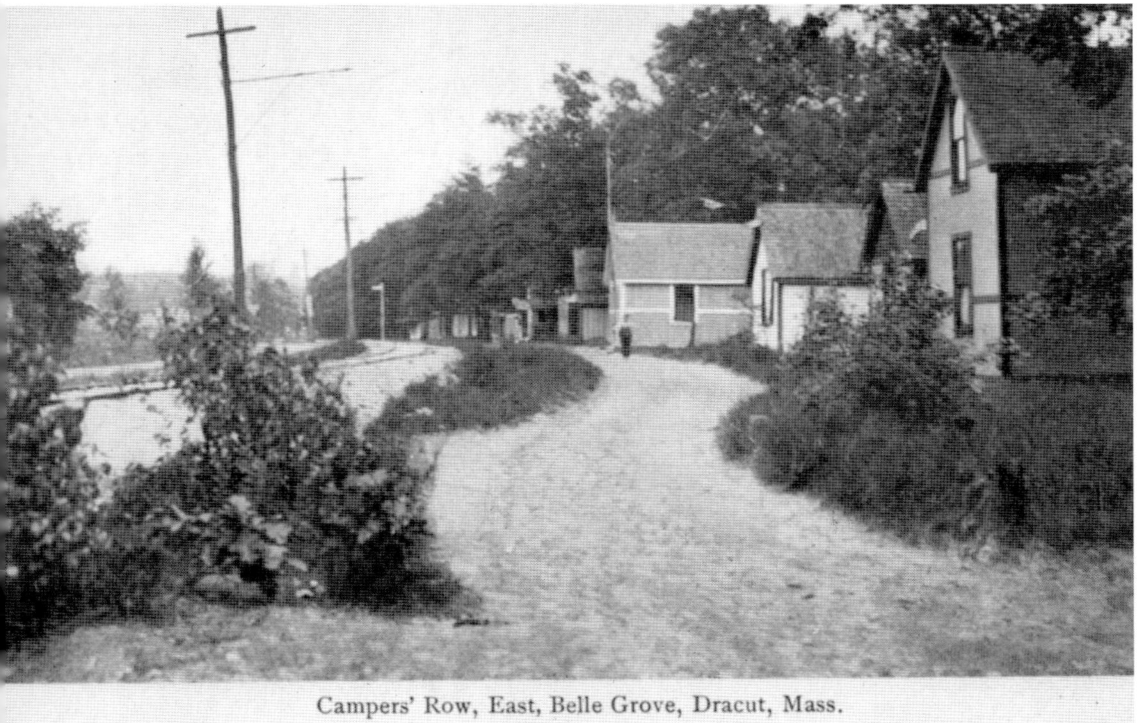

Campers' Row, East, Belle Grove, Dracut, Mass.

Wendell Corey

Dracut was the birthplace of Wendell Corey, who went on to star in numerous Hollywood movies. He is best known for his role in Alfred Hitchcock's 1954 film *Rear Window*, in which he played police lieutenant Thomas Doyle. Corey is pictured here at the 1960 Academy Awards with wife Alice Wiley, whom he married in 1939. Corey was born on March 20, 1914, and died on November 8, 1968, in Woodland Hills, California. (Courtesy Academy of Motion Pictures Arts and Sciences.)

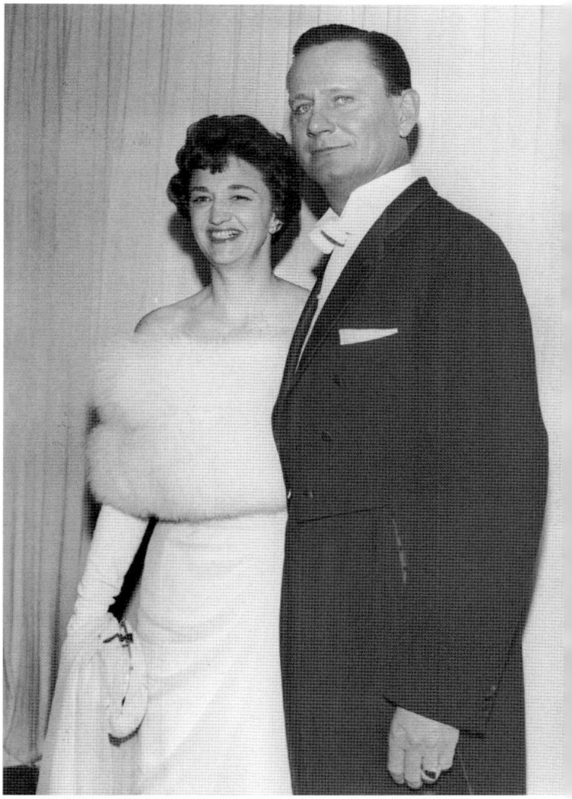

Andrea Grande

Andrea Grande taught as a music instructor in the Dracut Public Schools for over 30 years. Teaching in the elementary schools, she helped to instill a love of music in Dracut's schoolchildren at a young age. Andrea and her husband, Leon, have four children: Laura, Gina, Kate, and Christopher. According to the *Lowell Sun*, "Music in the Grande household came as naturally as breathing." The town owes much to Andrea Grande for sharing her passion for music with the town's students—future musicians and singers. (Courtesy Leon and Andrea Grande.)

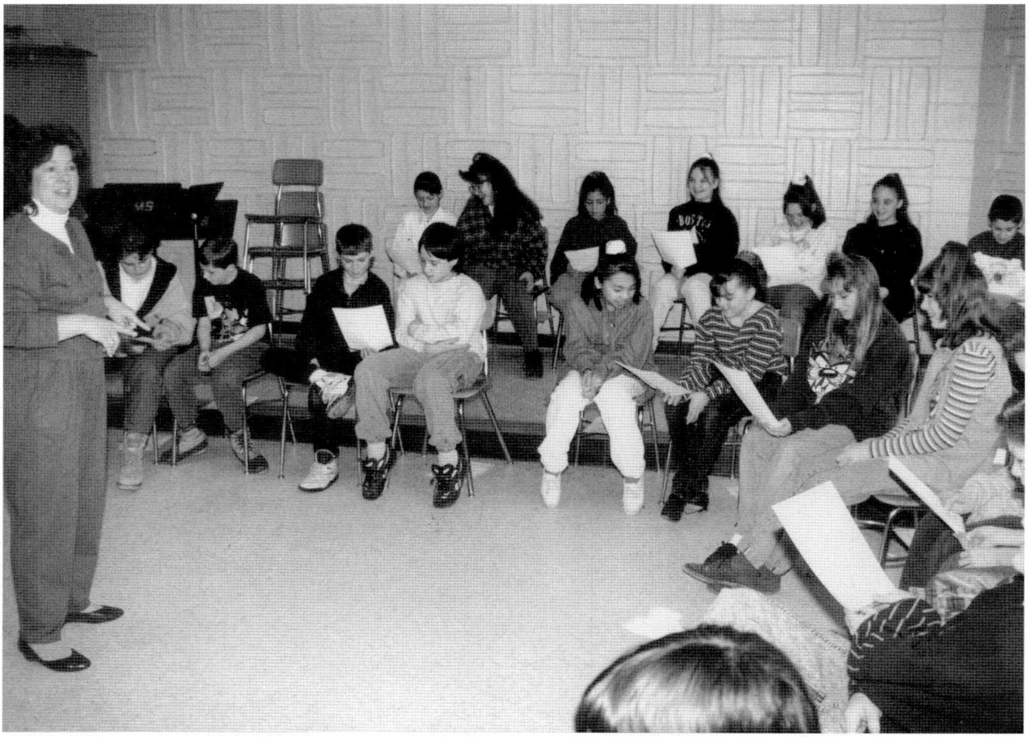

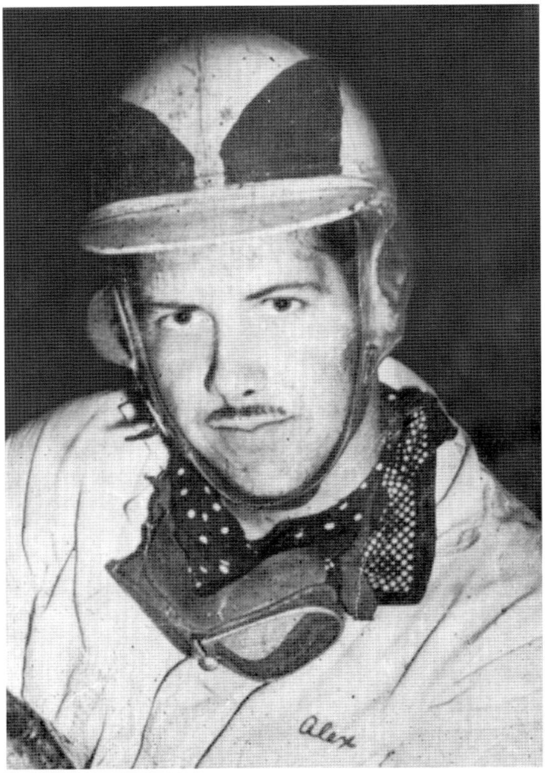

Alex Benoit
Born on May 24, 1923, Alexander Leon Benoit Sr. lived at 4 Broadway Road, where CVS is located today. He married Yvette Beaulieu, and they had four children. Benoit built and operated the Dracut Speedway, which was located on the corner of Broadway Road and Loon Hill Road. A quarter mile long, it was a popular spot until a tragic accident killed a spectator in the stands on June 9, 1955. Besides racing, the venue was used for other events like this visit from Ken Maynard, a rodeo performer and actor who appeared in more than 90 films. The Benoit family moved to Maine, and Alex Benoit passed away on January 17, 1983, after battling lung cancer. (Left, courtesy Lorraine Benoit Woolridge; below, courtesy Dracut Historical Society.)

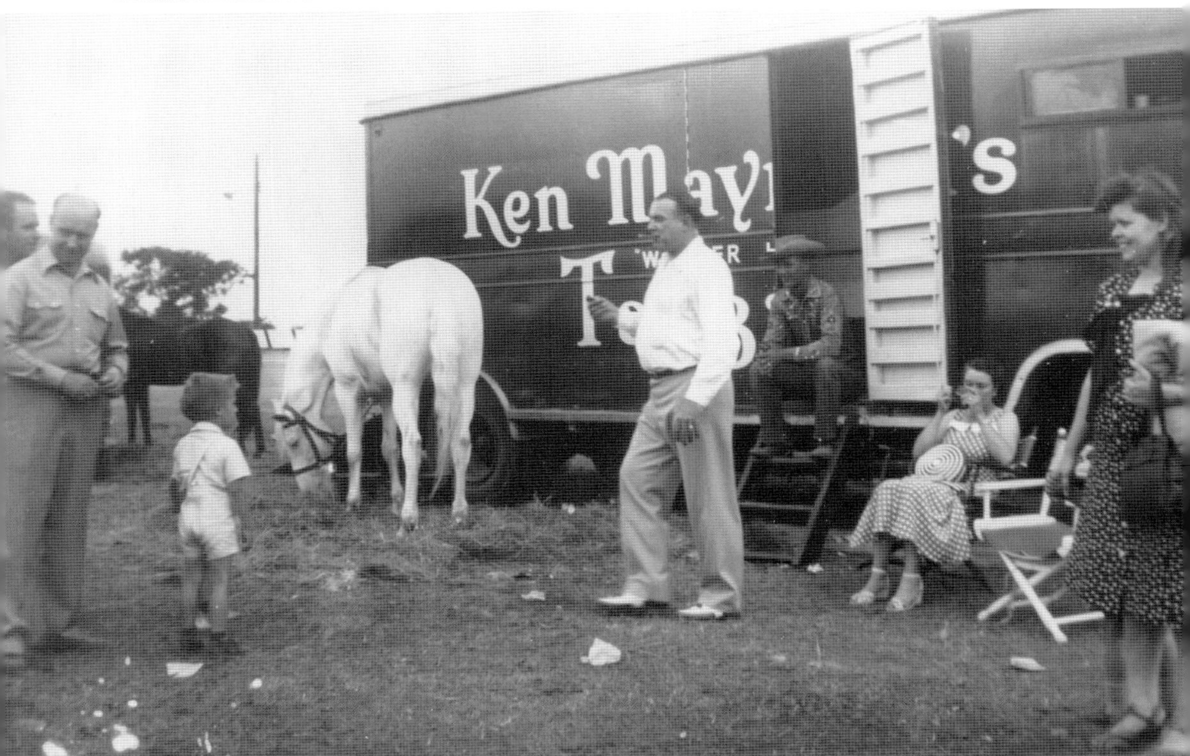

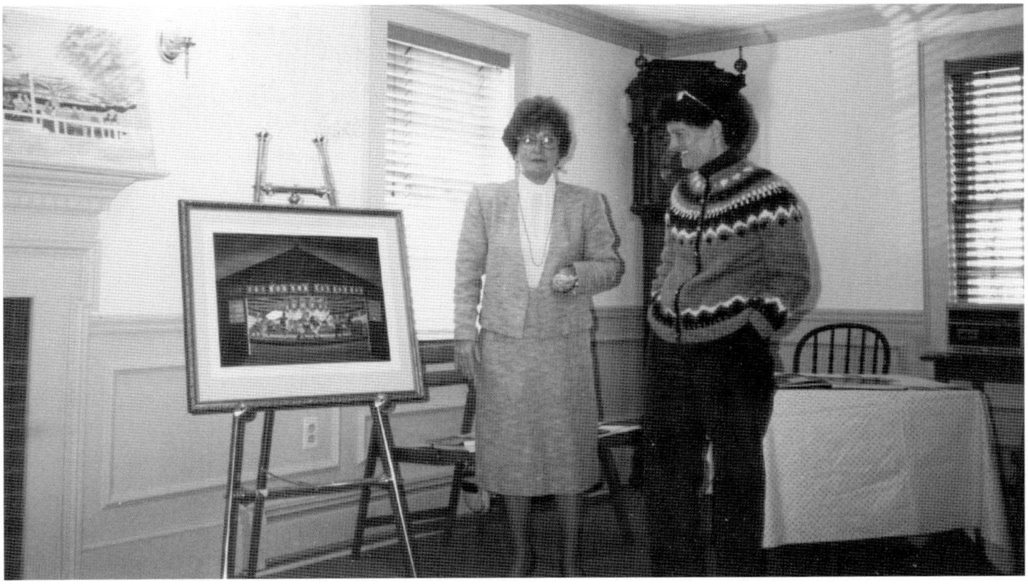

Betty Baroni

In the 1980s, interest in the history of the Lakeview Carousel sparked the search for Lakeview memorabilia. Dracut artist Betty Baroni was asked to paint a rendition of the Lakeview Carousel. Her research was the impetus for antique dealer James Keefe to ask his clients if they had, or knew of, any Lakeview memorabilia. When the eight original stained-glass windows were discovered, Baroni purchased two of them from Keefe. The find of the windows also helped Baroni with her painting of the carousel. Relying on memory as to what colors to use, she was pleasantly surprised when she discovered her colors were historically accurate. Betty Baroni is pictured above at the Dracut Historical Society standing next to her painting of the Lakeview Carousel. (Above, courtesy Dracut Historical Society; below, courtesy Paul Dumont family.)

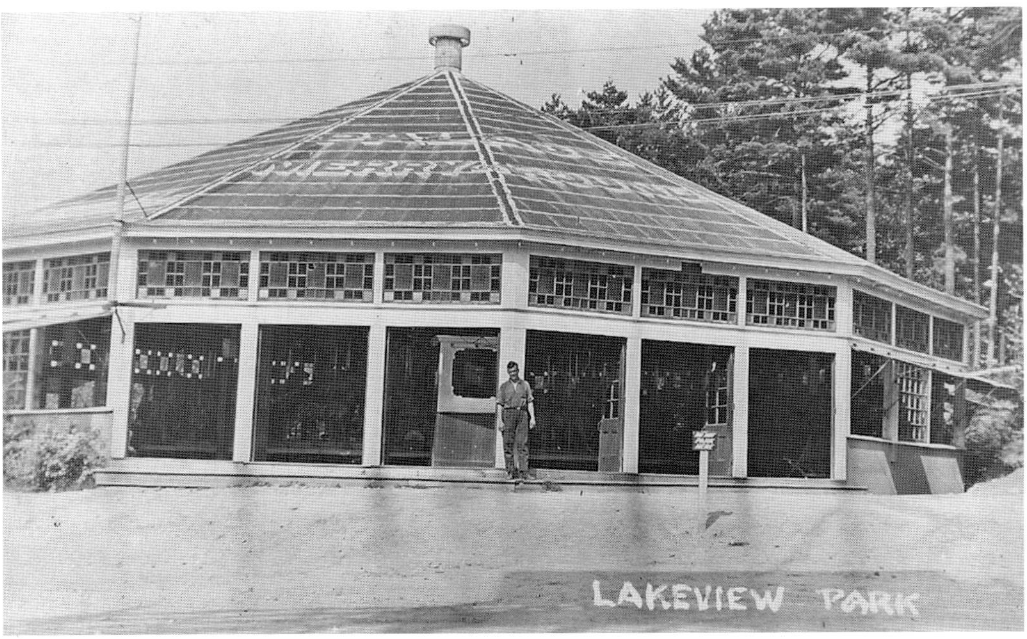

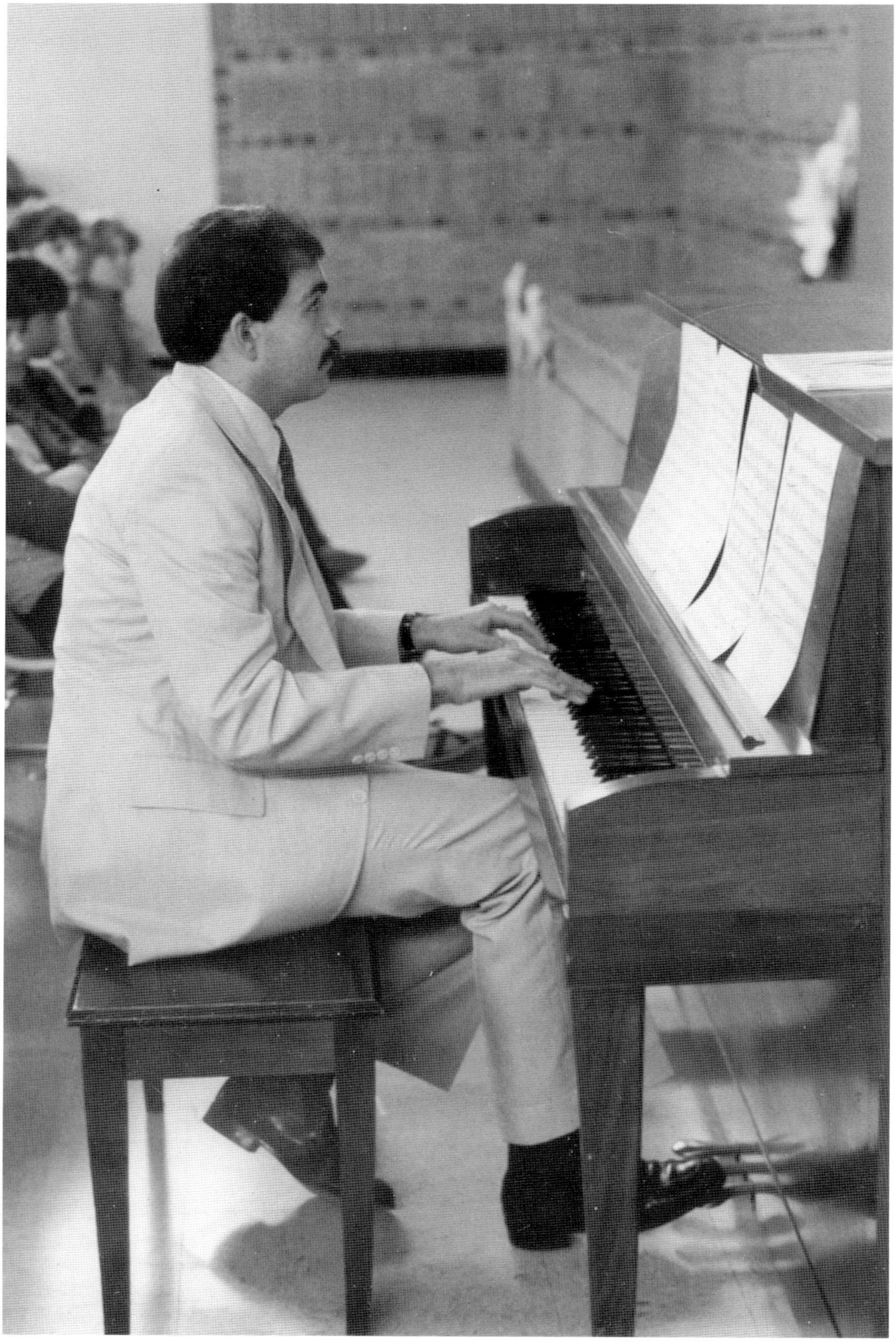

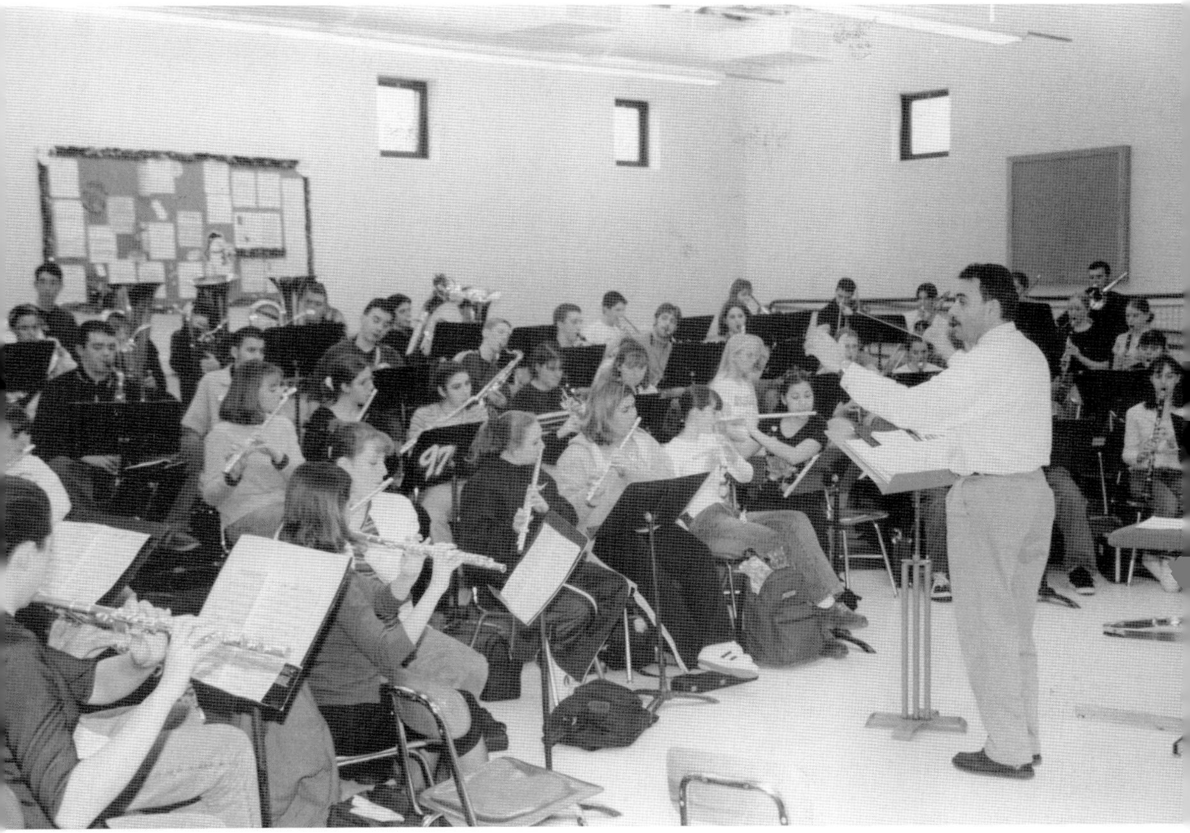

Leon Grande

When Leon Grande retired as the director of fine and performing arts for the Dracut Public Schools in 2011, the *Lowell Sun* called him "The Music Man." A more apt title could not have been given to Grande, who taught in Dracut for 30 years and was known for his spring musical productions from 1996 to 2011. When he became the program director in 1991, the chorus had 16 members, and the band had 50 members. By 2005, the program had grown to an astounding number, with 190 band members and 230 chorus members. In 2007, the high school spring musical *Fiddler on the Roof* won Best Musical at the second-annual Spotlight Awards at the North Shore Music Theatre. In addition coordinating Dracut's Community Chorus, Grande is a cofounder of the Greater Lowell Musical Theatre. Grande is pictured at left with students Kevin Dubuc and Jill Capodanno at the 2008 high school production of *Les Misérables*. (All, courtesy Leon and Andrea Grande.)

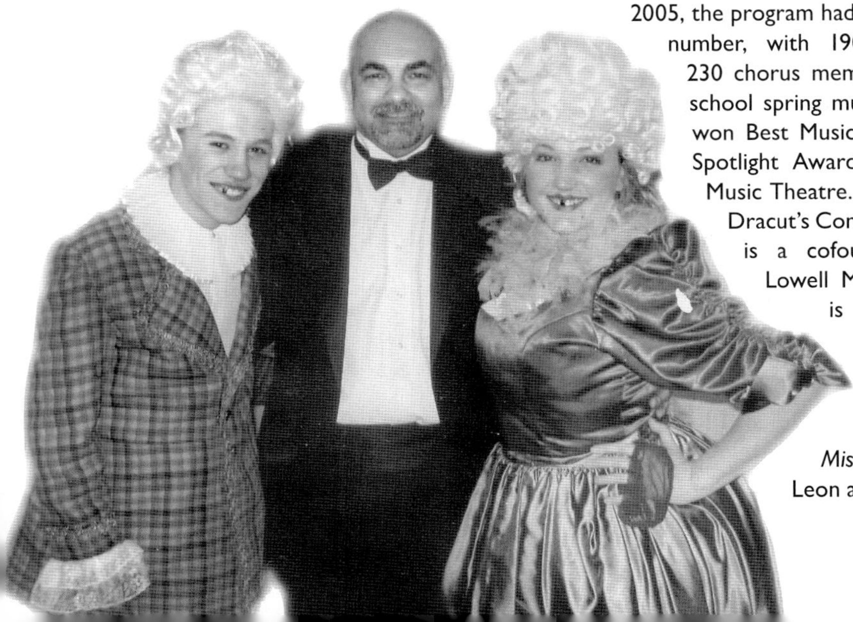

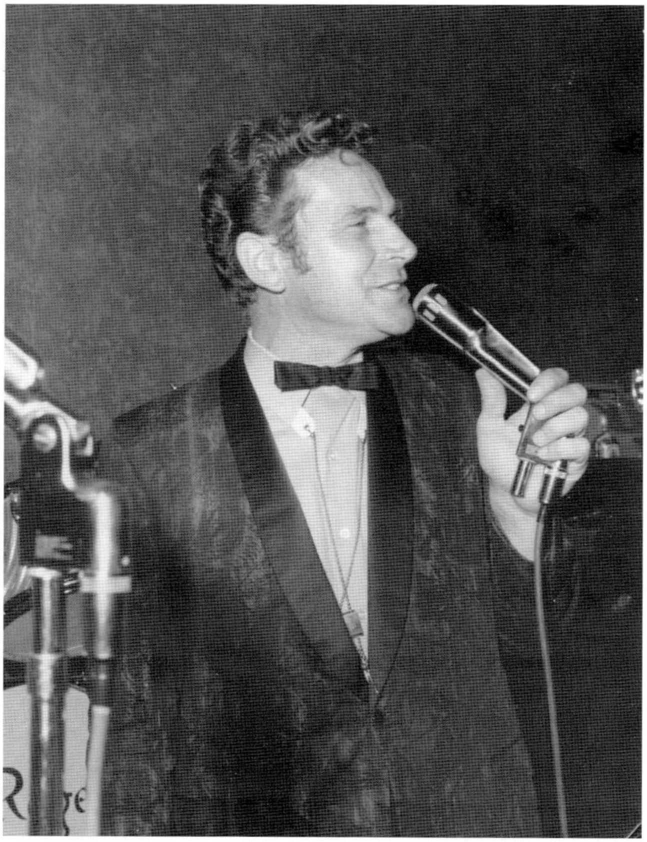

Frank Hickey
Supt. Christos Daoulas hired Frank Hickey in 1962, hoping Hickey would be able to create an instrumental music program in the schools. Daoulas had clearly found the right man for the job, as Hickey began building an instrumental program first for the elementary level and then the junior high school. Born in Dracut, Hickey graduated from Lowell State Teachers' College and served in Korea before joining the faculty in Dracut. He retired in 1994. The Dracut Music Department also has Hickey to thank for encouraging Leon Grande to join the school district. (Courtesy Frank Hickey.)

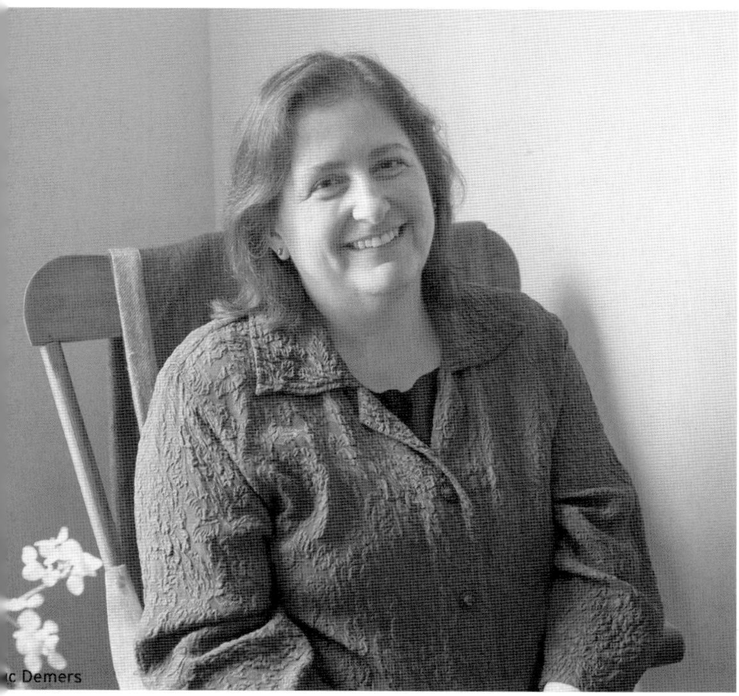

Jane Brox
Born to John and Antoinette Brox on September 4, 1956, Jane Brox found her passion not in farming, as had her father, but in writing. Earning a degree in English literature from Colby College and then a master of fine arts in poetry from Warren Wilson College, Brox has taught writing and poetry extensively at Lesley University, Harvard University, and Bowdoin College. She is a successful author, using her family farm as the basis for several of her works of nonfiction: *Here and Nowhere Else*, *Five Thousand Days Like this One*, and *Clearing Land: Legacies of the American Farm.* Brox currently resides in Maine. (Courtesy Luc Demers.)

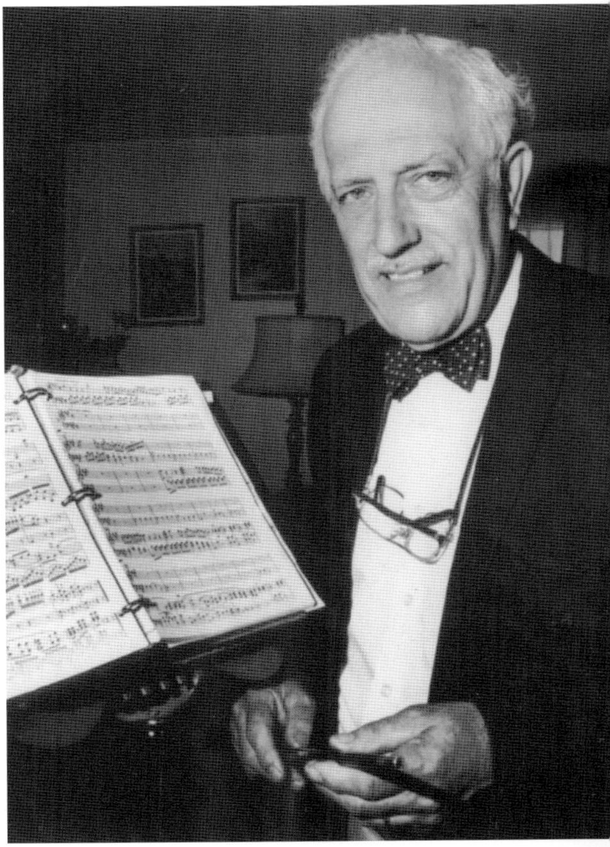

Maurice Pepin

Known as "Mr. Music" or, as the *Lowell Sun* wrote on his retirement, "Dracut's Music Czar," Maurice Pepin began teaching music in 1955 and was involved in all aspects of the music program in the schools. When Supt. Paul Phaneuf hired him, Pepin was charged with creating a music department, as virtually none existed in 1955. Over the years, Pepin started the first band, directed 25 musicals, organized two Elizabethan dinners, established the twirling corps, and taught the first television production classes, in addition to serving as band director, choir director, music department chair, and audiovisual director. Graduating seniors also have Pepin to thank for the bagpipes that lead their processional at graduation. He proposed the idea to principal Bruce Hutchins after seeing them at his son's graduation from Phillips Academy. Below, Pepin directs a 1964 spring concert in the high school courtyard. In 1985, he worked with businesses and community groups to have a gazebo constructed for summer musical performances, which the town has enjoyed ever since. (Both, courtesy Maurice and Diana Pepin.)

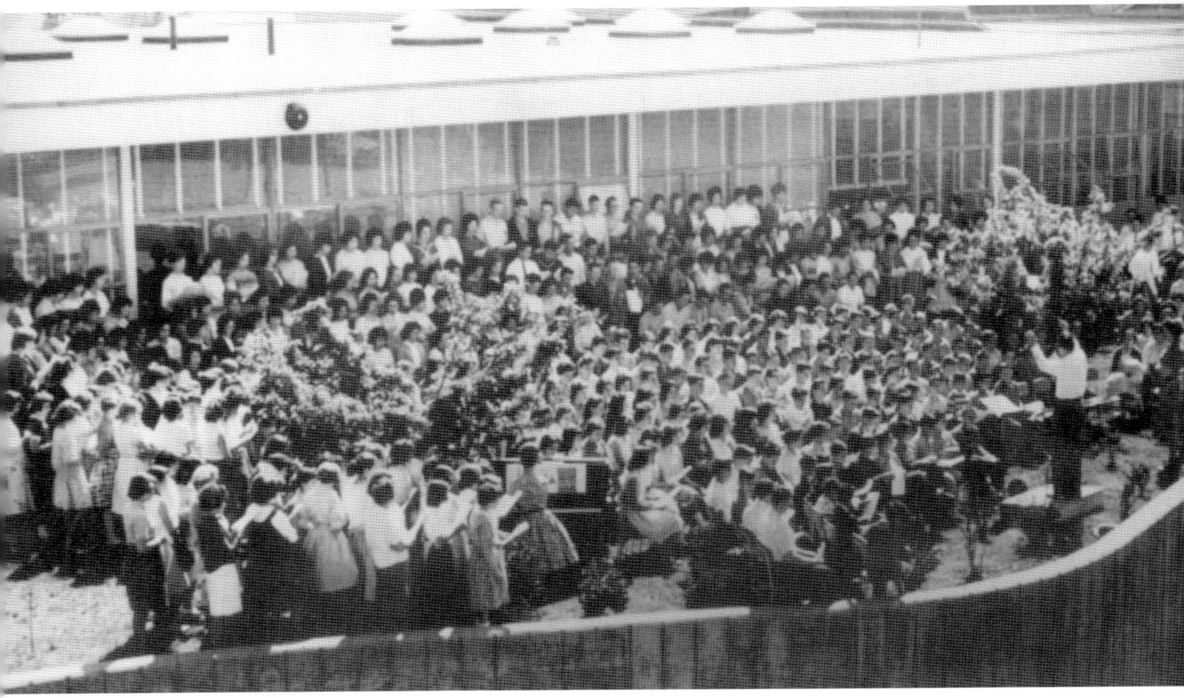

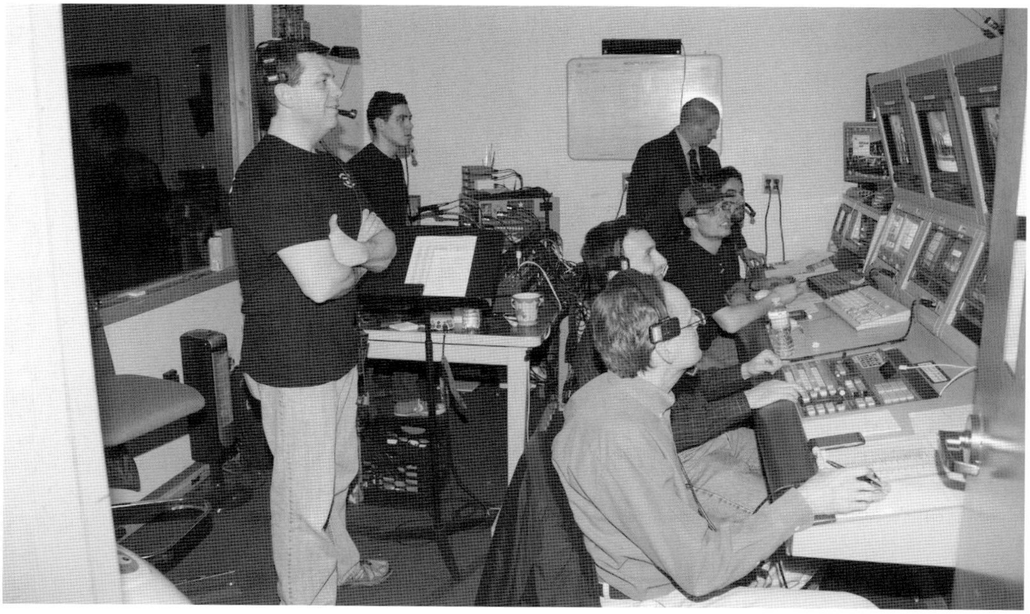

Gary Meuse
The annual Dracut Scholarship Foundation celebrated its 30th telethon in 2013, with the same person producing each of those telethons. Dracut High School alumnus Gary Meuse has been behind the scenes each March, ensuring everything is in place for the telethon, then running the control room each night. When not producing the telethon or doing other work for the Dracut Scholarship Foundation, Meuse is the executive director of Dracut Access Television. Meuse is pictured standing to the left overseeing a telethon production. (Courtesy Lenny Proposki.)

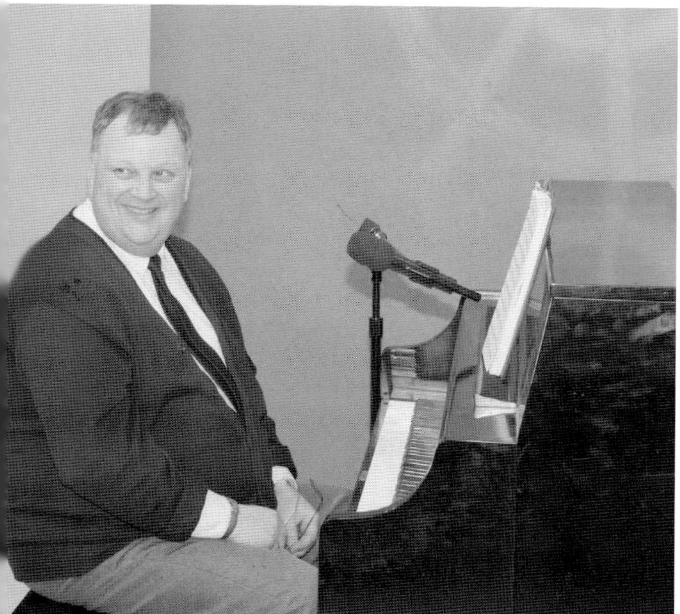

James Buxton
In 1978, James Buxton moved to Dracut with his wife and two children; a third child was born after the family moved to town. The Dracut Rotary invited Buxton to join in 1980. When the telethon was being organized, a Dracut Scholarship Foundation board member spoke to the Rotary, looking for volunteers to perform. Buxton volunteered since he was a member of a trio band and convinced the band's guitarist to perform with him. Together, they performed for the first two years; then Buxton sang solo with his guitar. For the past 10 years, he has performed on the piano. Buxton has been the opening act since the very first telethon. (Courtesy Lenny Proposki.)

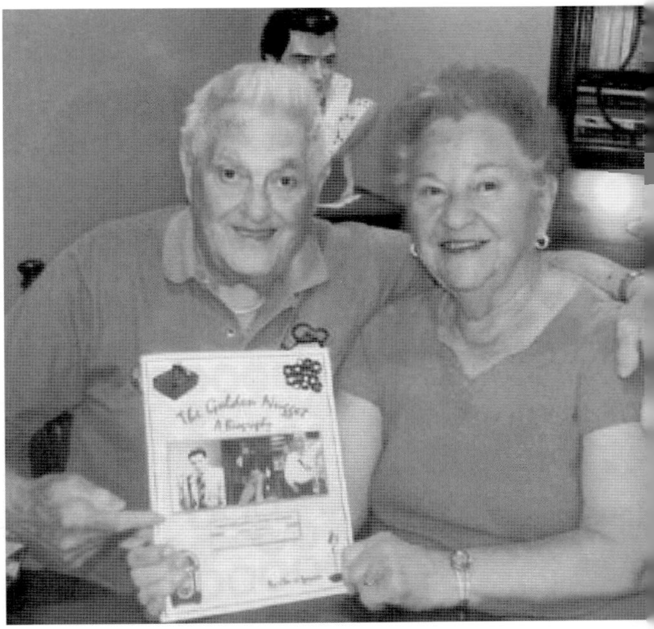

Claire Ignacio
Though a Lowell native, Claire Ignacio has lived in Dracut for over 50 years. During that time, she has authored several books, poems, and magazine articles. In the mid-1970s, she was a columnist for the *Massachusetts Out of Doors* magazine, and her columns were based on her fly-fishing experiences with her ex-husband and his friends. In 2012, she compiled her best columns into a book, along with a tribute to both former *Lowell Sun* sports editor Owen Flynn, who urged Ignacio to write the columns, and the Greater Lowell Fly Fishers Club. Titled *Rusty*, her first book is about a 12-year-old diagnosed with leukemia. Her latest and seventh book, published in 2014, is titled *The Golden Nugget: New England's Living Legend Jimmy "J.C." Camilli.* Claire is pictured here with J.C. Camilli. (Courtesy John Collins.)

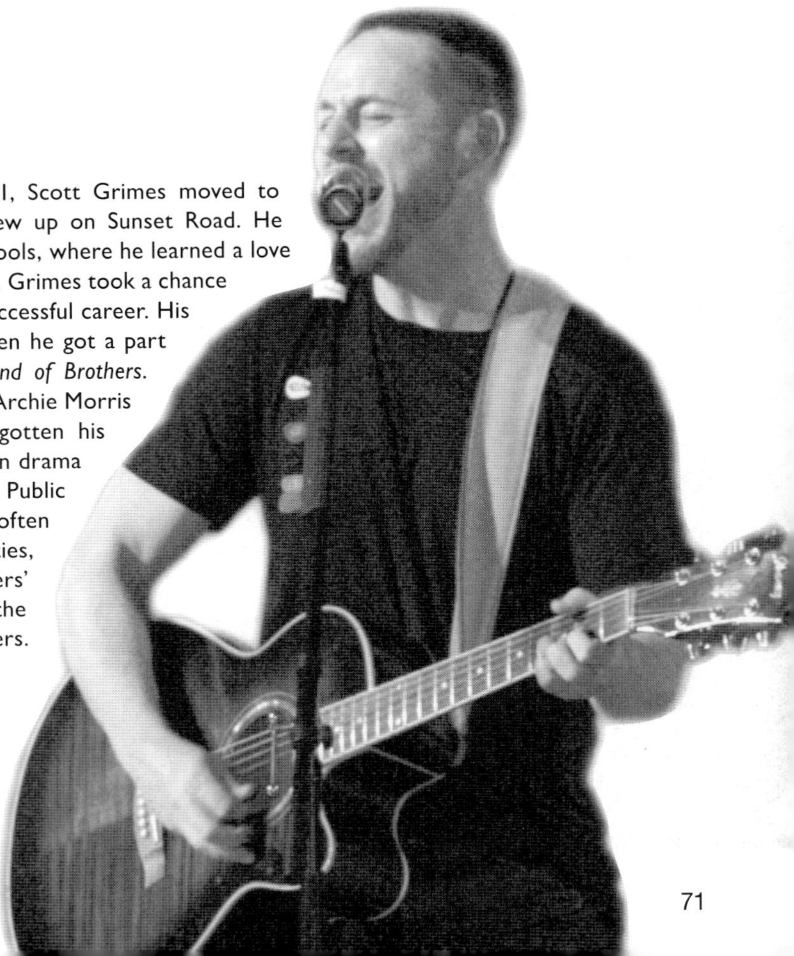

Scott Grimes
Born in Lowell on July 9, 1971, Scott Grimes moved to Dracut with his family and grew up on Sunset Road. He attended the Dracut Public Schools, where he learned a love of the arts. Like Wendell Corey, Grimes took a chance on Hollywood and has had a successful career. His first big break was in 2001 when he got a part in the television miniseries *Band of Brothers*. From 2003 to 2008, he played Archie Morris on *ER*. Grimes has never forgotten his roots or where his beginnings in drama and music started—the Dracut Public Schools. He returns to Dracut often to lend his talents to local charities, such as the Dracut Firefighters' Charity Golf Tournament and the Dracut Performing Arts Boosters. (Courtesy Rhonda Wojtas.)

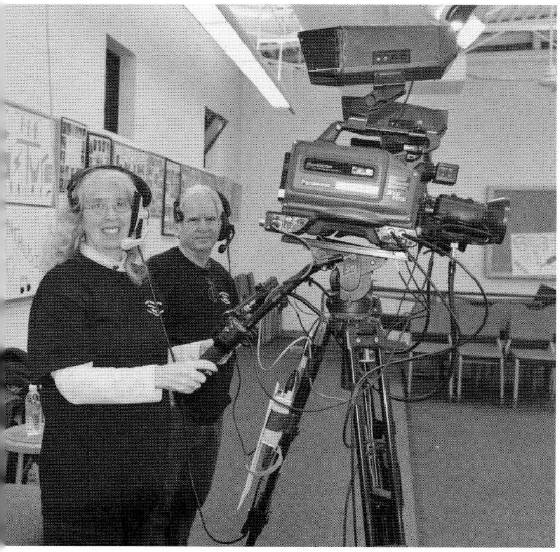

Bob and Gay Corey

Prior to being widely known due to the innumerable events they tape throughout town that are aired on Dracut Access Television, Bob and Gay Corey served in the military. From 1959 to 1963, Bob served in the US Air Force Security Force. This secretive branch of the Air Force was created during the Cold War to intercept and decode radio transmissions. Bob was stationed in Germany, and his code name was "Preakness." A civilian, Gay worked for the Air Force as an AUTOVON (Automatic Voice Network) operator at Okinawa from 1970 to 1972. Today, Bob also serves on the board of directors for DATV as chair of the membership and training committee. The Coreys' dedicated volunteering efforts have brought numerous locally produced shows to the town of Dracut. (Courtesy Lenny Proposki.)

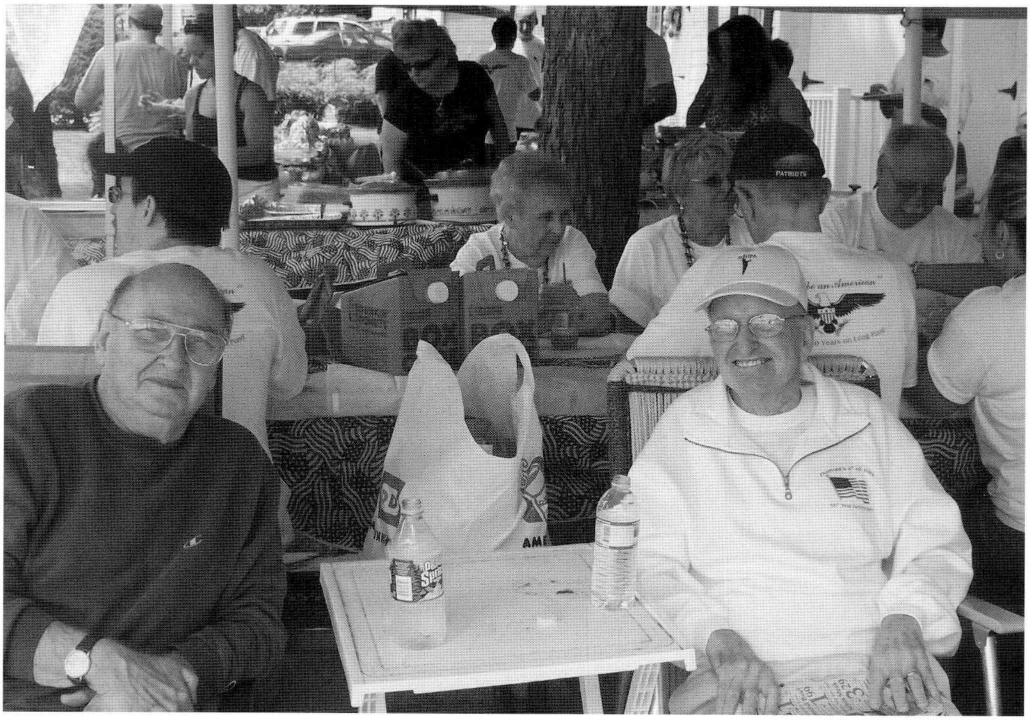

Annual Fourth of July Picnic

The Fourth of July would not be the same without the Dumont family annual picnic. Shown here are brothers Emile (left) and Paul Dumont with hundreds of family and friends along the shores of Long Pond in Pelham, New Hampshire. Paul and Irene Dumont purchased their summer camp in 1957, and the Dumont July Fourth tradition began. William Dumont, Paul and Irene's son, describes the family's Fourth of July celebration as follows: "Food, entertainment, dancing, the mini parade march of children waving flags and the rendition of the national anthem would culminate into a day full of memories for generations of people who would know no other place to be on July 4th." (Courtesy William Dumont.)

CHAPTER FOUR

For Love of Country

Veterans and Those Who Sacrificed All

Dracut has a long history of service and sacrifice to the nation. During the American Revolution, Dracut sent a third of its citizens off into battle. Dracut militia saw fighting at major battles such as Bunker Hill, Lexington and Concord, Monmouth, Saratoga, and White Plains, New York. After the war, these men returned home to Dracut to help build their community.

After fighting at Bunker Hill, Barzillai Lew settled on Totman Road. He was a farmer and cooper. Tony Clark, who fought at Saratoga and Monmouth, settled in what was known as Black North—the area along Route 113 near the Village Inn Restaurant.

When shots at Fort Sumter were fired marking the beginning of the Civil War in April 1861, a Dracut regiment marched down to Washington, DC, answering Lincoln's request for volunteers to protect the nation's capital. One of those men, Edward Coburn, was injured as the regiment marched through Baltimore and the riots in the city.

Most notable among the enlisted was Moses Greeley Parker, a Dracut native, who enlisted as an Army doctor in 1864 after graduating from Harvard Medical School. During the war, he helped supervise the construction of an Army hospital.

There were numerous men, not as famous as Parker, who left their farms and contributed to the war. Ira M. Cross's regiment fought at the Battle of Gettysburg. He was captured by the Confederates in the Battle of the Peach Orchard and was sent to the infamous prisoner-of-war camp Andersonville, where he died.

As people drive through the intersection of Mammoth and Lakeview Avenue, they may not realize that the stone monument in the square is for the three Dracut men who served in the Spanish-American War and enlisted from Dracut—Arthur E. Garland served in Cuba, Eden C. Walker served in the ambulance unit, and George H. Connell served in the infantry. Another Dracut man served during the Spanish-American War but did not enlist in Dracut: Joseph G. Eaton.

The list of Dracut men and women that have sacrificed in service to their country continues on and on, right up until the present day. The Kostoulakos family had six brothers serve the nation: Charles, George, William, Thomas, Stephen, and Arthur.

On July 16, 2014, the Dracut Garden Club dedicated the Air Force Sergeant Daniel Turner Blue Star Memorial By-way marker at the intersection of Hildreth Street and New Boston Road. Turner was killed in Vietnam on August 17, 1969.

Mathew G. Boule was the first Massachusetts casualty in Iraq. Born on December 7, 1980, Boule joined the Army in 2001 and had basic training in Fort Knox, Kentucky. He died on April 2, 2003, when his Black Hawk helicopter in Iraq crashed.

This chapter is just a very small sampling of the people who made themselves legendary locals through their service. The author thanks all servicemen and women for their sacrifices for our nation.

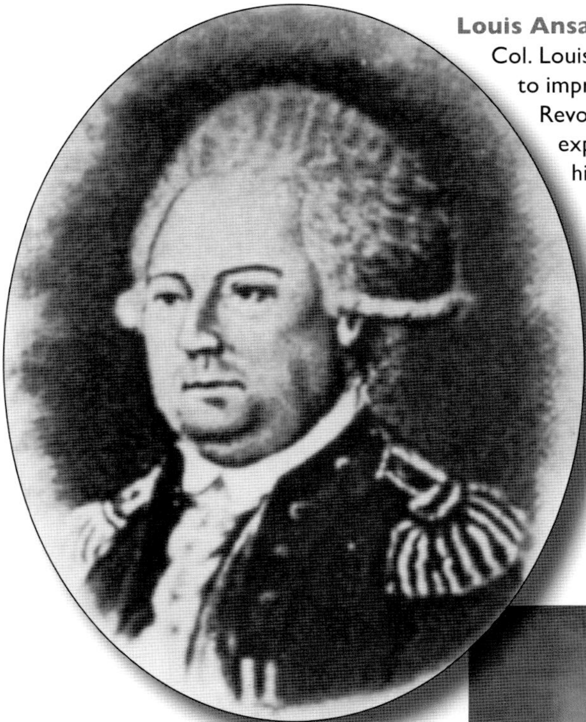

Louis Ansart

Col. Louis Ansart was a French nobleman who helped to improve American artillery during the American Revolution. Born in France in 1752, he was an expert in casting cannons—a skill learned from his father. He arrived in Massachusetts in 1776 and offered his help in forging cannons that would last longer than two firings, for which American cannons were notoriously poor. His help was invaluable during the Revolution. After the war, Ansart renounced his French title of nobility and settled in Dracut. He died in 1804 and is buried in Woodbine Cemetery. His house still stands on Varnum Avenue in Lowell. (Courtesy Dracut Historical Society.)

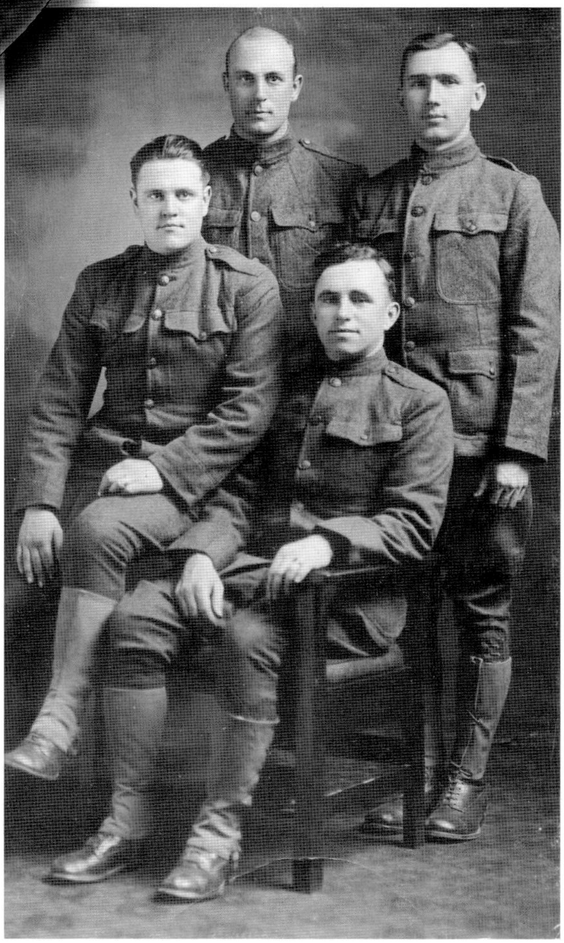

John Briscoe

This photograph was taken in 1918, when John Briscoe enlisted in the Army to serve during World War I. Briscoe is the man standing on the right. His service began on Saturday, January 12, 1918, when he arrived at Fort Devens. He kept meticulous records of his time in Europe, including a diary and maps. He fought in France, and as his diary indicates, he witnessed aerial dogfights and experienced bombing from German planes, as well as shelling from German artillery. Briscoe's son moved to Dracut in 1965, when he married, and taught for 40 years, both in the junior and high schools. John Briscoe passed away tending his beloved apple trees in 1973. (Courtesy John Briscoe Jr.)

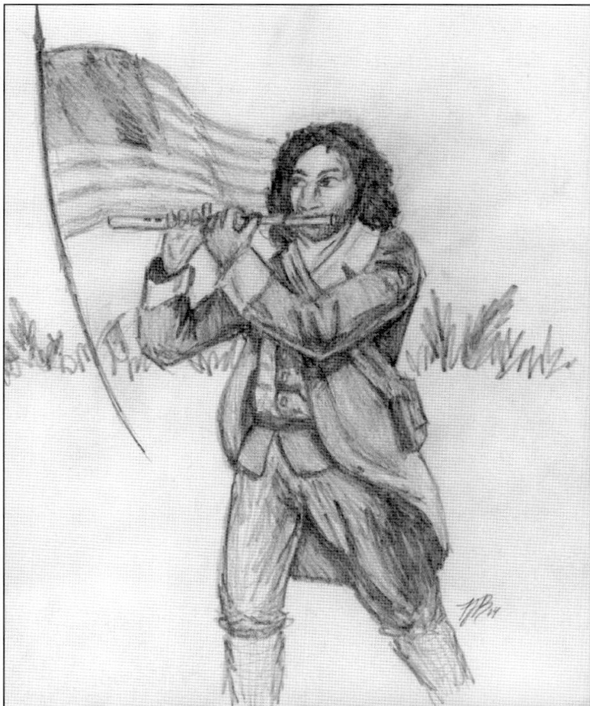

Barzillai Lew
The oldest son of Primus and Margaret Lew, Barzillai Lew was born in Groton on November 5, 1743. The sketch at left is an artist's rendition of what Lew might have looked like based on historical evidence. After the death of his parents, Lew was placed under the guardianship of Francis Blood until he was of age, as indicated by the document below. Lew married Dinah Bowman in 1767, when he bought her freedom for $400. During the American Revolution, Lew served at Bunker Hill as a fifer and at Fort Ticonderoga under Joseph Bradley Varnum. After the war, Lew and his wife settled in Dracut. Their farm was located on Totman Road in today's Pawtucketville section. Lew died in 1822. (Left, courtesy Tyler Bettencourt; below, courtesy Massachusetts State Archives.)

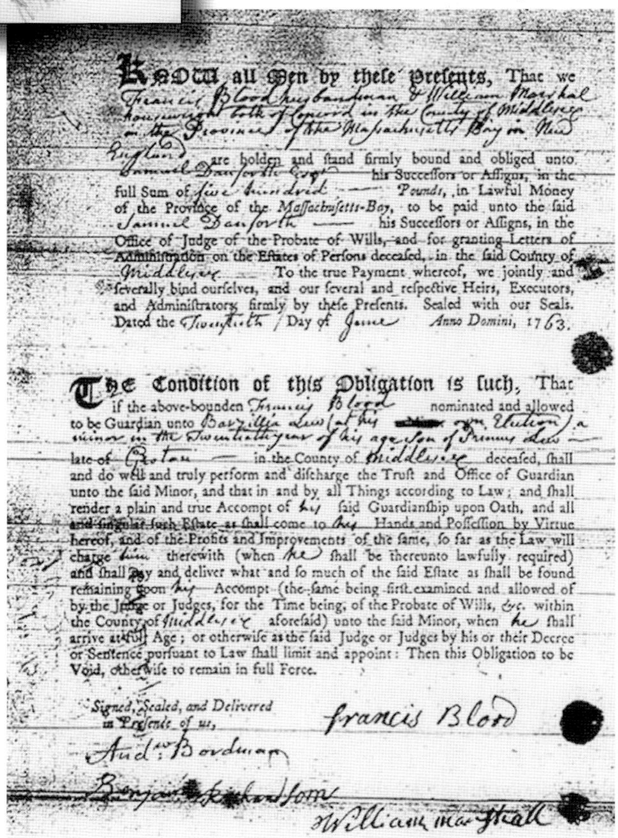

Know all Men by these Presents, That we Francis Blood husbandman & William Marshal housewright both of Concord in the County of Middlesex in the Province of the Massachusetts Bay in New England are holden and stand firmly bound and obliged unto Samuel Danforth Esqr his Successors or Assigns, in the full Sum of five hundred Pounds, in Lawful Money of the Province of the Massachusetts-Bay, to be paid unto the said Samuel Danforth his Successors or Assigns, in the Office of Judge of the Probate of Wills, and for granting Letters of Administration on the Estates of Persons deceased, in the said County of Middlesex. To the true Payment whereof, we jointly and severally bind ourselves, and our several and respective Heirs, Executors, and Administrators, firmly by these Presents. Sealed with our Seals. Dated the Twentieth Day of June Anno Domini, 1763.

The Condition of this Obligation is such, That if the above-bounden Francis Blood nominated and allowed to be Guardian unto Barzillia Lew (at his own Election) a minor in the Twentieth year of his age son of Primus Lew late of Groton in the County of Middlesex deceased, shall and do well and truly perform and discharge the Trust and Office of Guardian unto the said Minor, and that in and by all Things according to Law; and shall render a plain and true Accompt of his said Guardianship upon Oath, and all and singular such Estate as shall come to his Hands and Possession by Virtue hereof, and of the Profits and Improvements of the same, so far as the Law will charge him therewith (when he shall be thereunto lawfully required) and shall pay and deliver what and so much of the said Estate as shall be found remaining upon his Accompt (the same being first examined and allowed of by the Judge or Judges, for the Time being, of the Probate of Wills, &c. within the County of Middlesex aforesaid) unto the said Minor, when he shall arrive at full Age; or otherwise as the said Judge or Judges by his or their Decree or Sentence pursuant to Law shall limit and appoint: Then this Obligation to be Void, otherwise to remain in full Force.

Signed, Sealed, and Delivered in Presents of us,
Francis Blood
Andw Bordman
Benjamin Richardson
William marshall

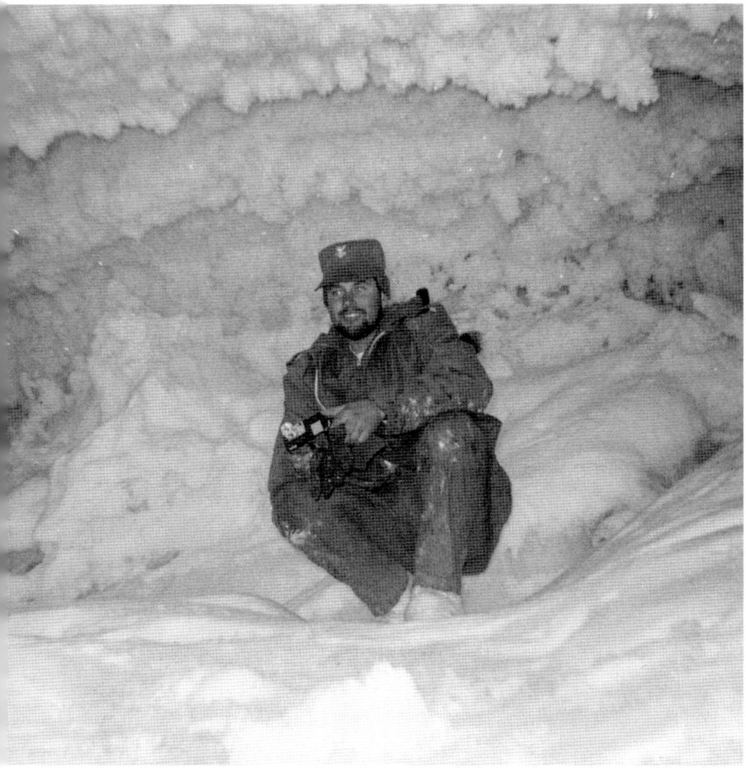

Bob Berube

Dracut native Bob Berube served in Vietnam for one year, from 1965 to 1966. When the Army activated him again, he served in the Reserves, but since he was reactivated so soon, the Army was precluded from sending him back to Vietnam. Instead, he was sent to McMurdo Station in Antarctica. For years, Berube has returned to Dracut schools to share his experiences in Antarctica with elementary students. As a result of Berube's visit to Maureen Riordan's second grade class in 2013, it was learned that a student had a cousin currently working at McMurdo, and a videoconference between Dracut students and scientist Neil Foley was organized. (Both, courtesy Bob Berube.)

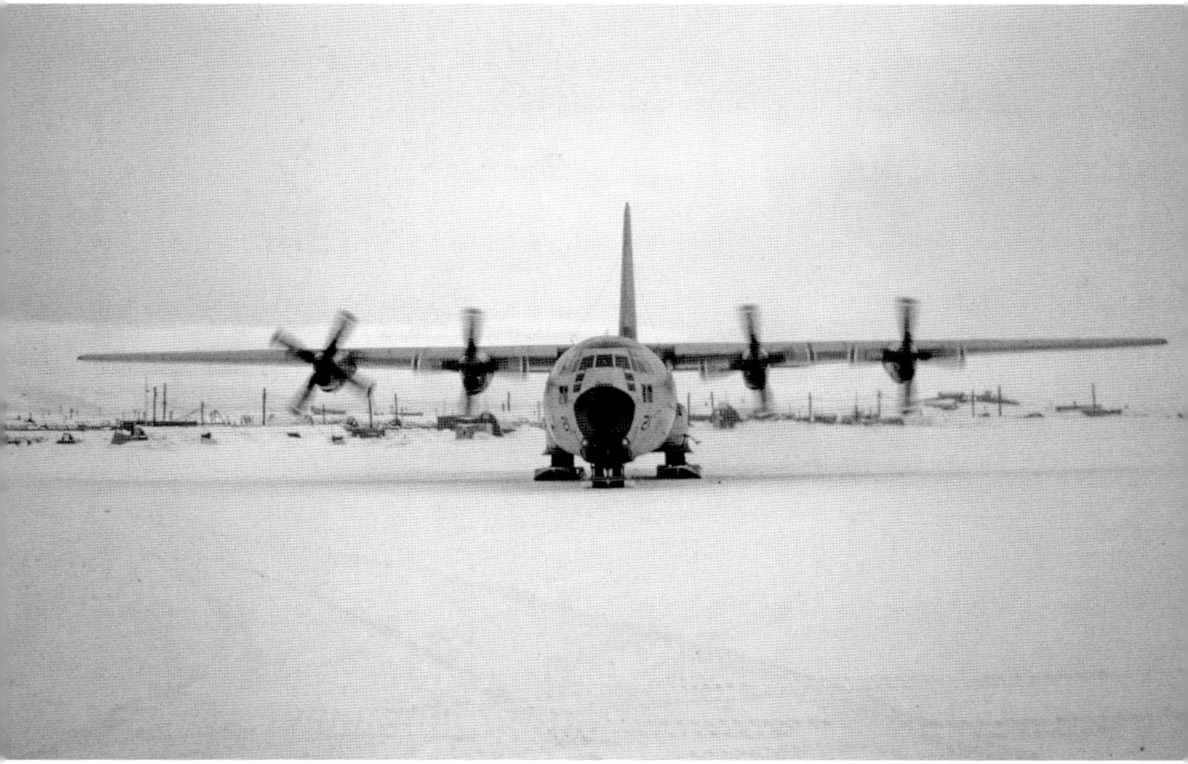

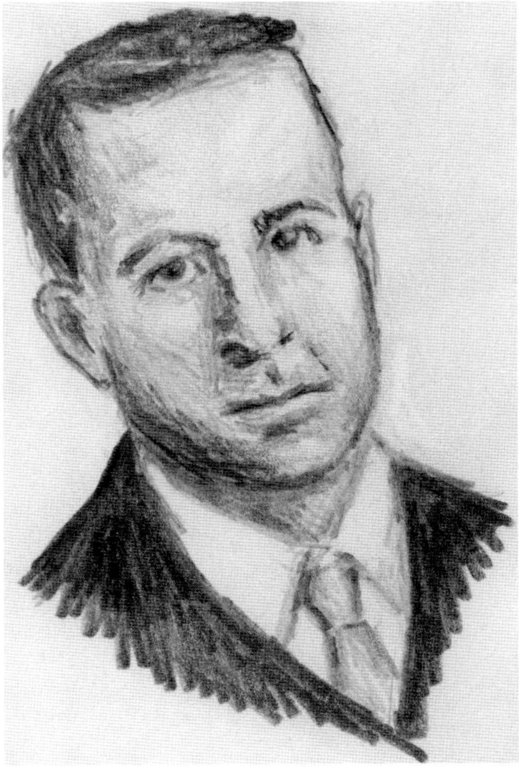

Leo C. Roth
Headed by Leo C. Roth, 16 World War I veterans gathered at the Dracut Navy Yard fire station to sign a petition to establish a chapter of the American Legion in Dracut. The petition was sent to the national office in January 1935, and the Dracut American Legion Post 315 was established officially in September 1935. Roth was also a 25-year member of the Dracut Center fire company and served several terms on the board of selectmen. The well-respected resident of 11 Huron Street passed away in February 1958, and the Dracut Post 315 was renamed in his honor. (Courtesy Tyler Bettencourt.)

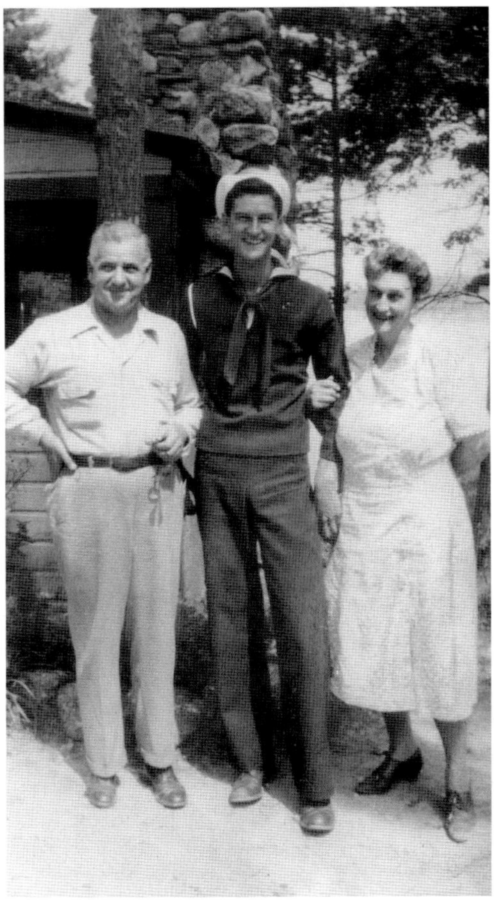

Richard R. Campbell
Richard Campbell is pictured here with his parents, E. Gaston and Idula Campbell. Born on June 7, 1927, Campbell served in the Navy during World War II. After the war, Campbell made his home in Dracut and worked in the construction business. During his retirement, Campbell was well known for his love of horseshoes, along with his good friends Paul Dumont, John Duffy, and Lee Ashford. Campbell passed away on May 16, 1994. (Courtesy Heather Santiago-Hutchings.)

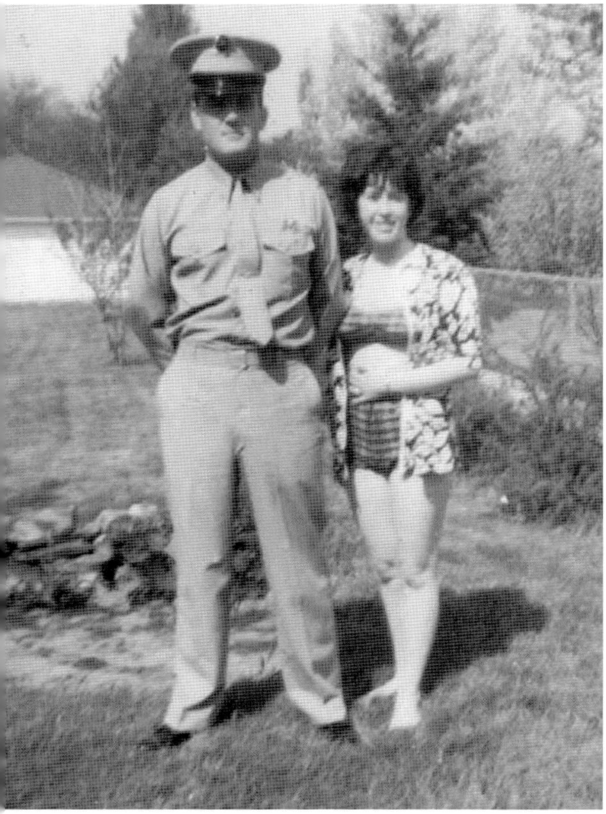

Michael Monahan

Michael James Monahan was born in Lowell Hospital on November 1, 1947, to James and Patricia Monahan of Malwood Avenue. Monahan graduated from Dracut's elementary and junior high schools, then Keith Academy in 1964. As a student at Boston College, he had aspirations to go on to medical school and become a physician. In March 1966, he left college in only his second year of studies to enlist in the Marines to serve during the Vietnam War. On September 1, 1966, he was deployed to Vietnam, where he was killed by enemy gunfire on October 26, 1966. He was only 19 years old. While in Vietnam, Pfc. Michael Monahan worked as a radio operator in the 3rd Marine Division. He is shown at left with his cousin Anne Kennedy before his deployment. (Left, courtesy Anne Kennedy; below, courtesy Dracut Historical Society.)

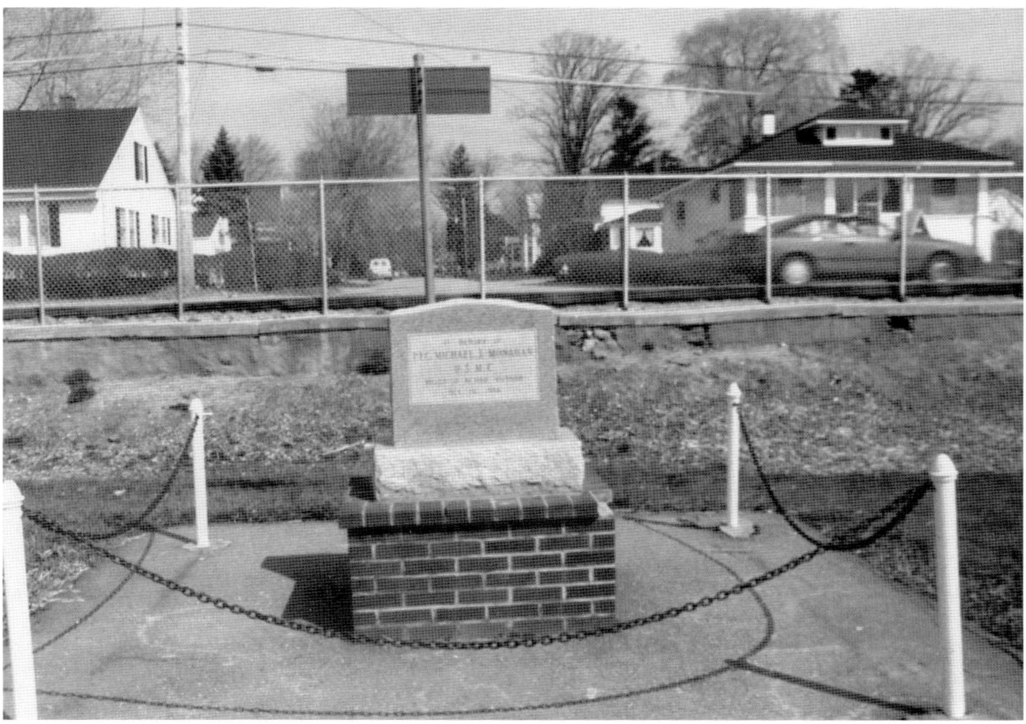

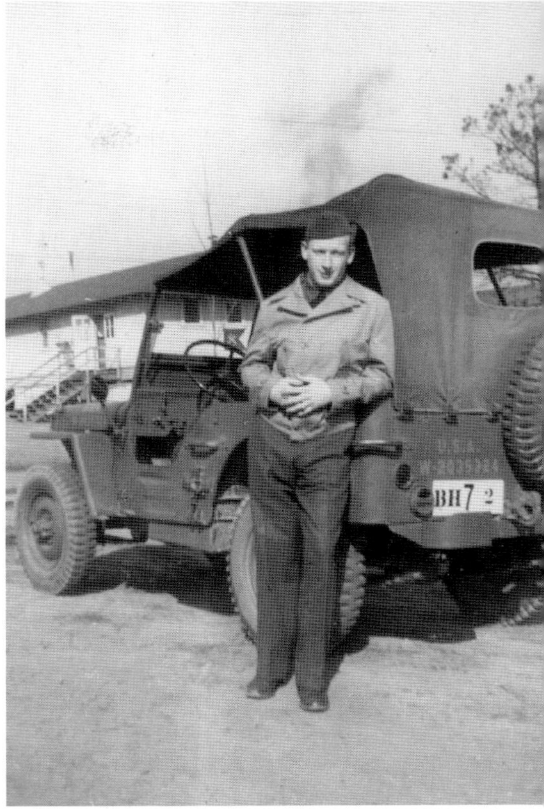

James V. Kiernan

Son of longtime Collinsville postmaster H. Francis Kiernan, James V. Kiernan served as an army captain in Battery B 1st Field Artillery Battalion during World War II, from August 18, 1942, until his discharge on April 1, 1946. Before being sent overseas, he was stationed at Fort Bragg and Fort Sill. Kiernan saw fighting at New Guinea and Luzon, for which he earned the following service awards: Asiatic Pacific Service Medal, World War II Victory Medal, Philippine Liberation Medal, and American Service Medal. (Courtesy Martha K. Wolfe.)

Irene Grondine

Irene Grondine (pictured below, second from left) volunteered in the Massachusetts Women's Defense Corps (MWDC) during World War II. The MWDC was established on April 2, 1941, as part of the Massachusetts Committee on Public Safety, which was responsible for civil defense during World War II. Approximately 18,000 women were trained as emergency firefighters, air raid siren wardens, medics, and communications personnel as part of the MWDC. (Courtesy William Dumont.)

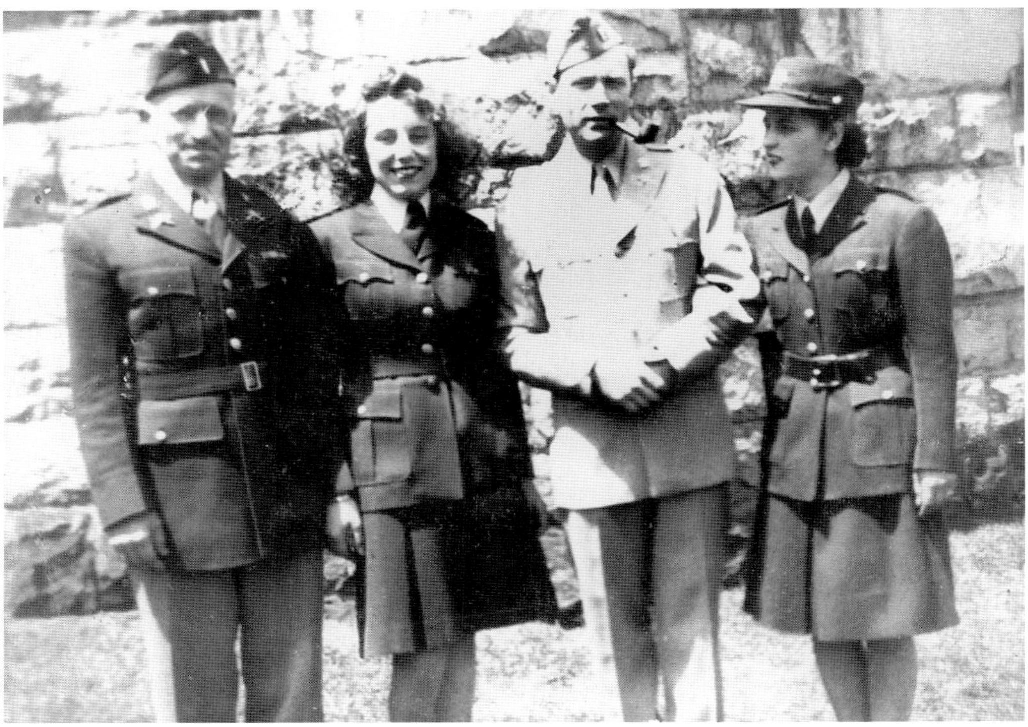

Christos Daoulas
Before Christos Daoulas joined the faculty at Dracut High School and served as superintendent for 38 years, he distinguished himself as a medic during World War II. In October 1942, he enlisted in the Army at Fort Devens, then was shipped to Camp Claiborne, Louisiana, to complete basic training and advanced training as a medic. Daoulas joined the 360th Engineer General Service Regiment as part of the medical detachment. His regiment participated in the Normandy landing, then fought throughout France and eventually in Germany. He was honorably discharged at Fort Devens on December 19, 1945. (Courtesy Arthur Daoulas.)

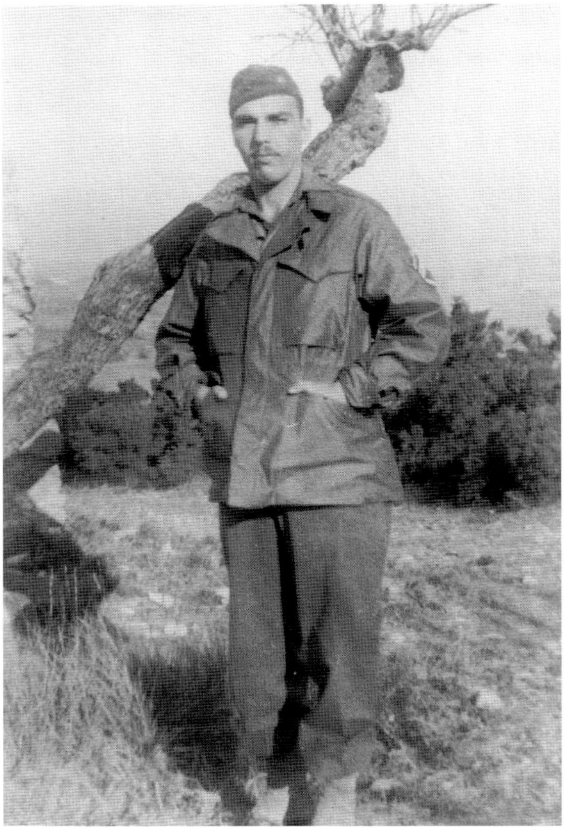

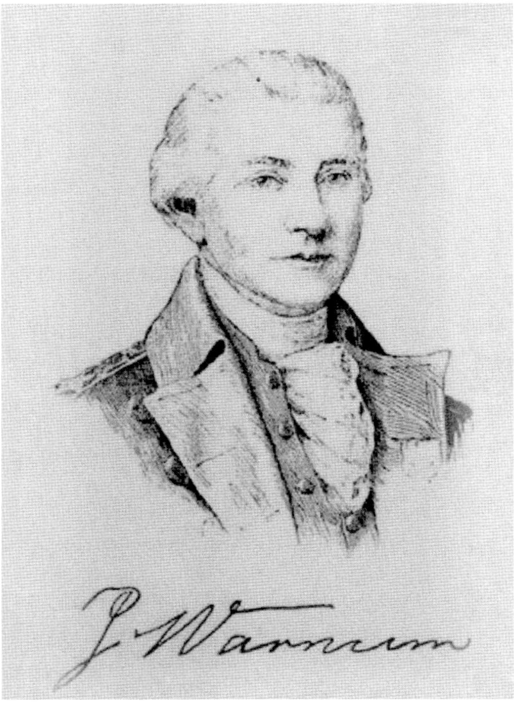

James Mitchell Varnum
James Mitchell Varnum was born in Dracut on December 17, 1748. He was the brother of Joseph Bradley Varnum, but unlike his brother, he did not make Dracut his home. He attended Harvard University and Rhode Island College (today's Brown University), where he was part of the college's first graduating class, and never returned to his hometown. He remained in Rhode Island. When the siege of Boston began after the Battles of Lexington and Concord in 1775, he went with his regiment to help the patriots. He went on to fight in White Plains and Long Island, New York, and rising to the rank of brigadier general, he had a headquarters at Valley Forge, which can still be visited. Varnum died at age 41 in 1789. (Courtesy Dracut Historical Society.)

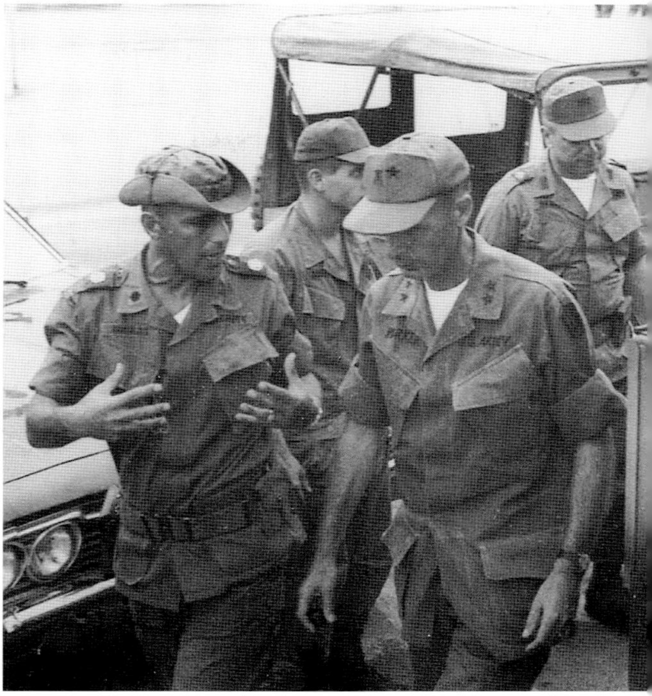

Arthur Daoulas
Brother of Christos Daoulas, Arthur graduated from Dracut High School in 1949. After completing the pre-engineering study program at Baldwin-Wallace College in Ohio, he returned to Dracut. In 1952, he was drafted into the Army and chose to make it his career. After multiple command and staff assignments in Europe and the Far East, plus military and civilian schooling, Daoulas retired with the rank of colonel in 1979. He then served under the Carter and Reagan administrations in two presidentially appointed positions: assistant secretary of the Army (research, development, and acquisition) and deputy assistant secretary of the Army (acquisition). As commander of the 864th Engineer Battalion, Daoulas is shown briefing Major General Parker, senior US Army engineer, in Vietnam around 1968. (Courtesy Arthur Daoulas.)

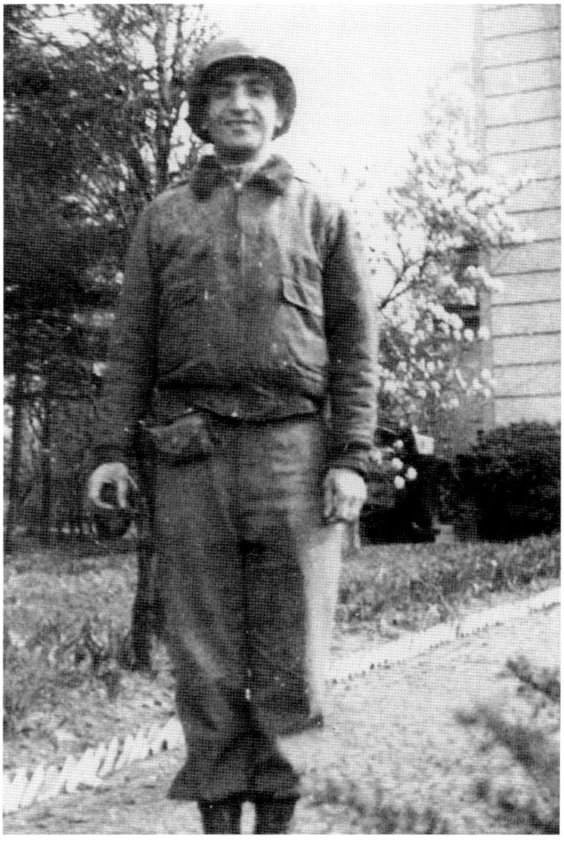

Costas L. Caraganis
Born in Lowell on August 15, 1910, Costas Caraganis moved to Dracut with his family when he was four years old. The family settled on Phineas Street, where there were several Greek families and farms. Caraganis graduated from the Massachusetts State College of Agriculture. Later, he joined the 4-H Club and won numerous awards for his work in agriculture. His army career was successful as well. In 1933, he held the rank of second lieutenant, and with the outbreak of World War II, he entered active duty in 1941. He left active duty in 1946, and while in reserve duty, he achieved the rank of brigadier general. Proud of his Greek heritage, he wrote *The History of Greeks in Dracut* in 1938. Caraganis died in 1998, and his military papers are part of the Norwich University archives. (Courtesy Nicholas Karas.)

Joseph Giles Eaton

Rear Adm. Joseph G. Eaton was born in 1847 in Greenville, Alabama. His first wife was Mary Ann Varnum of Dracut. Serving in the Navy for 33 years, Admiral Eaton was a hero during the Spanish-American War and commanded the *Resolute* during the Battle of Santiago. He retired in 1905. Eaton and his second wife, Jennie, adopted an infant in February 1909, but he died in August of that year. Jennie accused her husband of poisoning the baby, but an autopsy concluded the infant had died from natural causes. After several turbulent years of marriage, Eaton died suddenly on March 8, 1913. An autopsy showed that he had died from arsenic poisoning, and Jennie was charged with her husband's murder. She was acquitted. Admiral Eaton is buried in Oakland Cemetery with his first wife. (Courtesy Dracut Historical Society.)

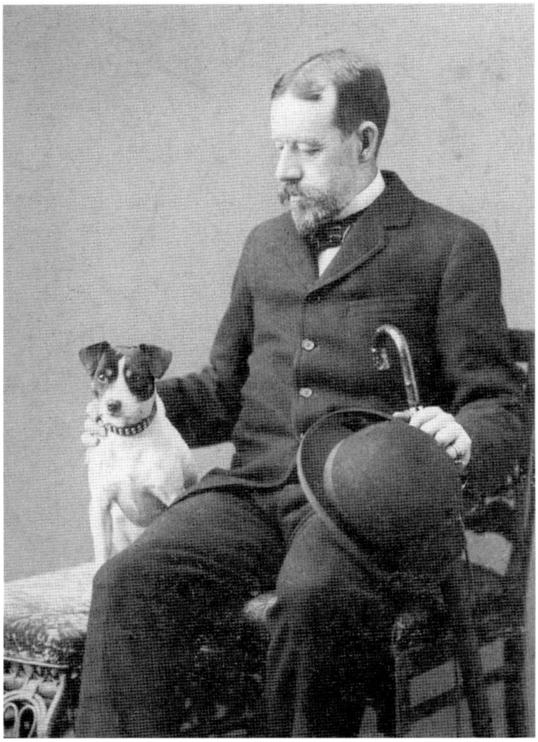

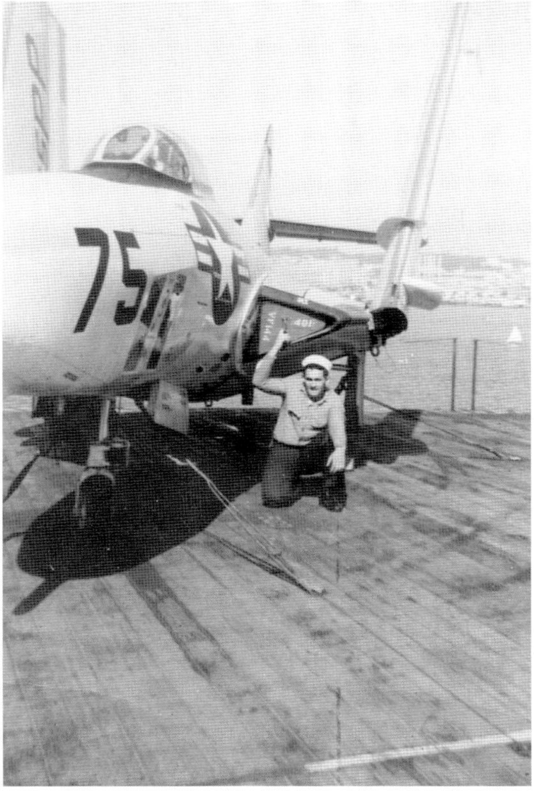

Albert Richard "Dick" Mercier

Known by many from his years as a Lowell police officer, Dick Mercier served in the Navy during the Korean War. He was honorably discharged in 1959. Born on November 19, 1938, Mercier was a graduate of Dracut High School and Northeastern University. He shared 50 years of marriage with his wife, Elaine. Mercier passed away on July 20, 2012. (Courtesy Rick Mercier.)

Arthur Elie
Born on June 5, 1919, Arthur Elie enlisted in the US Navy on June 28, 1943, and served as a Seabee in the Pacific Theatre, including time on the Solomon Islands. He was assigned to the 15th, 73rd, and 117th Naval Construction Battalions. Honorably discharged with the rank of carpenter's mate first class in 1945, Elie returned to Dracut, where he owned and operated the Golden Dairy Farm with his wife, Jeannette, until his death in 1963. (Courtesy Paul Elie.)

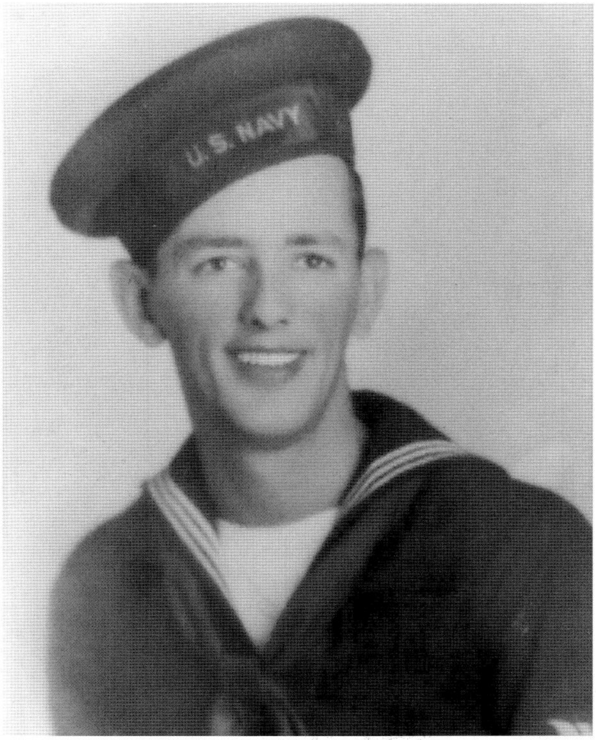

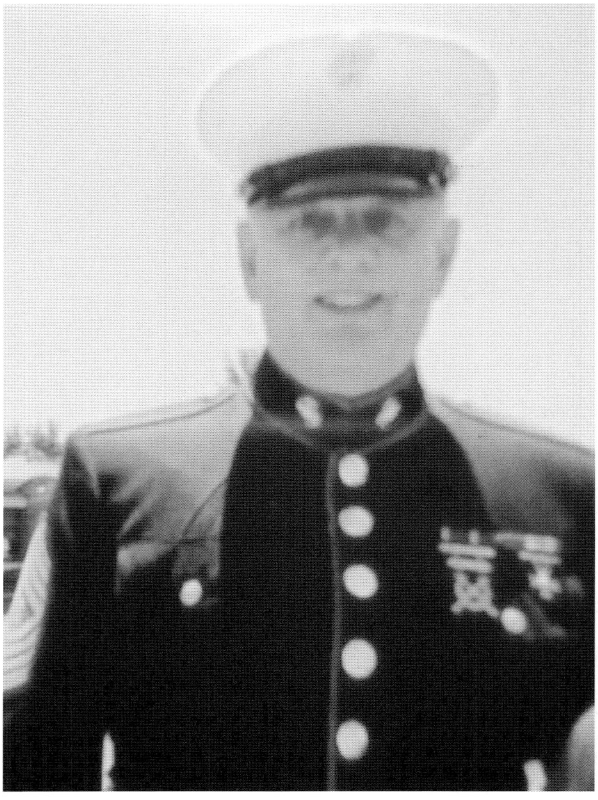

Paul Elie
Paul Elie was born in Dracut to Arthur and Jeannette Elie on March 24, 1947. Trained as an electrician and computer programmer, he enlisted in the US Marine Corps in May 1975, serving for 26 years. His tours of duty included Parris Island, South Carolina; Quantico, Virginia; Camp Lejeune, North Carolina; and Okinawa, Japan. In 2001, he was honorably discharged with the rank of master gunnery sergeant (E-9). After retiring from the Marine Corps, Elie worked as a programmer at Fort Devens. (Courtesy Paul Elie.)

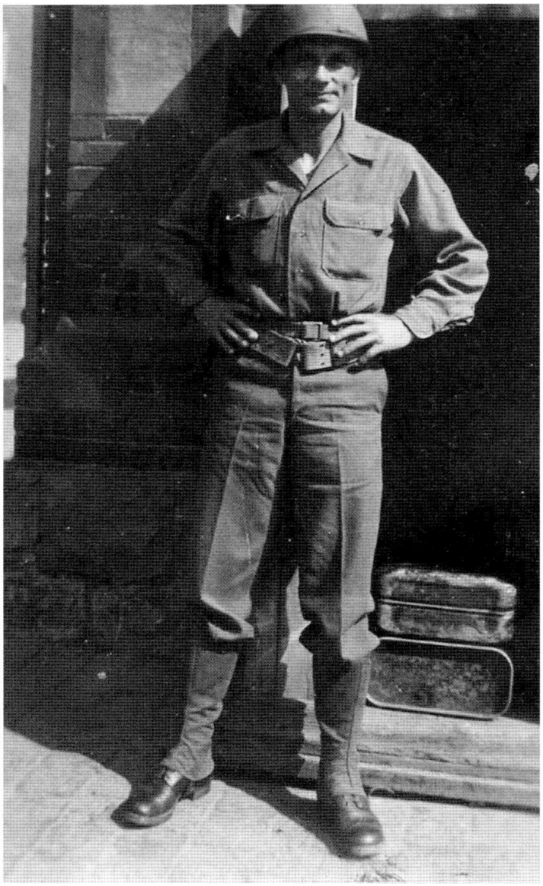

Charles Kostoulakos
Charles Kostoulakos was born in Dracut to Demetrios "James" and Marigo Kostoulakos. From 1942 to 1945, Kostoulakos served in the US Army. As an infantryman, he saw fighting in Africa, Italy, and Germany. He passed away at age 88 in 2001. (Courtesy Arthur Kostoulakos.)

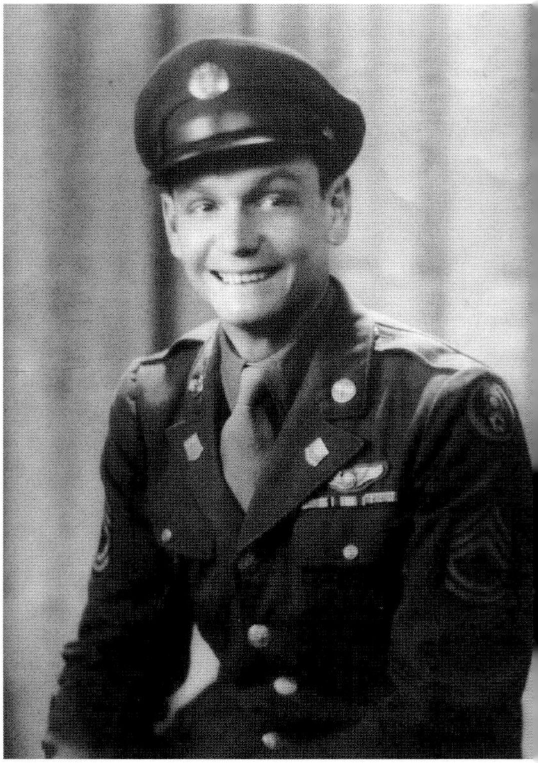

George Kostoulakos
Like his other three brothers who served during World War II, George Kostoulakos is an example of why his generation is called the "Greatest Generation." He was born on March 28, 1920, and graduated from Dracut High School as class valedictorian in 1937. During World War II, Kostoulakos served in the US Army Air Force. He was shot down over Germany and held as a POW from May 1944 until General Patton liberated him in April 1945. After the war, he returned to Dracut, where he owned and operated Kostoulakos Homebuilding. Later, he taught in the Lowell Public Schools. Kostoulakos passed away at age 93 on April 5, 2013. (Courtesy Arthur Kostoulakos.)

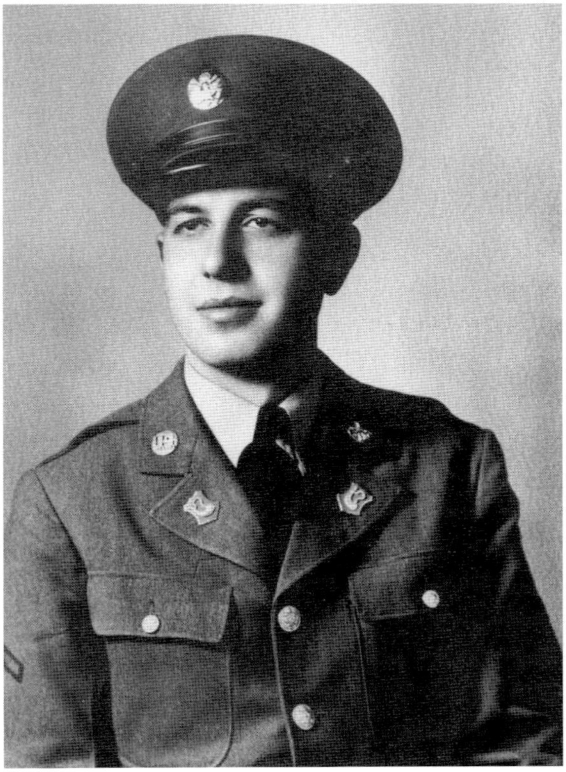

William Kostoulakos
Born in Dracut on July 21, 1918, William Kostoulakos was one of four brothers who served during World War II. In the Army, he was assigned to the Yankee Division Infantry. He trained at Camp Campbell in Kentucky, then was sent directly to France. His division fought at the Battle of the Bulge in France and then in Germany. Kostoulakos died at age 90 on September 17, 2008. (Courtesy Arthur Kostoulakos.)

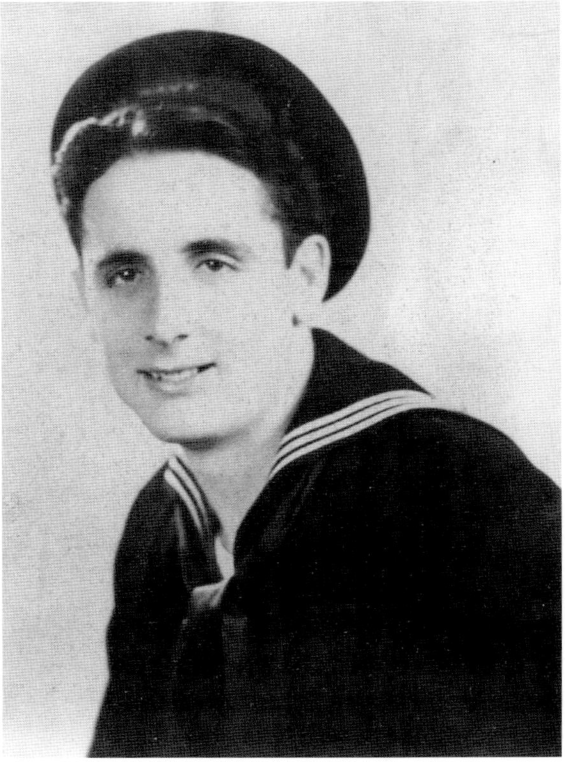

Stephen J. Kostoulakos
Born on August 28, 1921, Stephen Kostoulakos was the fourth Kostoulakos brother to serve in World War II. He graduated from Dracut High School in 1939, then served in the Navy as an aviation machinist's mate from 1942 to 1945. After the war, he returned to Dracut, where he owned and operated the first cab company in town. Kostoulakos passed away at age 92 on October 3, 2013, leaving his wife of 66 years, Irene. (Courtesy Arthur Kostoulakos.)

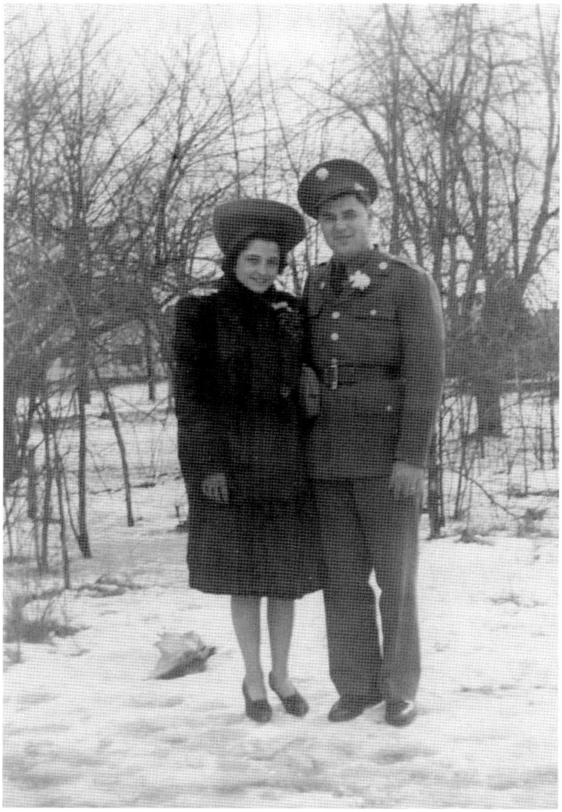

Ferdinando "Fred" Loffredo
The son of Thomaso and Maria Loffredo, Ferdinando Loffredo graduated from Dracut High School in 1939 where he was the co-captain of the football team. When World War II began, he enlisted in the Army and served as a corporal. He was sent to the South Pacific on the USS *Hawaiin Clipper* and spent time in the Philippines. The photograph below shows the destruction caused during the war in the Philippines, which Loffredo witnessed firsthand. After the war, he returned to the United States aboard the USS *Charles Carroll*. In December 1945, Loffredo and his wife made their home at 116 Sladen Street. He worked for Litchfield's Oil Company for 50 years. His daughter Elaine Robitaille describes her father as a "very positive person." Loffredo passed away on May 11, 2008, at the age of 88 leaving his wife of 66 years, Dorella. (Both, courtesy Elaine Robitaille.)

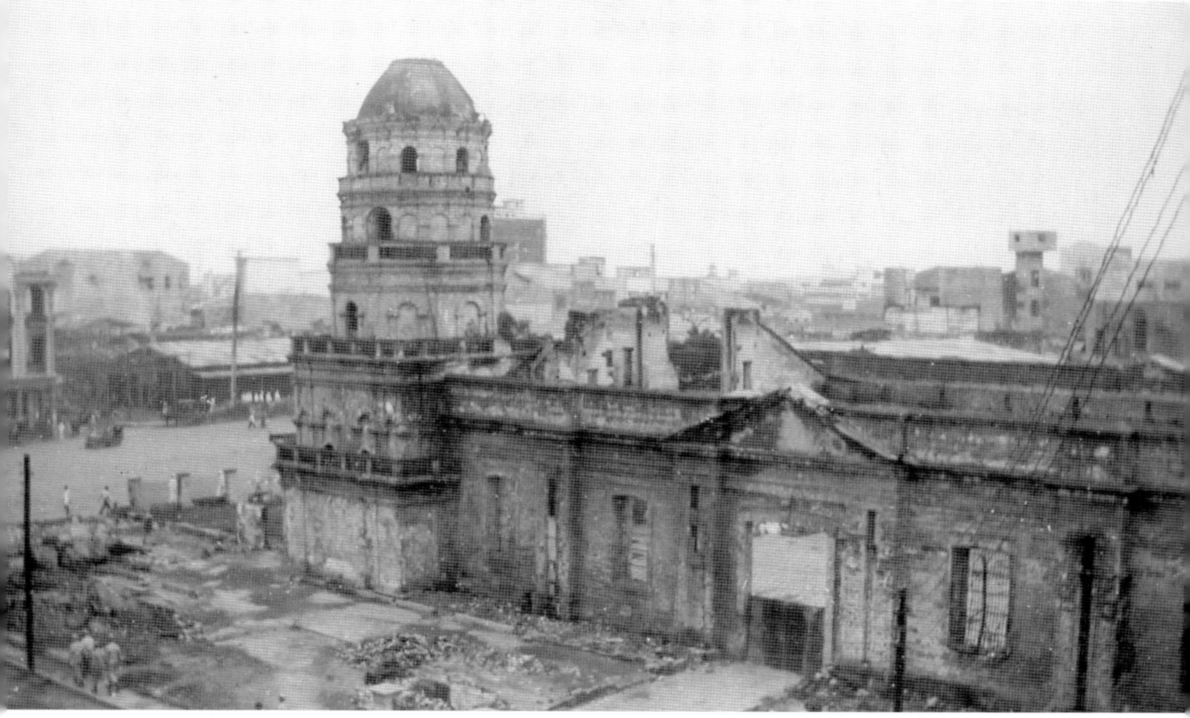

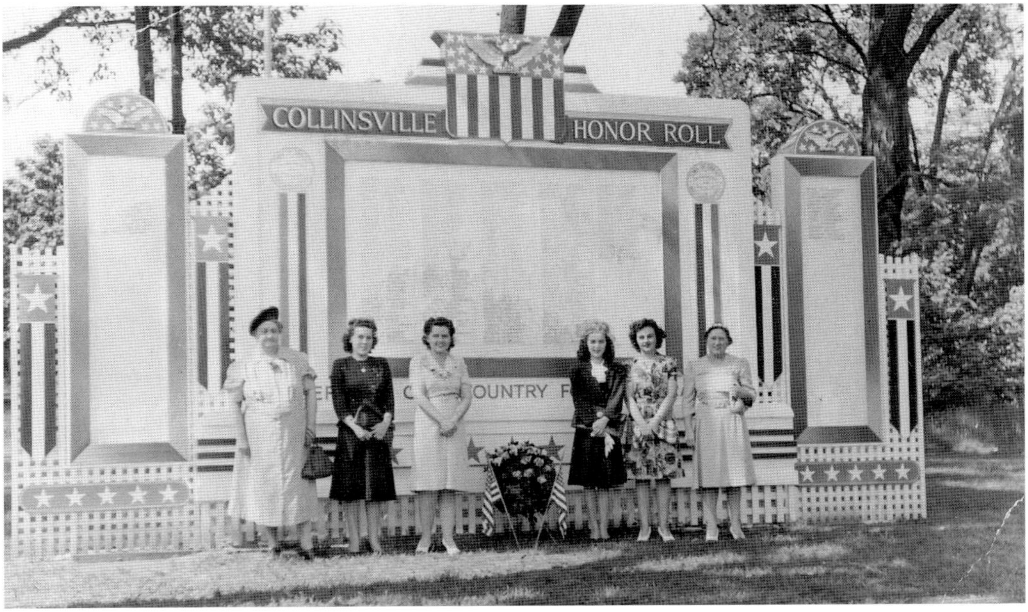

Collinsville World War II Memorial

During World War II, Collinsville residents erected an honor roll in Costello Square (the intersection of Lakeview Avenue and Mammoth Road) to recognize those from Collinsville who were off fighting in the war. The stone memorial in the foreground of the photograph below was dedicated in 1929 to honor the four Dracut men who fought in the Spanish-American War: Arthur Garland, Eden C. Walker, George H. Connell, and Joseph G. Eaton. The Collinsville Honor Roll was dedicated on November 14, 1943. Made of wood, the honor roll deteriorated over the years and eventually was torn down. A memorial honoring all Dracut men and women who fought in the nation's wars was erected on the grounds of Dracut High School. (Both, courtesy Dracut Historical Society.)

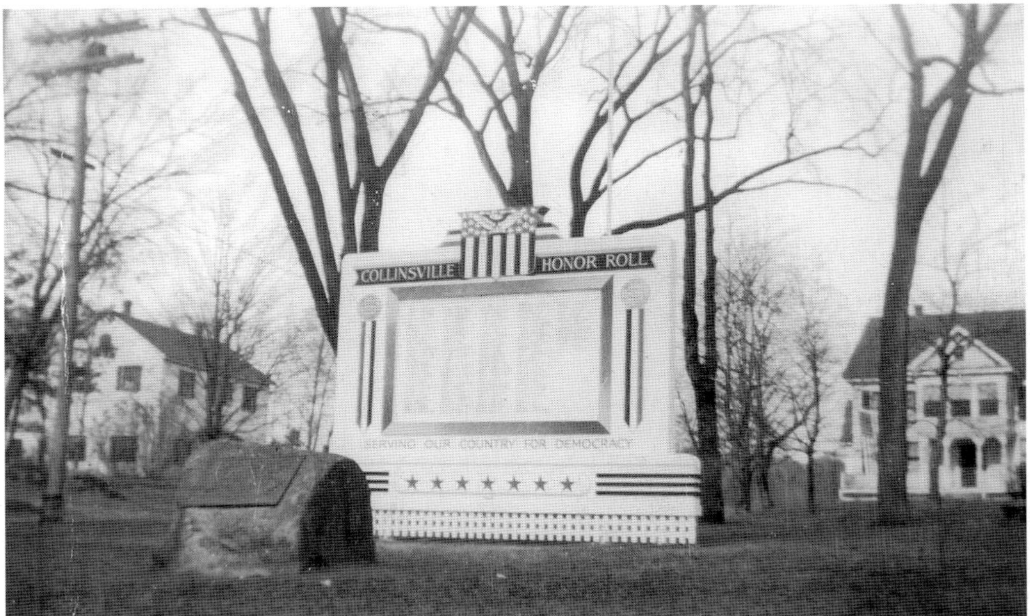

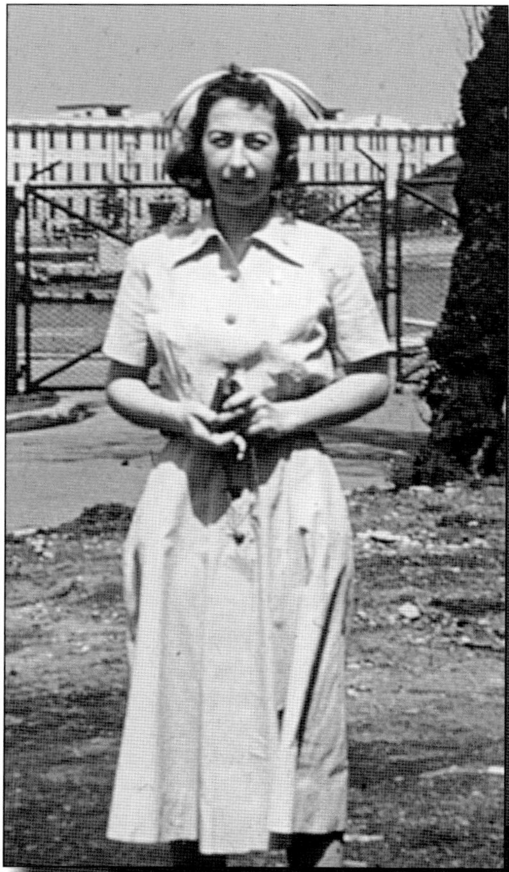

Stella Lambros
In 1927, Stella Lambros was born in her family home on Hildreth Street in Dracut. Lambros graduated from Dracut High School in 1942 and entered the US nurse program at Boston University. Upon graduation from Boston University, she joined the Navy, becoming one of the first female commissioned officers. The Navy had Lambros complete the Case Western Anesthesiology program. After becoming a nurse anesthetist, Lambros was stationed at Sangley Naval Station in the Philippines before being sent to Pusan as the Korean War intensified. For her service during the Korean War, Lambros was awarded the United Nations' Service Medal and the Presidential Unit Citation. She married Alfred Kurzenhauser in 1954 and passed away in 2009. (Both, courtesy the Stella Lambros family.)

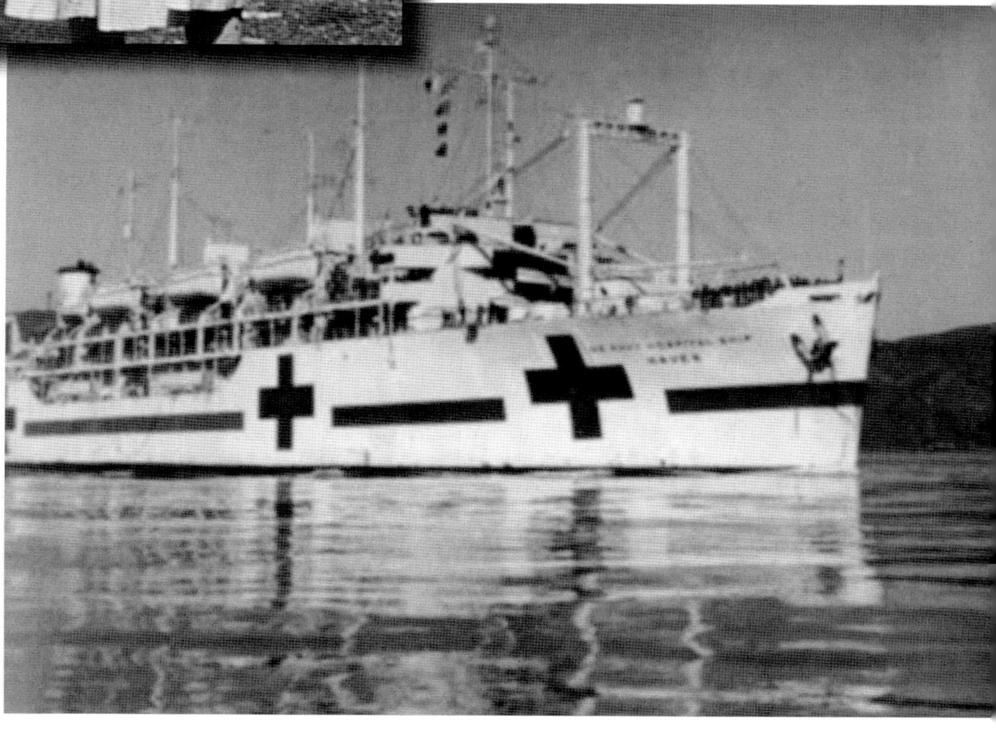

CHAPTER FIVE

Commerce

Farms, Factories, and Fortunes

Since its establishment in 1701, Dracut has been first and foremost a community of farmers: Ephraim Curtis had a farm on Broadway Road, which was a refuge for Acadians during the French and Indian War; Barzillai Lew had a farm on Totman Road; the Fox family had several farms in town, as they were one of the first families to settle in Dracut; Anthony Negro, a free African American, had a farm in the vicinity of Peter's Pond (named after his son Peter Negro); and Abraham Varnum built a home in 1736 that eventually would become the Beaver Brook farm on what is now Mammoth Road. This is by no means a complete list of the town's farms but, rather, an illustration of the numerous farms located in Dracut, as well as the town's diversity considering its isolated location in the 18th century.

In addition to farmers, there were other tradespeople like coopers and blacksmiths, along with sawmills and gristmills. One of the most well-known mill owners was Zachariah Goodhue, who built a house in 1790 at the corner of what is now Pleasant and Sladen Streets. The Goodhue mills were located along Beaver Brook, where the town had begun to see more industry emerge by the mid-19th century. In 1862, construction on the Merrimac Woolen Mills in the Navy Yard district began with a four-story brick mill. In 1886, Michael Collins built the Collinsville Mills, now known as the Beaver Brook Mills. At the other end of Lakeview Avenue, along Beaver Brook, the Goodhue family sold their property to Samuel Griffin and Darius Young in 1839, at which time a paper mill was established. Eventually, the property was sold to the Lowell Wadding and Paper Company in 1870. The M.L. Bassett Company then bought the business in 1877. The paper mill was profitable and expanded until a flood ruined the mill on February 27, 1900. By the time the company rebuilt, they had lost their business to neighboring paper mills in Lowell. The buildings were left vacant until a fire destroyed them on July 4, 1911.

Since that time, the Whitely Bleachery moved onto the property and operated until 1925. By the 1950s, construction of President Eisenhower's interstate highway system had begun. State representative John Brox worked to have Interstate 93 moved to the Dracut-Methuen line as opposed to the original plan to have the highway built farther east, near Haverhill. After World War II, farmers were selling out to developers, as they were facing competition from modern supermarkets, and the mills were closing, as the textile industry had moved to the southern United States. Once again, Dracut was evolving as a community. Today, it is a desirable community, with open space, a low tax base, numerous small businesses, and some remaining farms. As a headline in the August 12, 1912, *Lowell Sun* stated, "The Town of Dracut Is Quite a Busy Place." It was then and still is today.

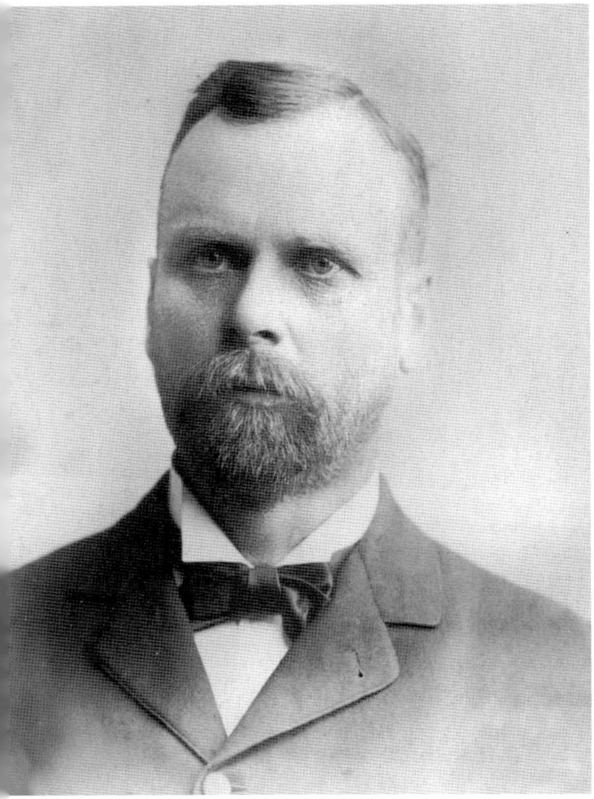

Michael Collins

Michael Collins was born in Dudley, Massachusetts, on June 6, 1839. After serving in the Civil War, Collins purchased the old Lawson mill in 1886. The photograph below was taken after a fire had destroyed the mill, and he had it rebuilt as a six-story structure. When the mills were operational again, Collins was known as "the largest individual woolen manufacturer in the US." Subsequently, he sold the mill to the American Woolen Company. It then became known as the Beaver Brook Mill, which operated until after World War II. The area in Dracut known as Collinsville is named after Michael Collins, who died at age 83 on October 8, 1922. (Both, courtesy Dracut Historical Society.)

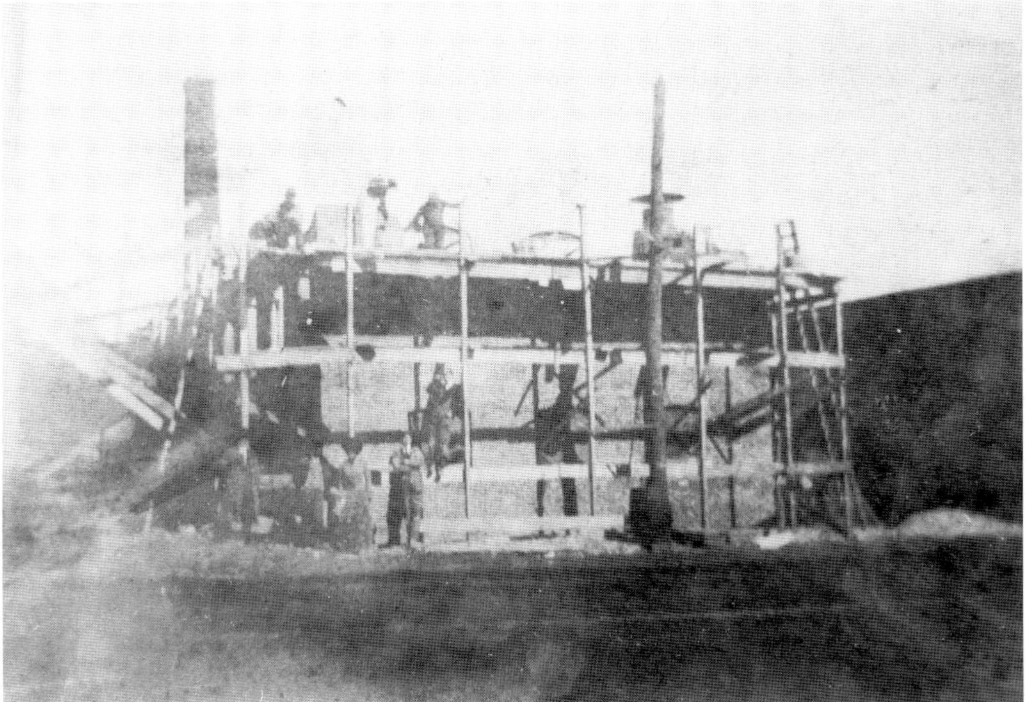

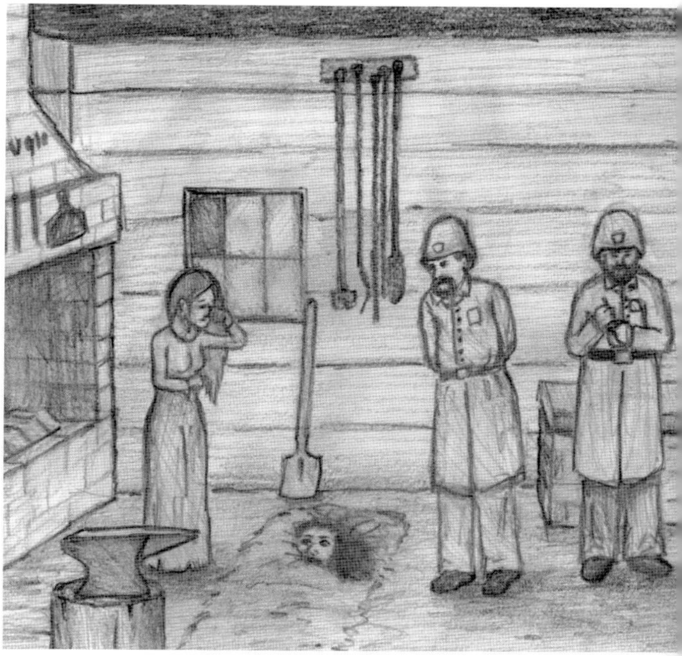

Joshua Heath

There were more than farmers and mill workers in Dracut. Joshua Heath was a blacksmith who lived along the border of Dracut and New Hampshire (today's Bridge Street area). On January 3, 1858, Heath's two adult children, Francis and Miriam, followed through on their plan to murder their father. First, they poisoned him, but that did not kill him. Francis then shot his father and took his body to his blacksmith shop next to the house, where he buried him in the floor. When neighbors came looking for Heath, the children confessed. Francis was even wearing his dead father's clothes. Their trial was held in Boston in June 1858. Francis and Miriam claimed they had murdered their father due to years of abuse. They were both found guilty and sentenced to life in prison. (Courtesy Tyler Bettencourt.)

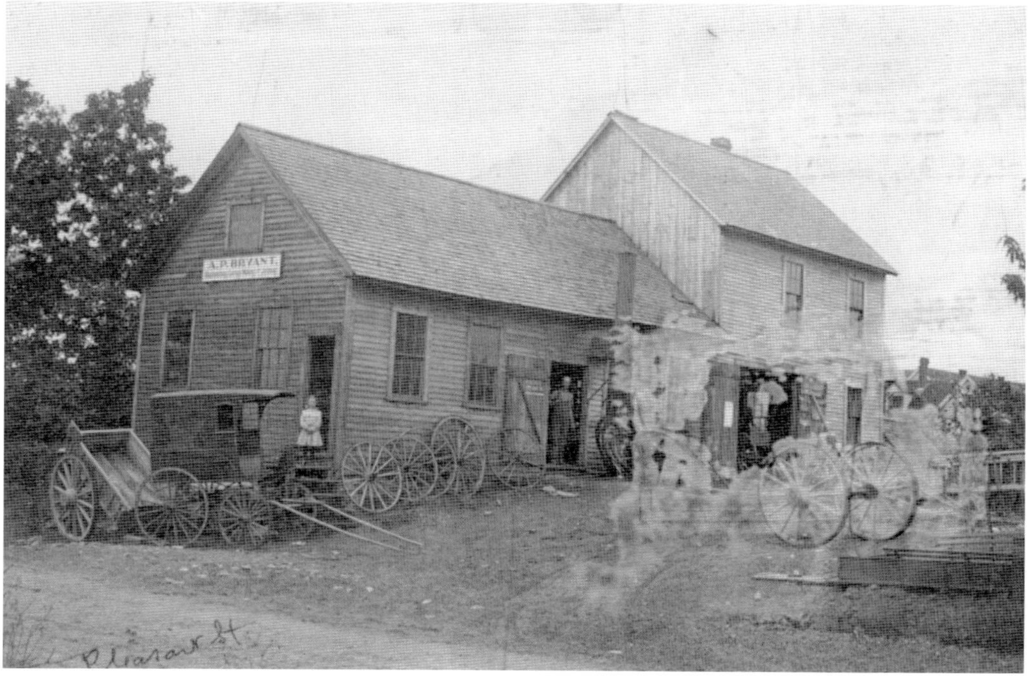

Adelbert P. Bryant

Adelbert P. Bryant was Dracut's first chief of engineers, serving from September 1907 to May 1908. His home was located at the corner of Delbert and Pleasant Streets; Delbert Street is named after him, and Pleasant Street is the dirt road in foreground. He is pictured here with his daughter at his wheelwright shop, which was his primary occupation. The title for chief of engineers was changed to fire chief in 1957. (Courtesy Willard Hibbard.)

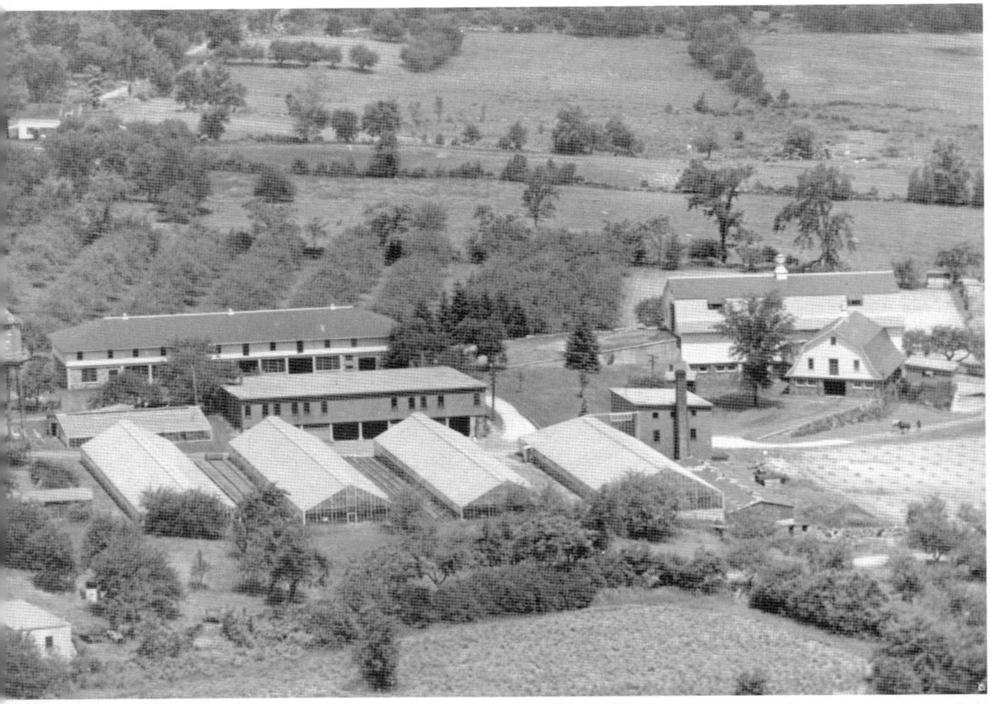

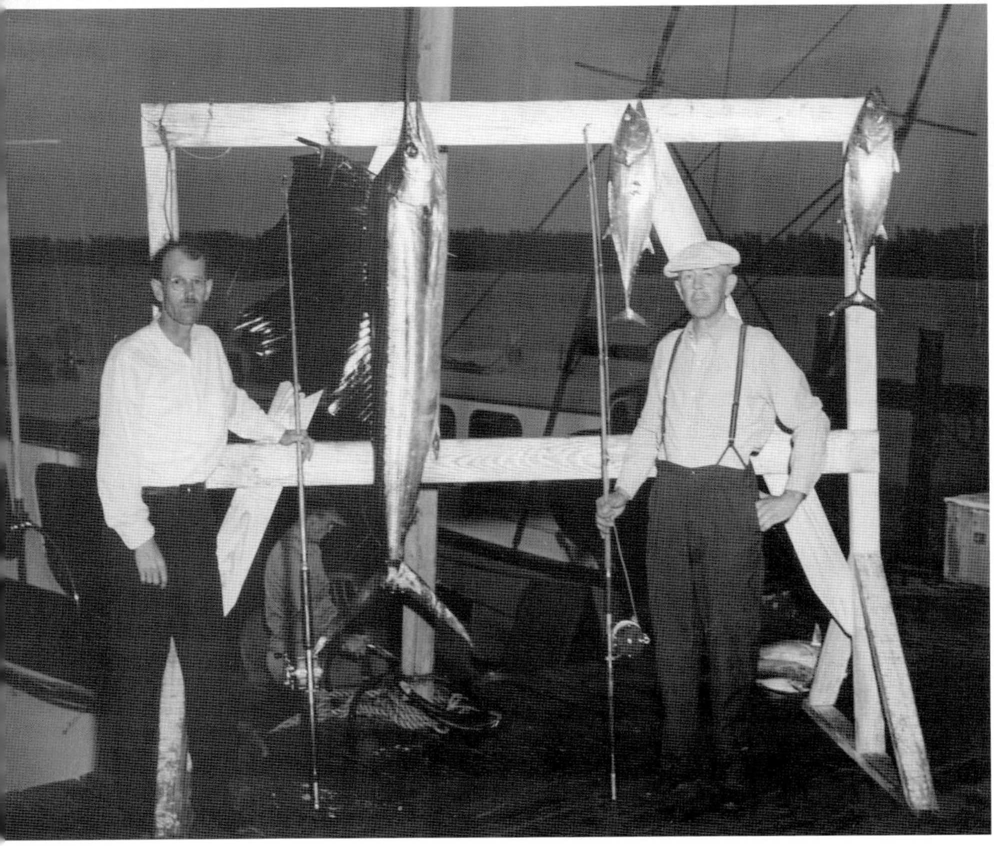

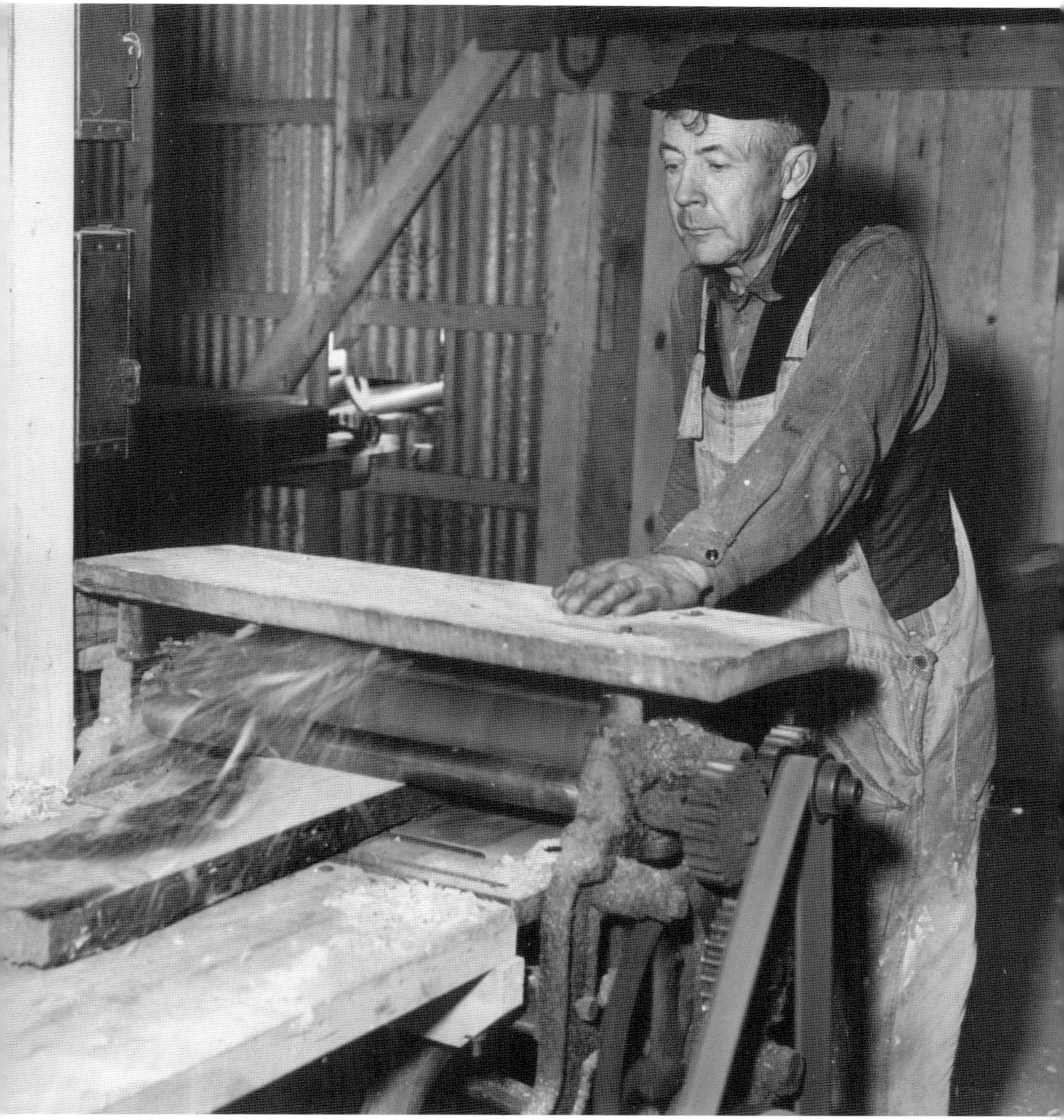

Beaver Brook Farm

Dracut was, and still is, known as a farming community. Justus C. Richardson owned and operated one of the most successful farms—Beaver Brook Farm on Mammoth Road. Richardson was famous for his blue Hubbard squash and his innovation in growing rhubarb. In 1903, the farm's first greenhouse was built. It had a furnace that allowed for the growing of seedlings during the winter. Richardson passed away in 1968. The photograph on the opposite page, above, shows Beaver Brook Farm in 1939. The photograph on the opposite page, below, shows Richardson fishing in Florida with friend Max Cherburn in 1944. Above, Richardson is working in the farm's wood shop. (All, courtesy Peter Richardson.)

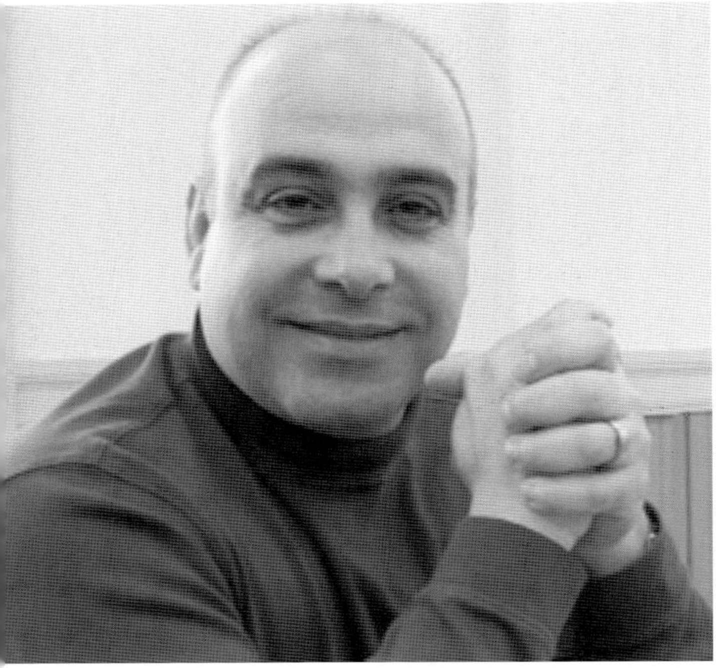

Kal Hamze

Seeking an education and escaping a brutal civil war in his native Lebanon, Kal Hamze arrived in the United States in 1987, found a job as a gas attendant, and began saving money for college. In 1989, he entered Northeastern University, where began studying to become a pharmacist. He bought his first gas station in Salem, Massachusetts, in 1992, then his second, Dracut Shell, in 1993. After graduating from Northeastern in 1994, Hamze decided to pursue his true passion—cars. He focused on building his business at Dracut Shell. By 2012, Hamze's business had grown, and he needed to expand. He purchased Roussell Marine on Bridge Street and opened Kal's Automotive in January 2013. (Courtesy Kal Hamze.)

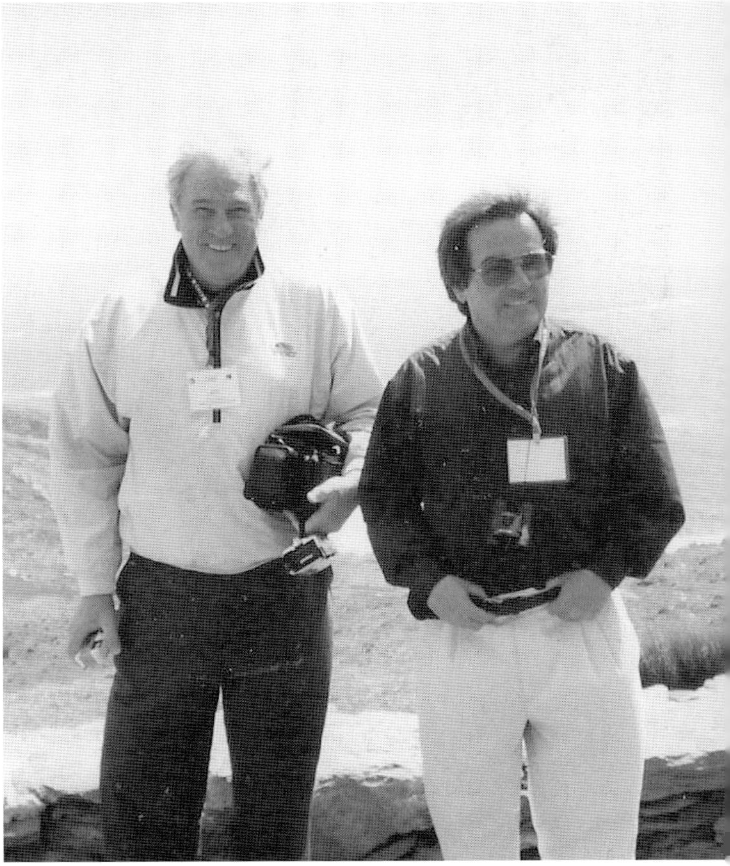

James Gookin

James Gookin (left) was born on June 6, 1935, and graduated from Dracut High School. After serving in the Navy during the Korean War, Gookin became a police officer in Dracut, then Lowell. He was well known as the owner of the popular Dracut Irish pub, O'Hara's Tavern on Lakeview Avenue. Gookin owned O'Hara's for 17 years, selling it in March 2013. He enjoyed traveling to Ireland and is shown here with his good friend Dennis McNamara on one of their many trips to the Emerald Isle. Gookin passed away on October 10, 2013. (Courtesy Michael F. McNamara.)

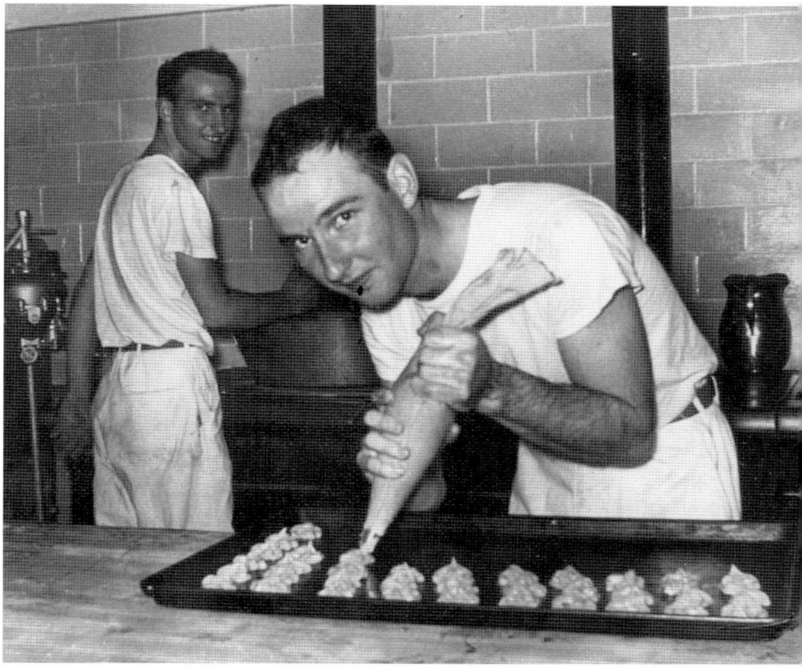

Emile Dumont
Pictured here are identical twin brothers Emile (foreground) and Paul Dumont (background) at Foot Hood, Texas. The Dumont brothers served in the Army during the Korean War, then returned to Dracut after the war. Emile established the Tasty Pastry Shop located in the strip mall next to Dracut Hardware on Lakeview Avenue. (Courtesy the Paul Dumont family.)

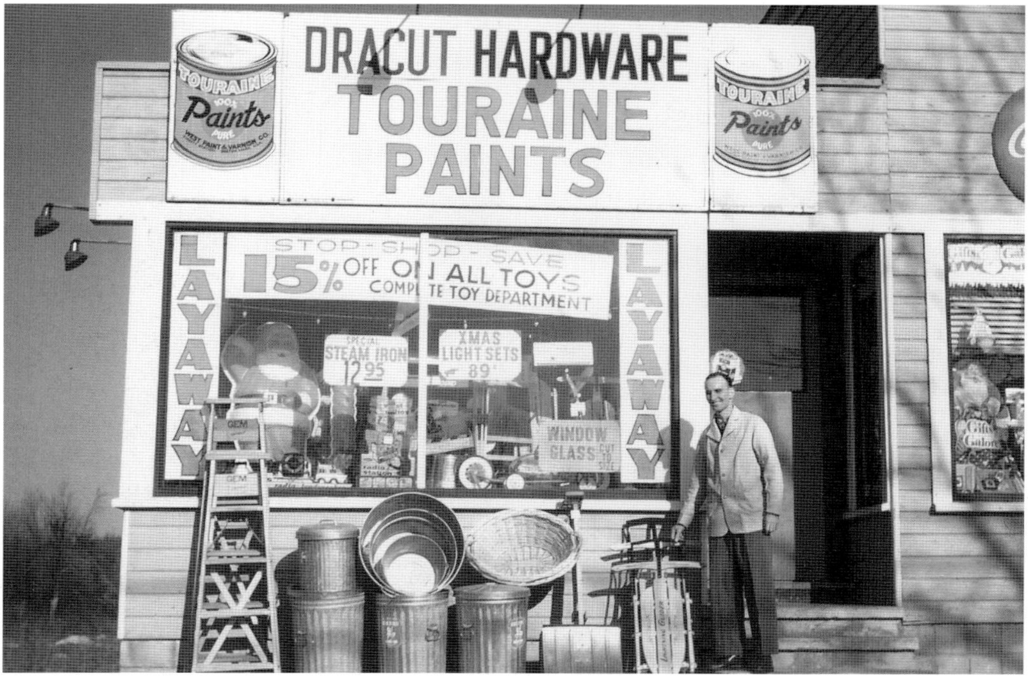

Dracut Hardware
Paul Dumont was born in Arlington on June 1, 1928. In the mid-1940s, the Dumont family moved to North Chelmsford. In 1953, Paul established Dracut Hardware in the Navy Yard district, at what is now Gorman's Plaza. Eventually, it was moved down Lakeview Avenue, across from St. Therese's Church, then relocated again to its current location at 1982 Lakeview Avenue in 1959. The Dumont family still owns and operates the store. (Courtesy the Paul Dumont family.)

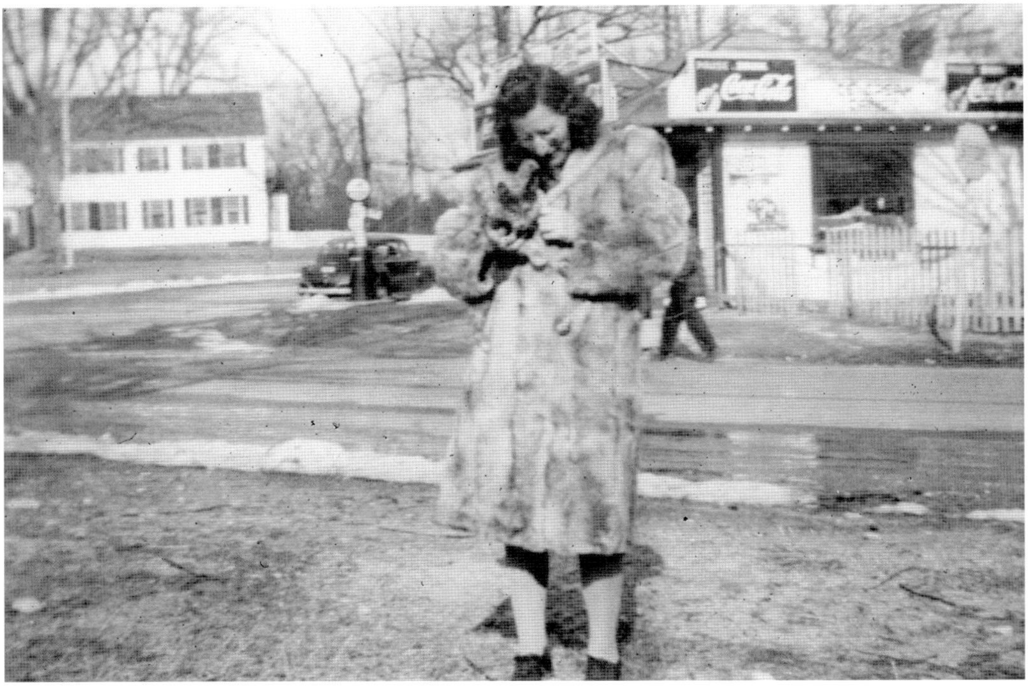

Pauline "Polly" Urquhardt

When Polly Urquhardt passed away at age 91 in 2006, selectman Doug Willett said, "This town will never see another Polly. We have lost an outstanding citizen." Anyone who remembers Polly would agree. Born in Dunstable to Matthew and Ida Urquhardt on September 26, 1904, Polly and her family moved to Dracut when she was a young girl. Her father was the caretaker at Lakeview Park. In the 1930s, Polly and her aunt Minnie rented a small store at the corner of Mammoth Road and Lakeview Avenue. By 1946, Polly had saved enough money to purchase the store. She delivered newspapers to her 100-plus customers until she was 84. She retired in 1991 and deeded the store to the town so the land could be turned into a park. Polly is shown above in 1938. (Above, courtesy the Paul Dumont family; below, courtesy Dracut Historical Society.)

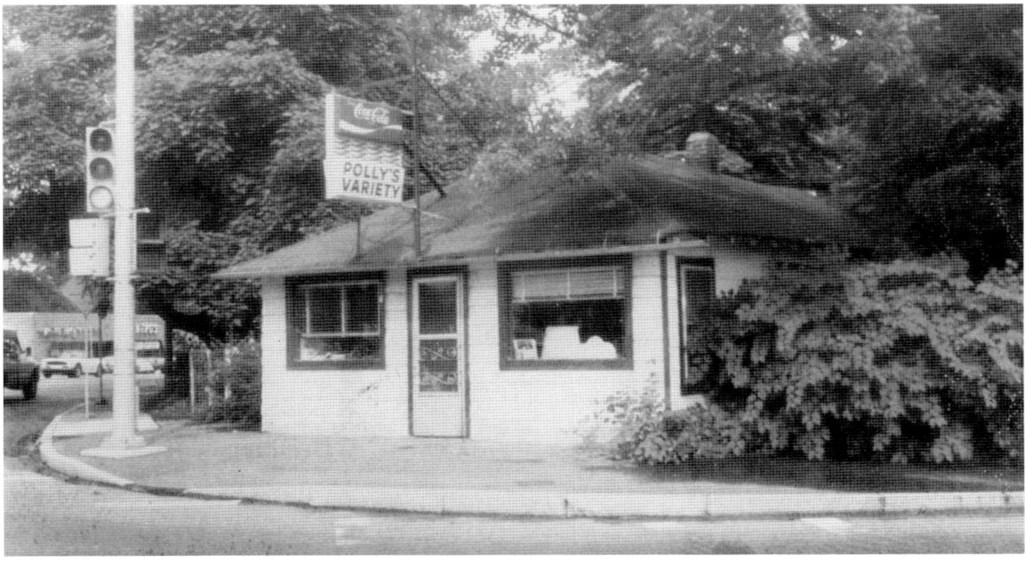

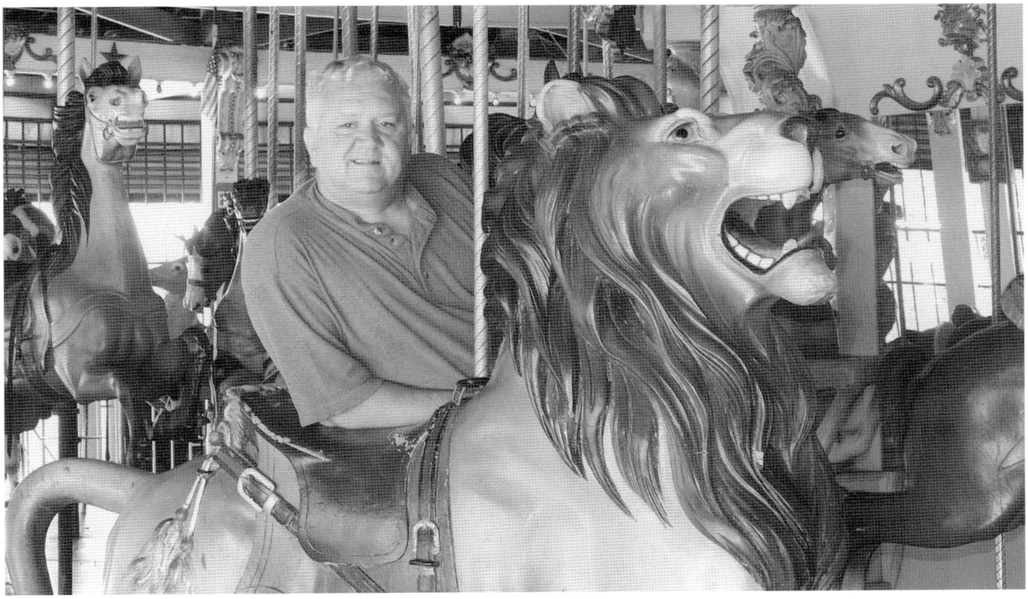

Lenny Proposki

This photograph was taken at the restored Lakeview Carousel in Forest Park, New York. Pictured on the carousel is Lenny Proposki, who has visited the merry-go-round numerous times to photograph it. Born in Lawrence, Proposki has been a professional wedding photographer for 40 years, in addition to working for local newspapers. For 29 years, he was a photographer for Honeywell Information Systems. He is the author of *Boston after Midnight*, a series of black-and-white posters of Boston landmarks. Proposki has served on numerous town boards, including that of appeals. In 1964, Proposki married Doris Brunette, with whom he has three children. (Courtesy Lenny Proposki.)

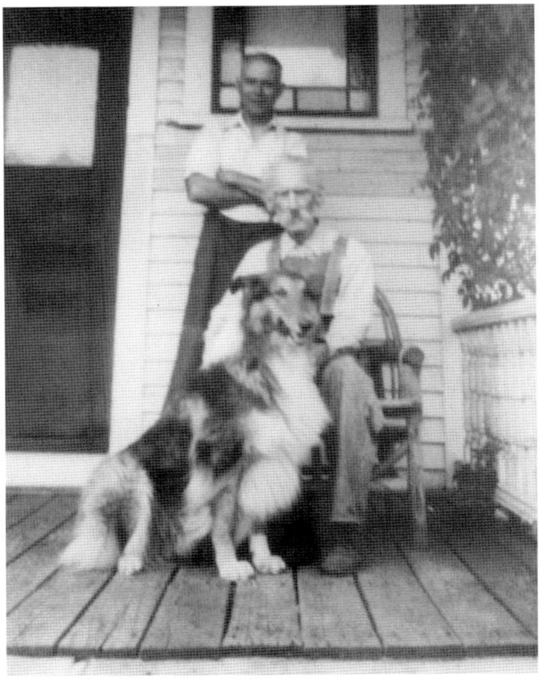

James L. Costello

When James L. Costello passed away at age 92 on November 5, 1952, he was the oldest resident of Collinsville. Born in Lowell, Costello was a resident of Collinsville for 73 years, along with his wife, Rose Ann. Together, they made their home at 1064 Mammoth Road. Costello worked at the American Woolen Company (Beaver Brook Mills) for 57 years, retiring at age 76. The intersection at Lakeview Avenue and Mammoth Road was dedicated to the Costellos' son James F., who was killed in France during World War I in October 1918. The intersection is known today as Costello Square. Costello, or Pop, as he was called, is pictured sitting with his dog Lance and Charles Rogers. (Courtesy Martha Collins.)

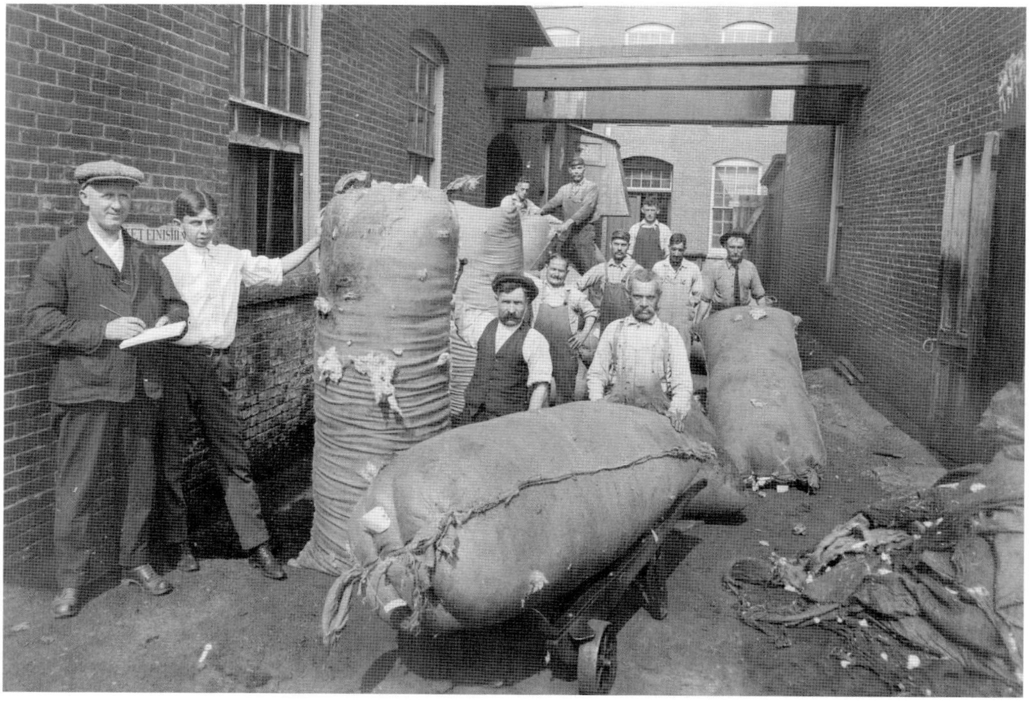

Mill Workers

This photograph was taken at the Beaver Brook Mills, where workers are moving bales of wool. When Michael Collins owned the mills in the late 19th century, he built a canal system utilizing the waterpower of these falls. The canal ran under the mills on the north side of Lakeview Avenue, then under Lakeview Avenue, and into the mills on the south side. The water from the canal reenters Beaver Brook about a half mile downstream from the mills. Homes built for the mill workers can still be seen on Mill Street and Primrose Hill. (Courtesy Dracut Historical Society.)

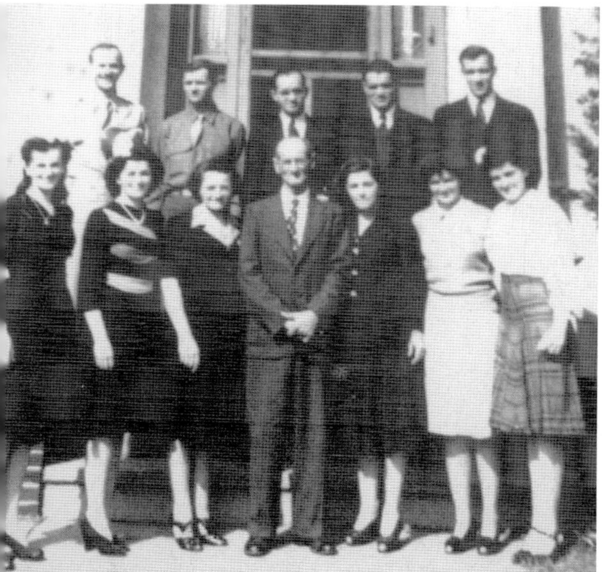

Zoel Houle

Zoel Houle was born in Sainte Brigitte de Saults, Quebec, in 1880. He moved to Dracut around 1900 and married his wife, Pamela Desureault. Together, they had 14 children. Houle was president of the Zoel A. Houle General Contracting Company, which was well known in the area. In addition to their chicken farm on Arlington Street, Zoel and his brother Henri made the first commercial cement blocks in Dracut. Zoel Houle died unexpectedly at age 73 on May 12, 1953. Houle is shown here with 11 of his children. From left to right are (first row) Lucille Webster, Bernadette Matte, Noela Dumond, Zoel Houle, Blanche Vigeant, Rita Gorman, and Gertrude Bouffard; (second row) Emile Houle, Ray Houle, Gilbert Houle, Leo Houle, and Louis Houle. (Courtesy Marietta Paquette.)

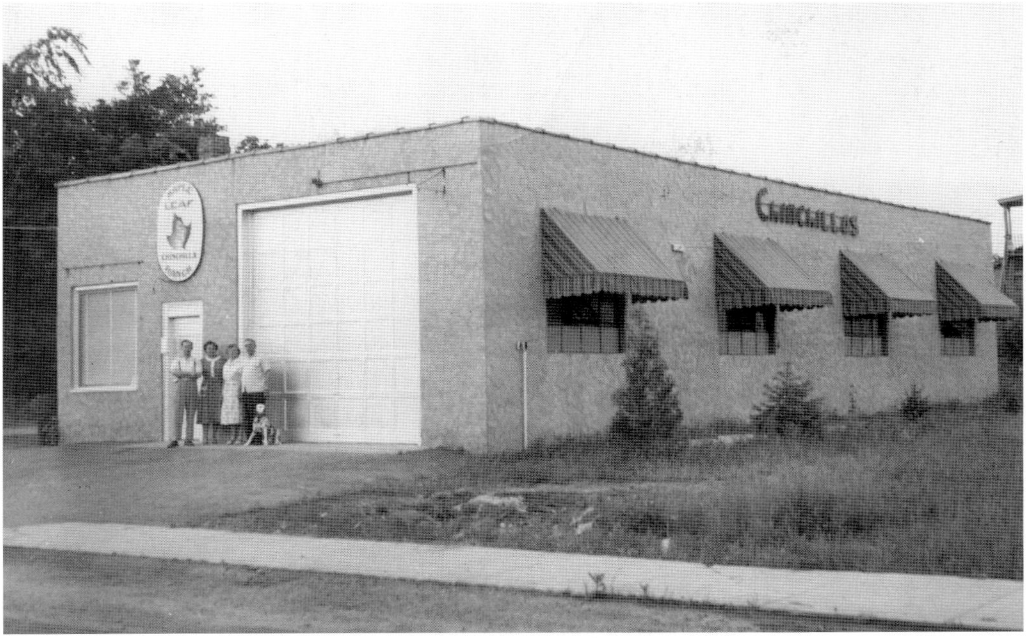

The Houle Family

By the 1950s, the Houle family had begun investing in the chinchilla fur industry and established the Maple Leaf Chinchilla Ranch, pictured here at 101 Arlington Avenue. Indigenous to South America, chinchillas are prized for their soft, beautiful fur. The thickness and color of the fur makes it unique, as each strand has three colors: deep blue at the root, then white, and dark brown at the tip. Chinchilla fur was used for trim on ladies' evening gowns, as well as stoles, jackets, and capes. To make a full-length coat from chinchilla fur, about 200 pelts are necessary. (Both, courtesy Dracut Historical Society.)

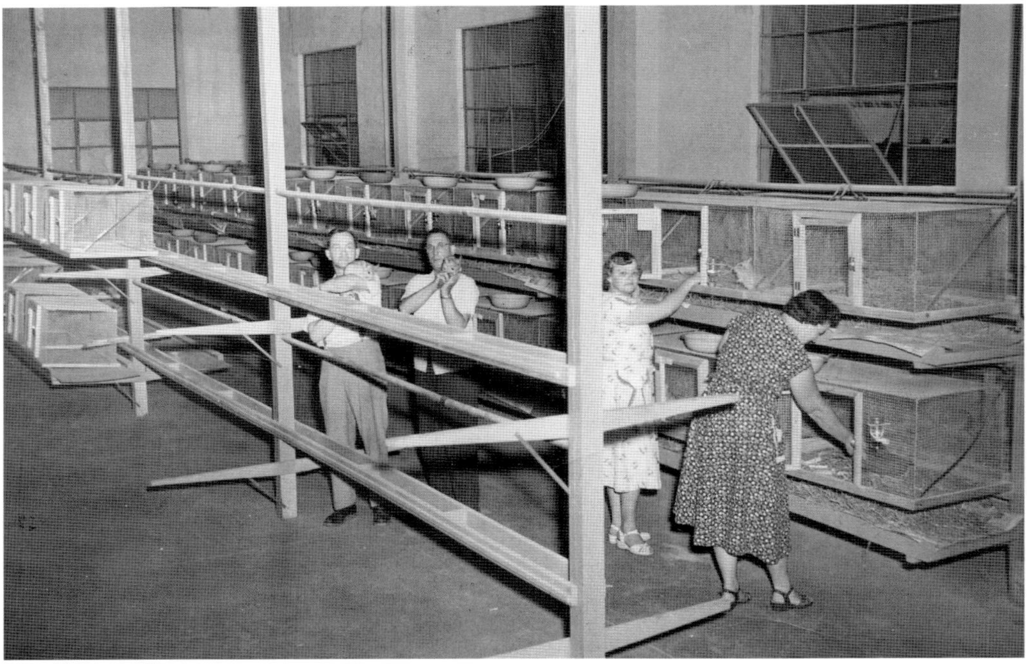

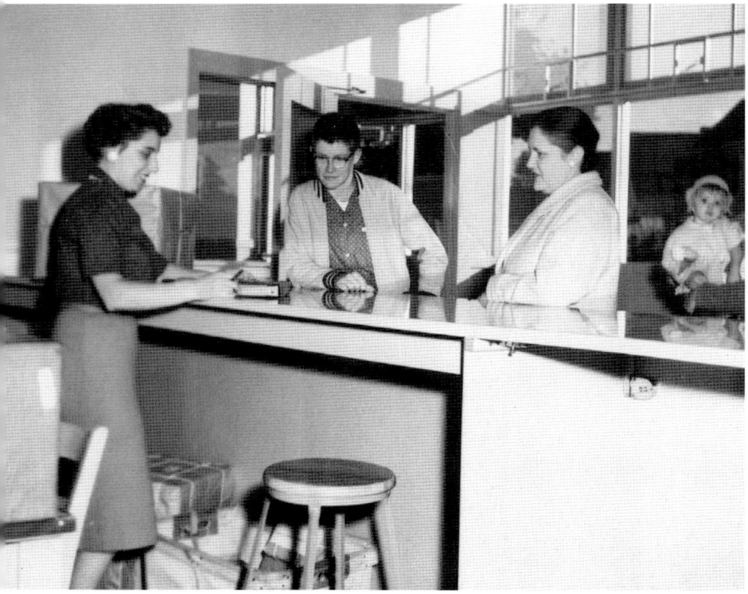

Navy Yard Post Office
Irene Grondine was born in Dracut on November 21, 1928. After graduating from high school, she worked in the Collinsville Post Office for longtime postmaster H. Francis Kiernan. Grondine (left) is shown here at the opening of Dracut's second post office, located at 10 Dinley Street. She opened this post office with postmaster Hubert McAnespie. Grondine married Paul Dumont, the well-known proprietor of Dracut Hardware. The Navy Yard Post Office building is now home to Kashin Garden Restaurant. (Courtesy William Dumont.)

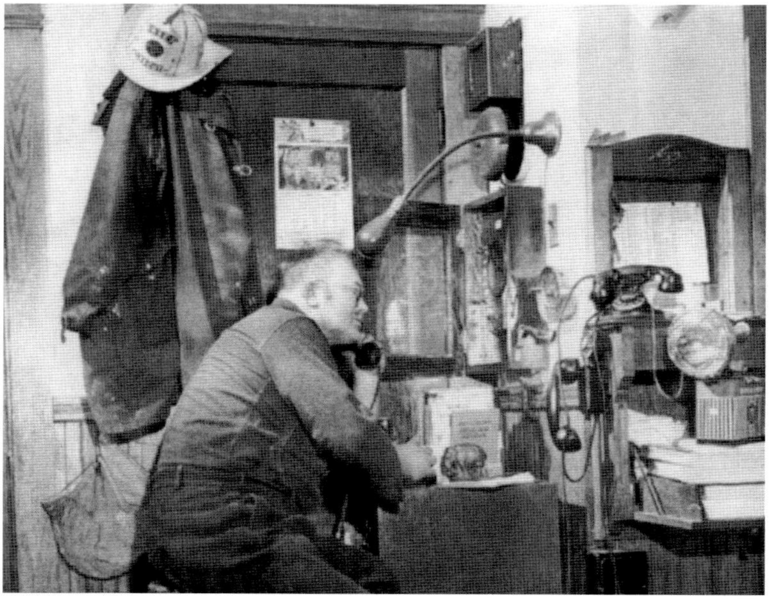

Ernest H. Gunther Jr.
Born in Dracut on February 17, 1902, Ernest Gunther served as fire chief for 33 years. He was first appointed as chief of engineers on May 1, 1934, and tragedy struck the fire department less than four months later. A Dracut fire truck with nine men tipped over on First Street in Lowell on its way to a call. Of those nine men, John Dillon and Robert McAnespie lost their lives. In 2010, the town named the Dillon-McAnespie Park in Collinsville in their memory. Gunther married Katherine Kiernan, daughter of postmaster H. Francis Kiernan, and she faithfully answered calls for the department for 25 years. Gunther is pictured below answering a call in his home. Calls went to the Gunther home until 1961, when a radio was installed in the Navy Yard Station. That same year, the fire department went from an all-volunteer force to a full-time department. Gunther retired in 1967 and passed away on March 1, 1978. (Courtesy Dracut Historical Society.)

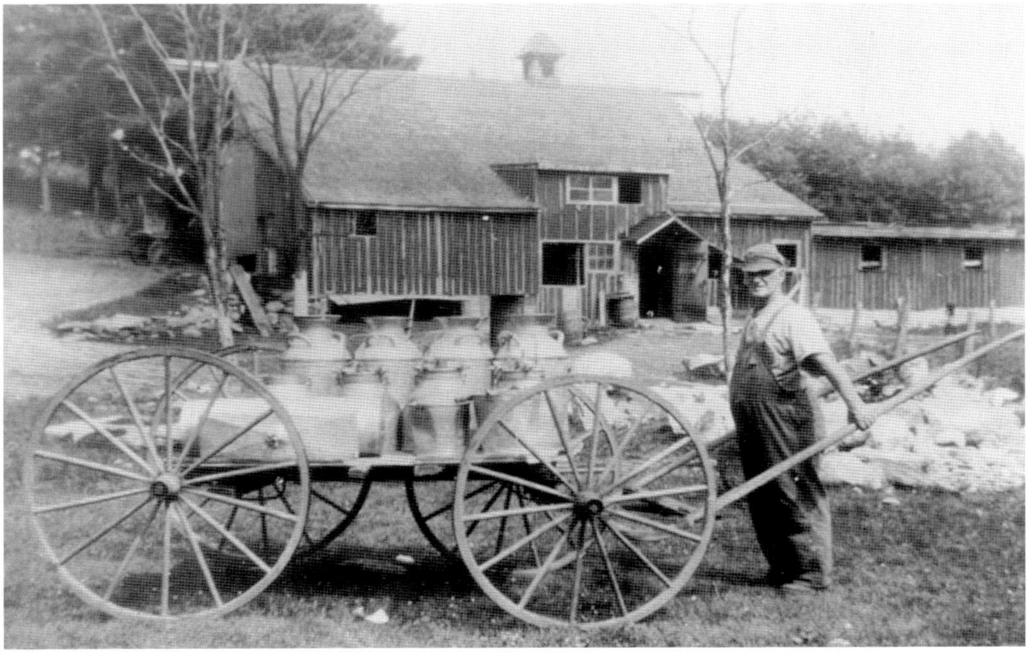

M.L. Shaw Sr.

Mark L. Shaw Sr. (pictured above) and his wife, Annie, of Nova Scotia, were married on November 27, 1889. They had three children: Mark Jr., Albert, and Gladys. Prior to establishing the Shaw Dairy Farm in 1908, they operated the Shaw-Hutchinson Bakery. In 1908, Mark and Annie purchased a plot of land at 195 New Boston Road and built a house, barn, and milk house. In 1912, Mark Jr. began delivering milk for the Oliver J. Coburn Farm, where the Dracut Historical Society is now located. When the Coburn farm went out of business, Mark Jr. had the opportunity to retain the home delivery customers he had served while working for Coburn. (Above, courtesy Warren Shaw; below, courtesy Dracut Historical Society.)

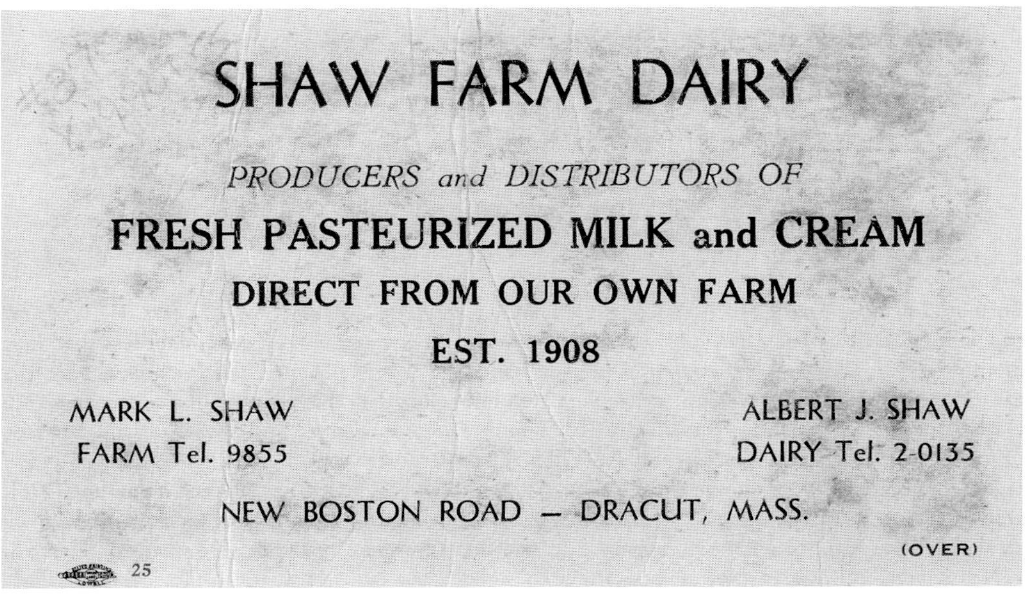

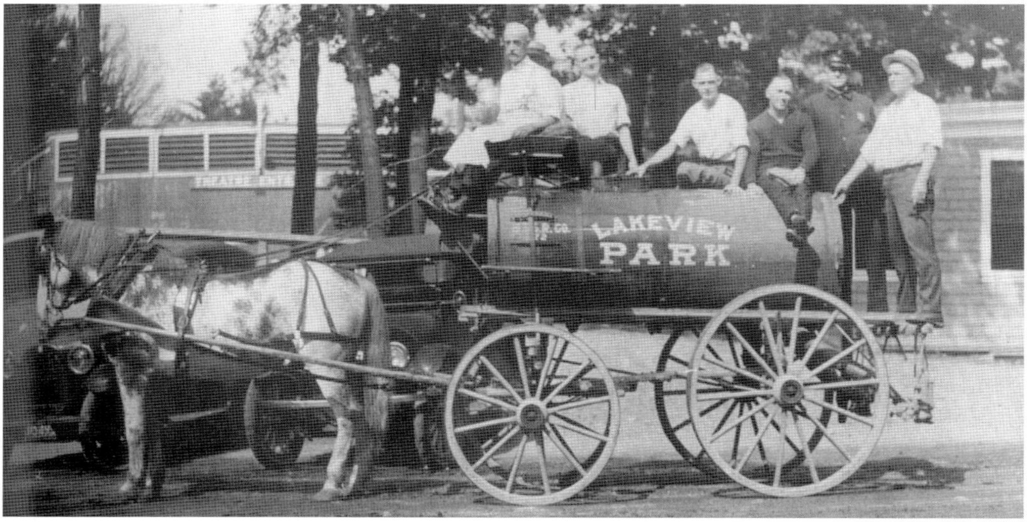

Matthew Urquhart

This photograph was taken in 1921 at Lakeview Park, and anyone who visited Lakeview at that time would have known the man at the reins of the wagon. As caretaker of the park, Matthew Urquhart lived on the grounds for 25 years. Hired in 1918, he remained caretaker until his death at age 66 on November 29, 1943. Later Dracut residents would come to know and love one of Matthew's three daughters, Polly, whose store was at the corner of Lakeview Avenue and Mammoth Road. (Courtesy Dracut Historical Society.)

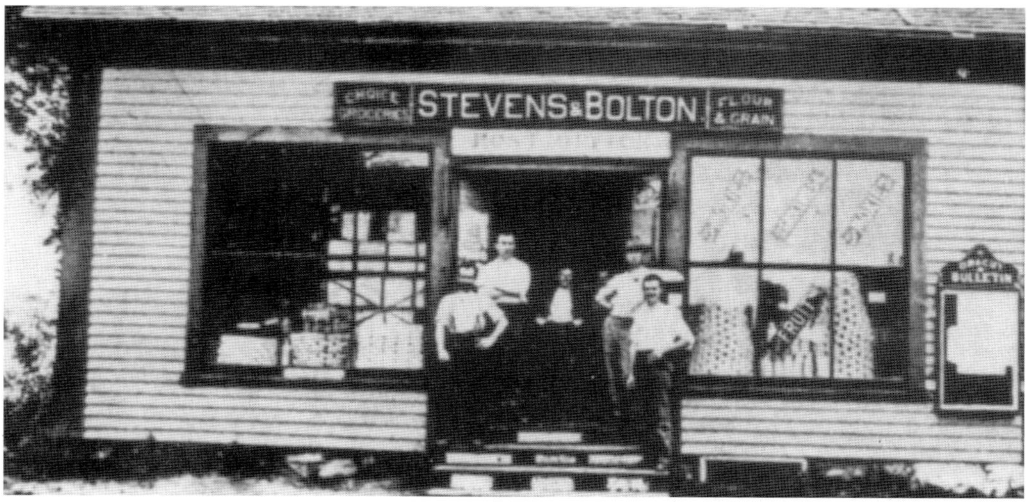

Stevens & Bolton Store

Countless Dracut High School students have gone to this store when prom season arrives. Today's residents know it as A's Tux Formal Center, run by proprietor Dot Ambrosino. However, this building has been the site of business for almost 200 years. Originally owned and operated by the Wilson family as a blacksmith shop and then as dry goods store, it was then operated as the Stevens-Hodge Grocery and Provisions. George Stevens was later involved in the historical society and held numerous town positions. Stevens's aunt helped get him into the grocer business. His first partner was Charles L. Hodge. Hodge sold his share of the partnership to Peter Bolton, and the store became known as Stevens & Bolton, as shown in this photograph. (Courtesy Dracut Historical Society.)

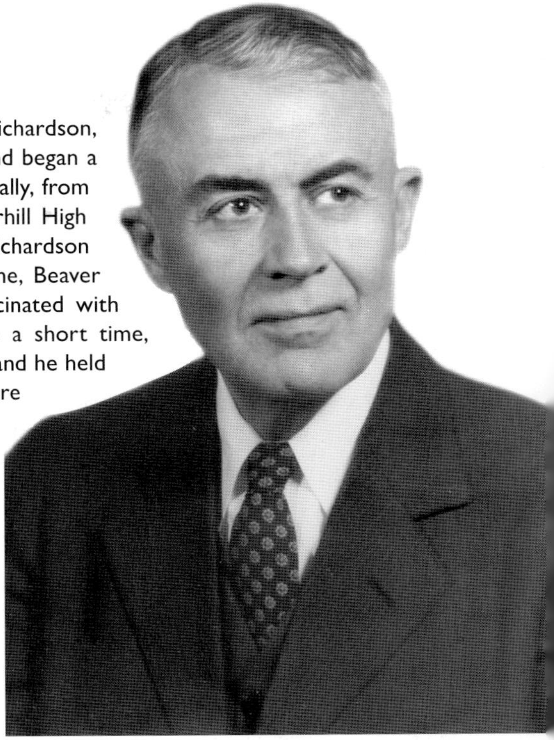

Lester G. Richardson

Born in Dracut to George A.H. and Julia (Cutter) Richardson, Lester Richardson graduated from Harvard University and began a teaching career first in Maynard, then Leominster, and finally, from 1909 to 1913, as the science department chair at Haverhill High School, where he earned $1,500 annually. Illness forced Richardson to retire from teaching and convalesce at his family home, Beaver Brook Farm (below). While bedridden, he became fascinated with the New York Stock Exchange and began investing. In a short time, Richardson's initial investments had grown to $1 million, and he held stock in several large national companies, two of which were Paramount Pictures and the Public Theatre Corporation. When these two companies wanted to merge in 1930, company representatives had to visit Richardson at his home to have the merger approved due to the large amount of stock he held in both. However, tragedy struck on October 20, 1950, when a speeding car hit Richardson while on his nightly walk along Mammoth Road. He died at the scene. He was 68. The Dracut High School auditorium is dedicated to Richardson. (Right, courtesy Peter Richardson; below, courtesy Dracut Historical Society.)

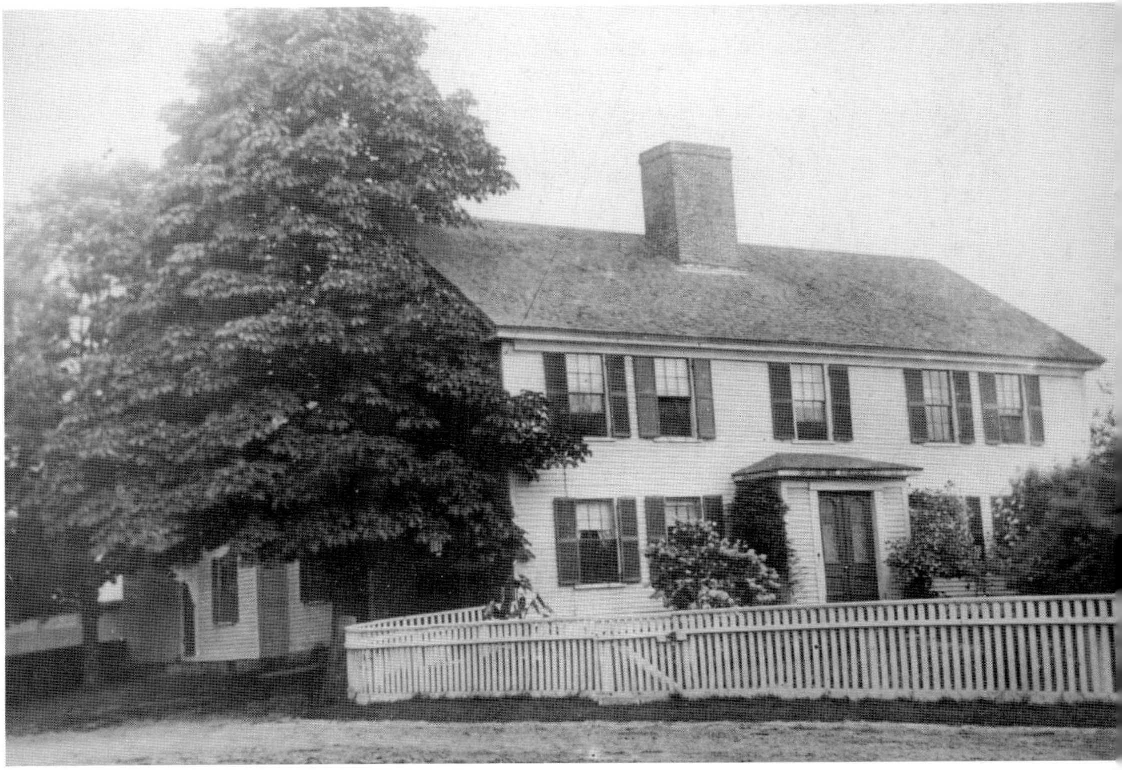

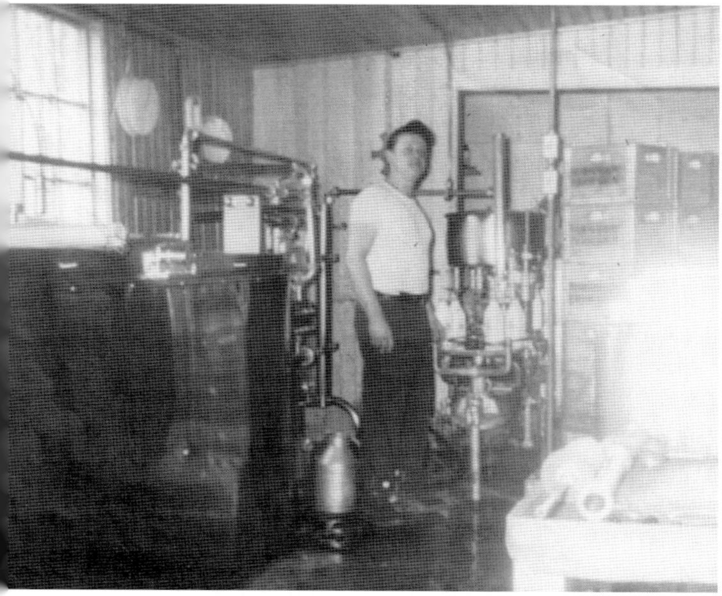

Walter "Wally" Beidron Sr.
Wally Biedron Sr. is pictured here in the Shaw Farm milk bottling plant around 1952. He lived on Old Road when he began working for Shaw Farm until his retirement in 1994. He eventually became the milk-processing manager. His son Walter Biedron Jr. still works on the farm as the herdsman. (Courtesy Warren Shaw.)

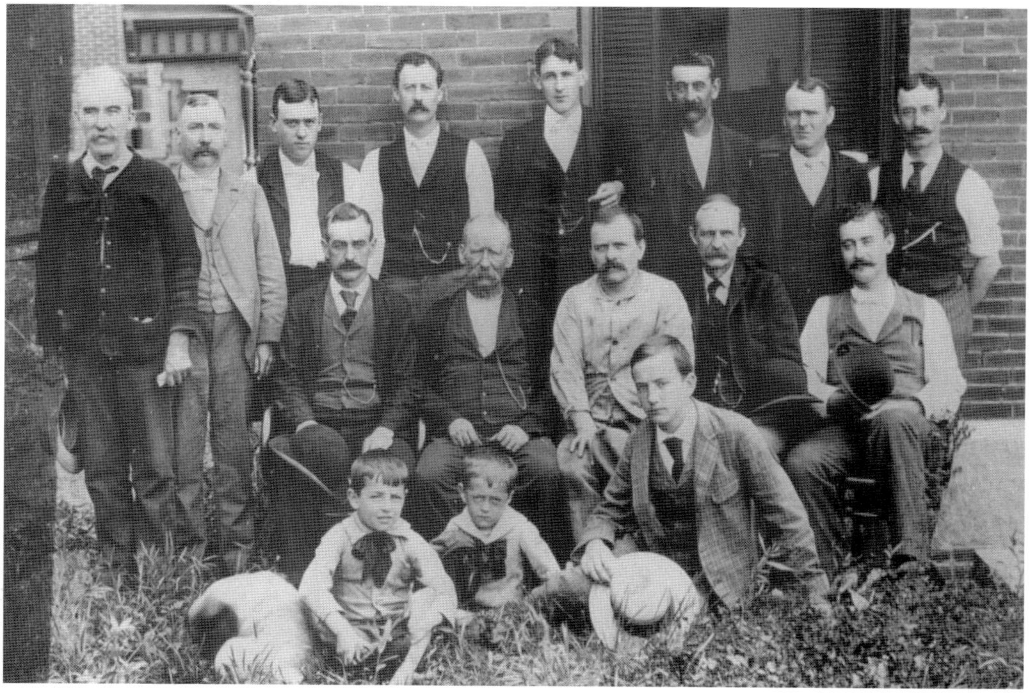

William Bromley
Known throughout Collinsville for his straw hat and for keeping the mills' master clock working, William H. Bromley retired as superintendent of the American Woolen Company (Beaver Brook Mills) in December 1952. His retirement marked the end of an era. For 74 years, a Bromley had worked in the mills. His father started there as a boss spinner. Bromley was a four-term selectman who retired from the board in 1966. Bromley is shown in the first row seated (with his straw hat). His father, Edward, is seated second from the left. This photograph was taken around 1899. (Courtesy Dracut Historical Society.)

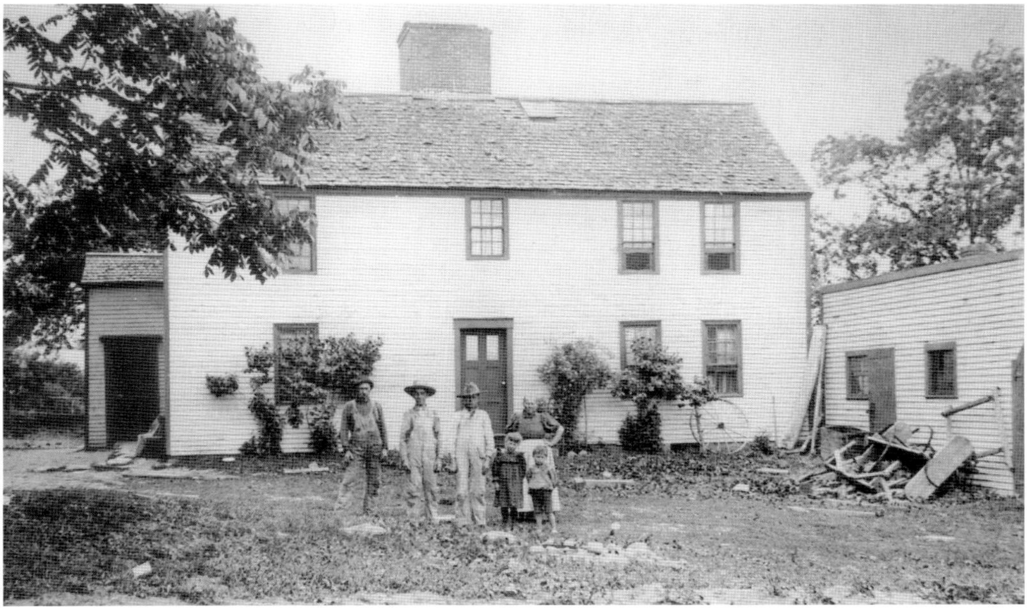

Ephraim Curtis

Built in 1737, the Ephraim Curtis farm was located on Broadway Road (where Dunkin' Donuts is today). During the French and Indian War, the English forced the French Acadians out of Nova Scotia. Several displaced Acadian families came to Dracut looking for assistance as they traveled south out of Canada, one of whom, the Landerie family, stayed at the Curtis farm. The farm continued until 1930, when the house was razed. Members of the Curtis family are pictured above. (Courtesy Dracut Historical Society.)

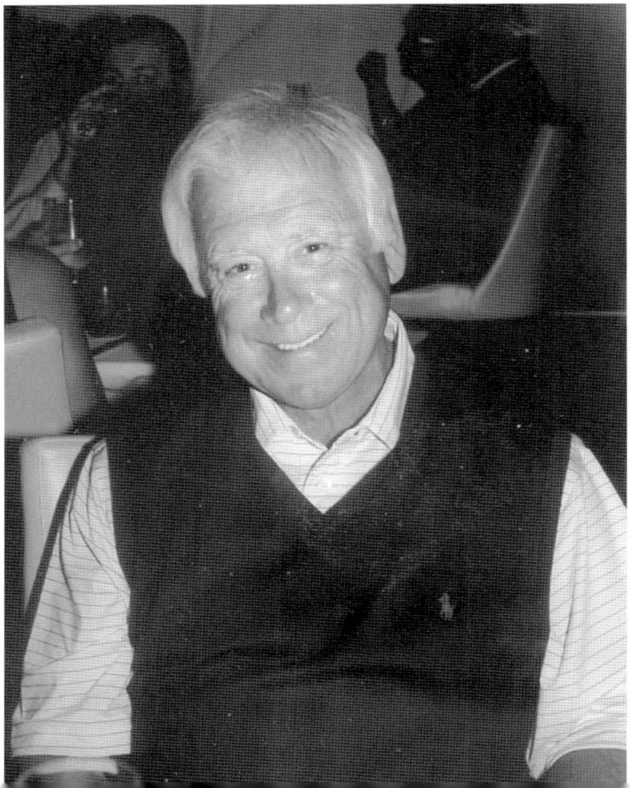

Andrew Graham

The Blue Angus Café located at 34 Broadway Road was established in 2006. Andrew Graham, one of the proprietors, not only helps run this successful Dracut eatery but has also worked for the town for 40 years in several capacities. Most recently, he has served as the supervisor of building and grounds for the public schools. During this time, he has overseen the building of the Lakeview Junior High School (now the Richardson Middle School) and the current renovation of Dracut High School. (Courtesy Judy Enis.)

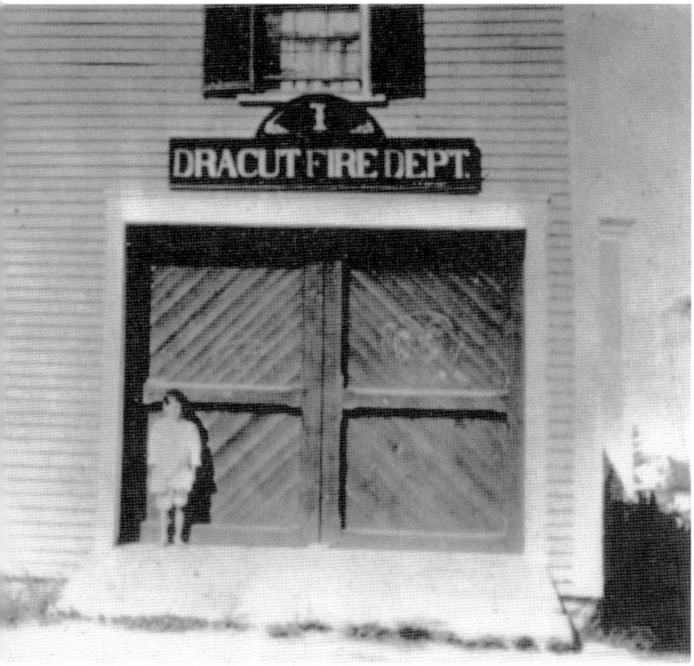

Thomas Dinley

Born to Michael and Mary Dinley in 1903, Thomas Dinley came from a well-known family. The Dinleys owned a popular store in the Navy Yard. Thomas Dinley was a Navy Seabee who spent time in Guam before working in Dracut's highway department for many years. He passed away in 1986. In this photograph, Dinley is standing in front of the Navy Yard fire station. Originally, there were four stations throughout town: the first was in Kenwood, which was near the Kenwood School; the second was in the Dracut Center, which was near the library, but the building is now gone; the third was in the Navy Yard, which was the old central station on Pleasant Street; and the fourth was in Collinsville, which is still in use. (Courtesy the Paul Dumont family.)

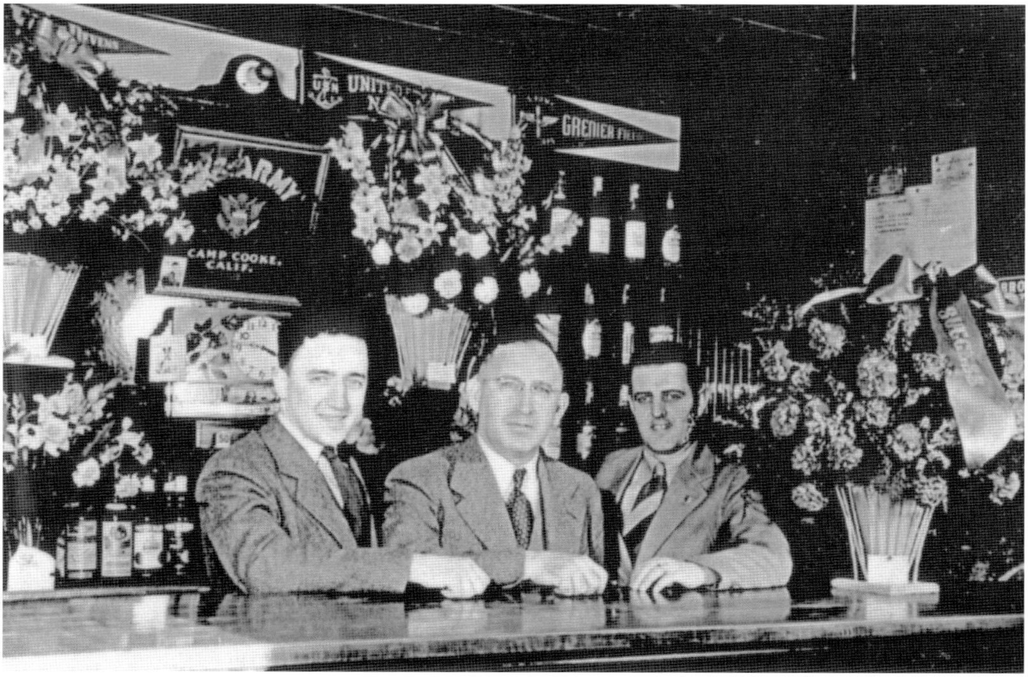

Arthur H. Beauregard

This photograph was taken inside the Fleur de Lys Club, which has been a popular spot in Dracut for many years. From left to right are Bill McDermott, Emile Daigle, and Arthur Beauregard. Beauregard was born in Lowell on June 6, 1911. A naval veteran of World War II, he lived at 320 Varnum Road with his wife, Ethel. For 18 years, he owned and operated Town and Country Dry Cleaners in Dracut. The Fleur de Lys Club is still in operation. (Courtesy the Paul Dumont family.)

CHAPTER SIX

Preserving Dracut

Past and Future

Our communities are a direct result of the hard work of those who came before us. It is our responsibility to continue what was started before us and build upon it. Dracut's past is full of men and women who have worked to preserve the town's history and heritage: John Bailey, George Stevens, Silas Coburn, John Pendergast, Donat Paquet, Betty Baroni, and Harvey Gagnon, just to name a few. Their collective efforts have contributed books, museums, videos, civic buildings, monuments, research papers, and paintings.

It is not just historians who preserve the past, however. Throughout this book—or any book—on Dracut, the importance of farming is mentioned. Though most farms were lost to developers after World War II, the town has been able to maintain its rural appeal. This was made possible due to the efforts of one woman—Marjorie Dunlap. Her desire to preserve her farm and not lose it to developers marks the beginning of land preservation in Dracut. So while she did not write a history of Dracut farms, she took action that preserved the actual land, laying the groundwork for a future in which the rural character of the town would continue to exist.

In 1982, Dunlap asked Warren Shaw for his help in protecting her farm. Shaw describes that day on Ed Pomerleau's neighboring property where he was haying as "easily the most significant moment in town history," because it marked the beginning of the land preservation movement in Dracut. Three people were primarily responsible for this part of the town's history: Marjorie Dunlap, John Ogonowski, and Warren Shaw. Because of a simple idea Marjorie Dunlap had to preserve her family farm, the following land has been preserved in Dracut: Veterans Memorial Park, a 48-acre site adjacent to the Dunlap farm acquired during the golf course approval; part of the Shaw farm; the Pomerleau farm, which abuts the Dunlap farm; the Lyzinski property; and the Saja farm.

The efforts of Dunlap, Ogonowski, and Shaw have not gone unnoticed by those in the agricultural and civic communities. Dracut renamed the annual Earth Day celebration in April as Marjorie Dunlap Day, the Massachusetts Farm Bureau Federation (MFBF) established the John Ogonowski Award, and Shaw was awarded the Ogonowski award in December 2012. The MFBF annually presents the Ogonowski Award to a farm bureau member who has "shown distinguished service to the organization and to the agricultural community as a whole."

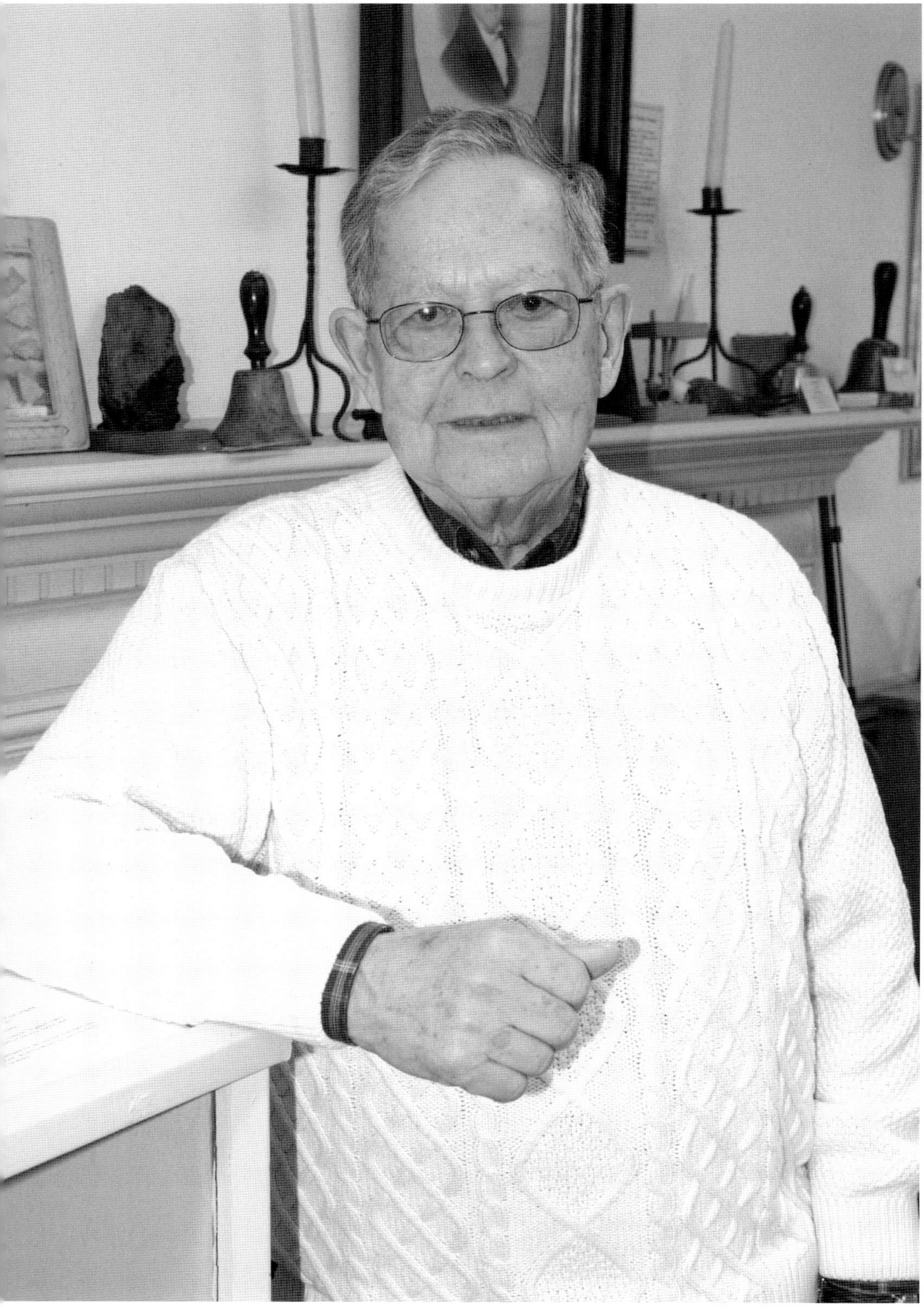

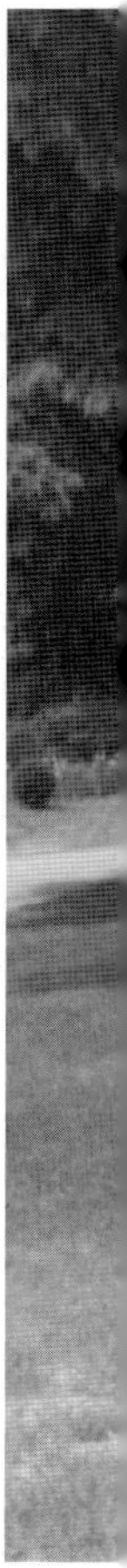

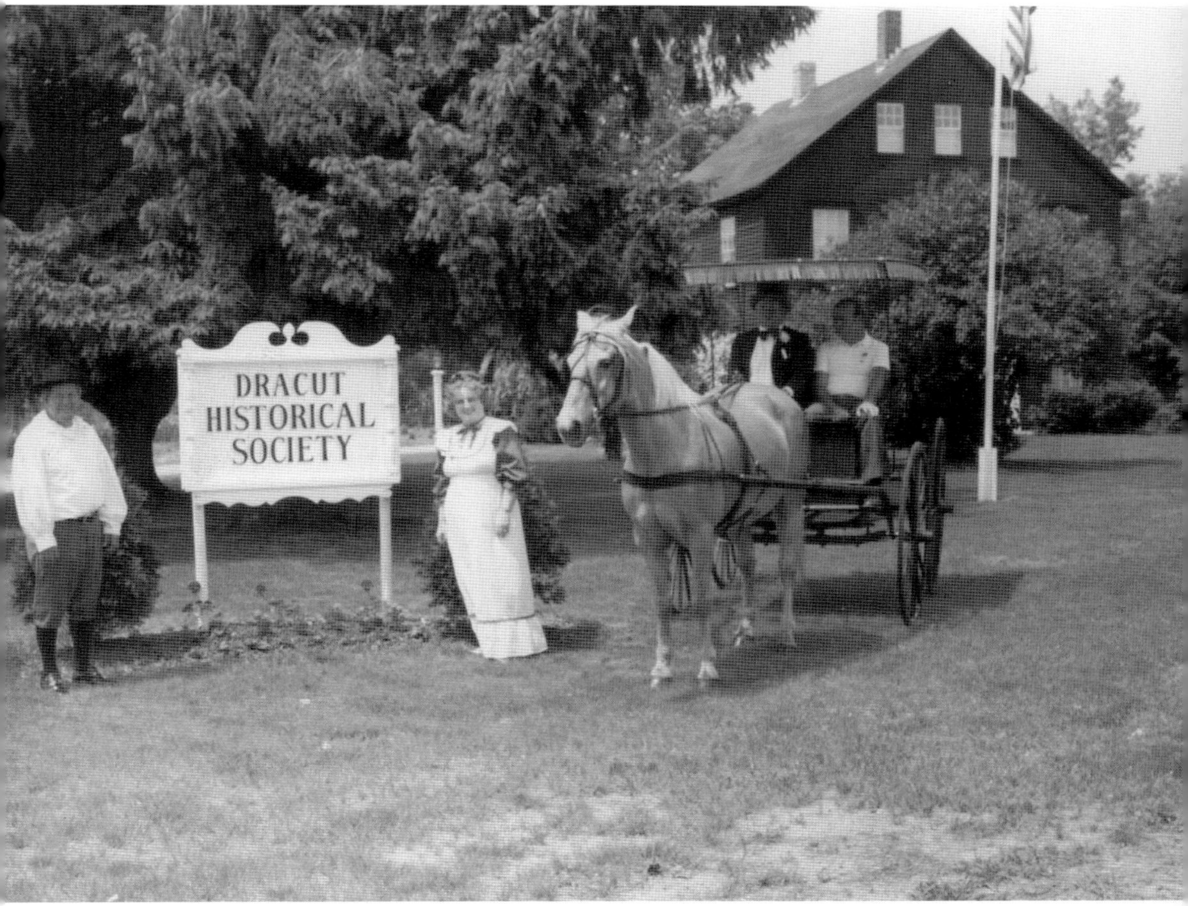

Harvey J. Gagnon

No discussion about Dracut would be complete, or accurate, if it did not include Harvey J. Gagnon. The oldest of 10 children, Gagnon was born to Albert J. and Corine B. Gagnon of Chelmsford on March 25, 1931. Gagnon's grandparents lived in Dracut, where they made their first home on Goodhue Avenue, now the site of St. Marguerite D'Youville. Eventually, they sold that farm and moved to the corner of Parker and Lakeview Avenues. Albert and Corine moved their young family from Chelmsford to Dracut in 1938, and Harvey entered second grade in the Dracut Public Schools. He graduated from Dracut High School in 1949 and married Loyce E. Thomas in 1953. Through the years, Gagnon has been active in numerous town organizations and boards, beginning with the Dracut Alumni Association. He served on the Dracut Scholarship Foundation for 40 years, until stepping down to serve on the Community Preservation Committee in 2001. Gagnon joined the Dracut Historical Society in 1978 and has been an active member ever since, including serving as president of the society. He is also a member of the Dracut Grange, Dracut Historical Commission, and Permanent Building Committee. In 1994, Gagnon's initiative was the driving force behind the preservation, and relocation, of Harmony Hall. In 1997, Harmony Hall (now handicap accessible) was reopened at its current location for town use. In regard to his town service, Gagnon humbly says, "Loyce and I are very grateful in having the opportunity to participate in our community." In the c. 1980 photograph above, from left to right are Harvey Gagnon, Priscilla Daigle, Whitey Baldwin, and Leon Litchfield. (Opposite page, courtesy Lenny Proposki; above, courtesy Dracut Historical Society.)

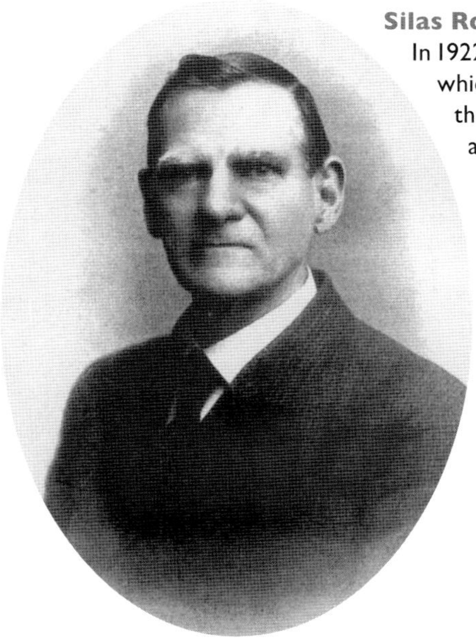

Silas Roger Coburn

In 1922, Silas R. Coburn published *History of Dracut, Massachusetts*, which covers all aspects of the town's history. He dedicated the book as follows: "The people of Dracut, Mass. And to all descendants of those sturdy pioneers who were the early settlers in this vicinity. Wherever their lot is cast This Memorial is dedicated with respect and affection." Anyone who is interested in learning more about Dracut owes much to Coburn and will refer to his work at one point or another, as his book is the first significant history of the town. Coburn died in 1932. (Courtesy Dracut Historical Society.)

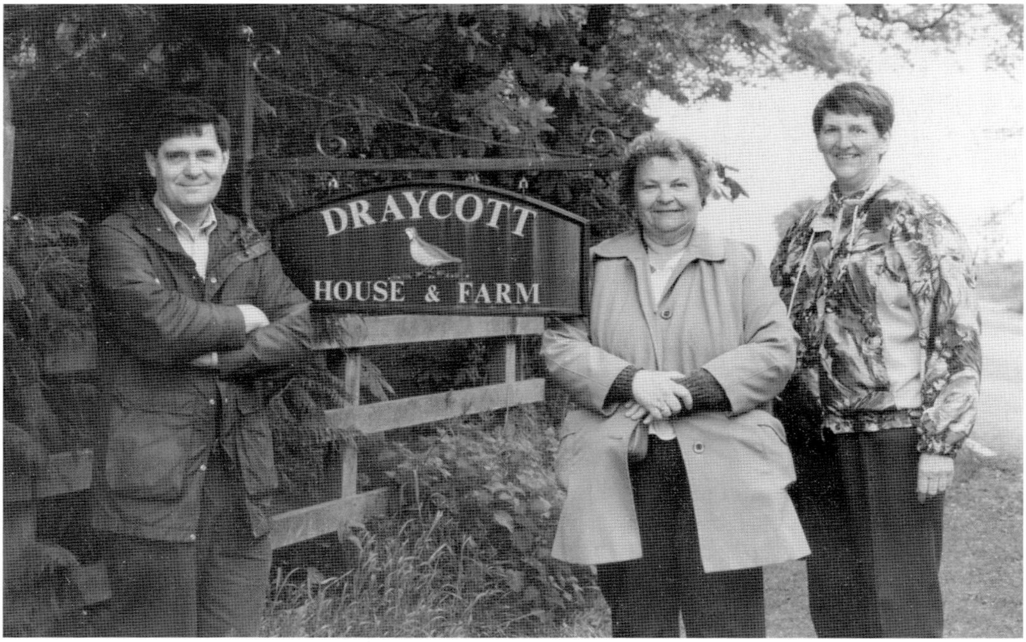

Esther Garland and Norma Taplin

As longtime members of the Dracut Historical Society, Esther Garland and Norma Taplin have been invaluable to the organization, volunteering many hours to provide tours on Sundays, serving as officers, or answering inquiries from the public about the town's history. Esther (left) and Norma (right) are pictured here with Larry Zimmerman on Sunday, May 26, 1996. They were traveling with about 15 others, mostly from Dracut. The group was interested in locating the village of Draycott Foliat. The town had virtually disappeared, but this manor house bearing the name still existed. John Evered Webb, Dracut's first settler, had come from this area of England. There is no other town, anywhere, with the name *Dracut*. (Courtesy Larry Zimmerman.)

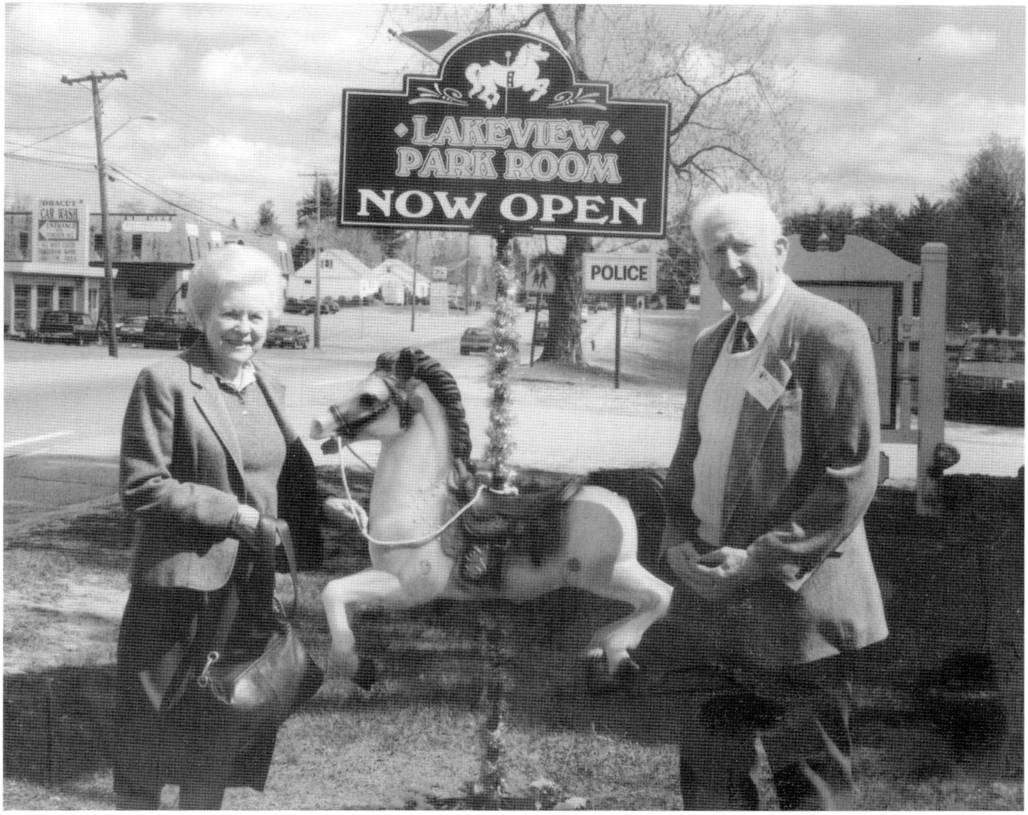

James V. and Dorothy G. Kiernan Coincidentally born on the same day, July 27, 1917, James and Dorothy (Grondine) Kiernan were dedicated members of the Dracut Historical Society, where they are shown above at the opening of the Lakeview Park Room in the 1980s. James Kiernan was determined to revitalize the organization in the early 1960s. He worked tirelessly to incorporate the society, and when a new charter was written in 1963, he served as the first president. Kiernan then served on the board of directors and was one of the people involved in securing the Oliver Coburn house as a permanent home for the society. In addition, he and his wife donated the mailboxes, which are still on display, from the original post office in the Kiernan store. At right is the Kiernan home on Lakeview Avenue. (Above, courtesy Dracut Historical Society; right, courtesy Martha K. Wolfe.)

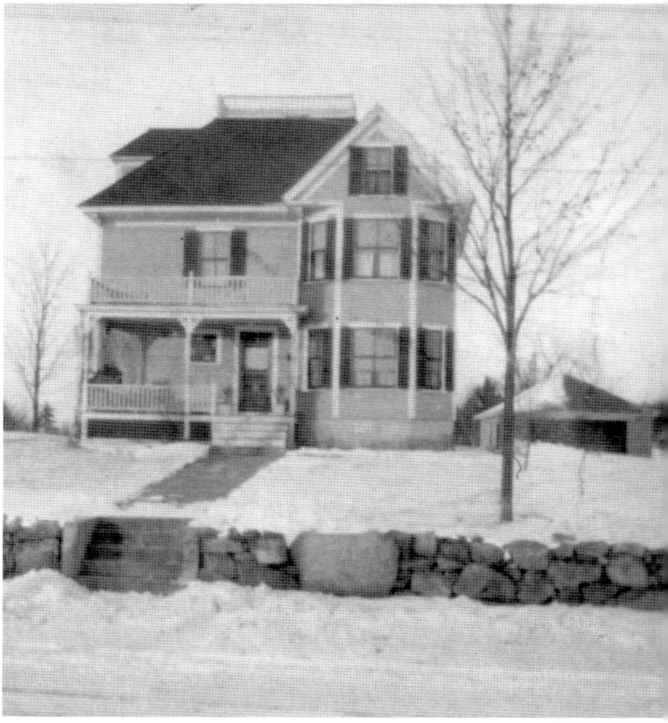

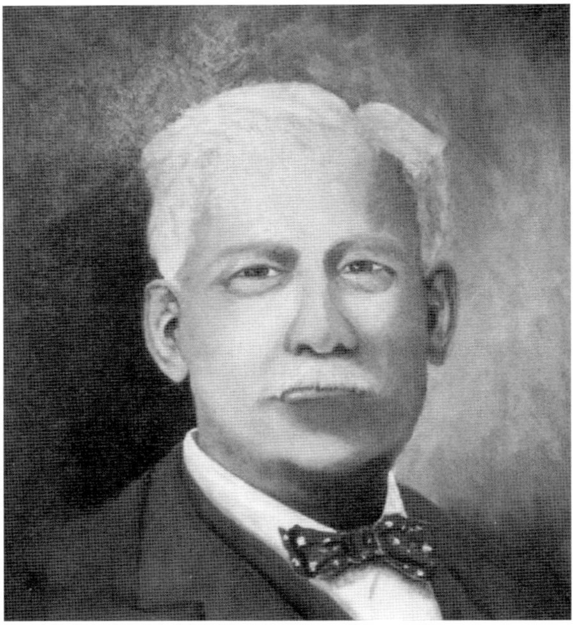

John Bailey
The historical society owes much to John Bailey, who moved to Dracut when he was 74 years old. He realized that the town's early museum, then housed in the town offices on Arlington Street, was in need of attention, and he worked diligently to archive and collect important town records and documents. Officially organizing the Dracut Historical Society in June 1928, Bailey was elected as the society's first president, and today, the Research Room at the historical society is named in his honor. This portrait by Betty Baroni hangs in the historical society, located in the former Oliver Coburn house. (Courtesy Dracut Historical Society.)

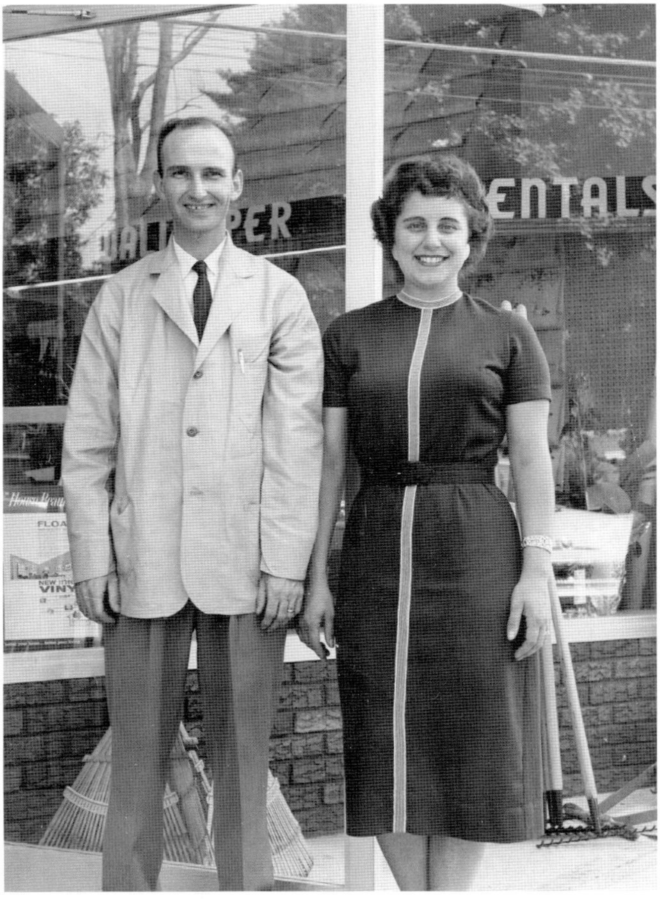

Paul Dumont
Paul Dumont is shown here with his wife, Irene (Grondine) Dumont, in front of Dracut Hardware on Lakeview Avenue, which they owned and operated for 50 years. Dumont had a passion for history. Over the years, he amassed an extensive photograph and postcard collection that has become an excellent source for local historians. (Courtesy the Paul Dumont family.)

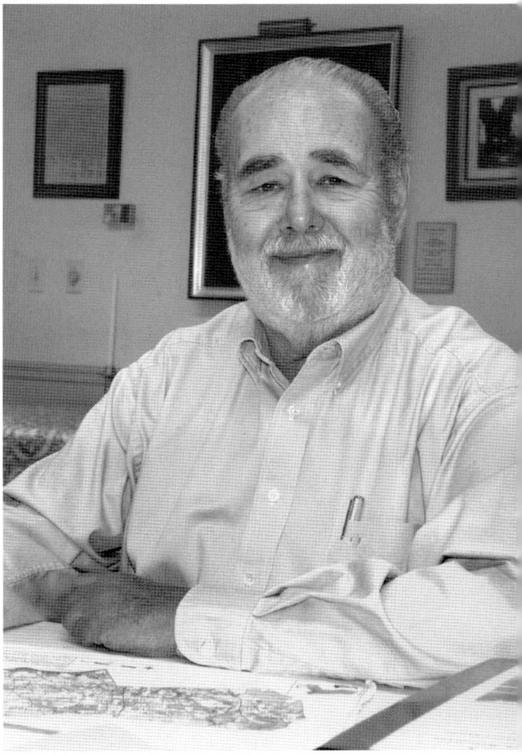

David Paquin

Over the past 20 years, David Paquin has been involved in numerous preservation efforts and historical events, serving as chairman of the following organizations: Dracut Historical Commission, since 1994; Old Home Day Committee, from 2001 to 2011; and Dracut Tercentennial Committee, from 1999 to 2002. Of all his projects, he is most proud of his work in creating the 9/11 memorial at the Jones Avenue Fire Station. When Paquin first heard that municipalities were able to apply for a piece of the steel infrastructure from the fallen World Trade Center, he approached town manager Dennis Piendak, who fully supported the idea. Paquin submitted the request to the Port Authority of New York and New Jersey, and Dracut was approved as a recipient. Paquin then designed the memorial and oversaw its construction. The memorial was dedicated in July 2011. (Right, courtesy Lenny Proposki; below, author's collection.)

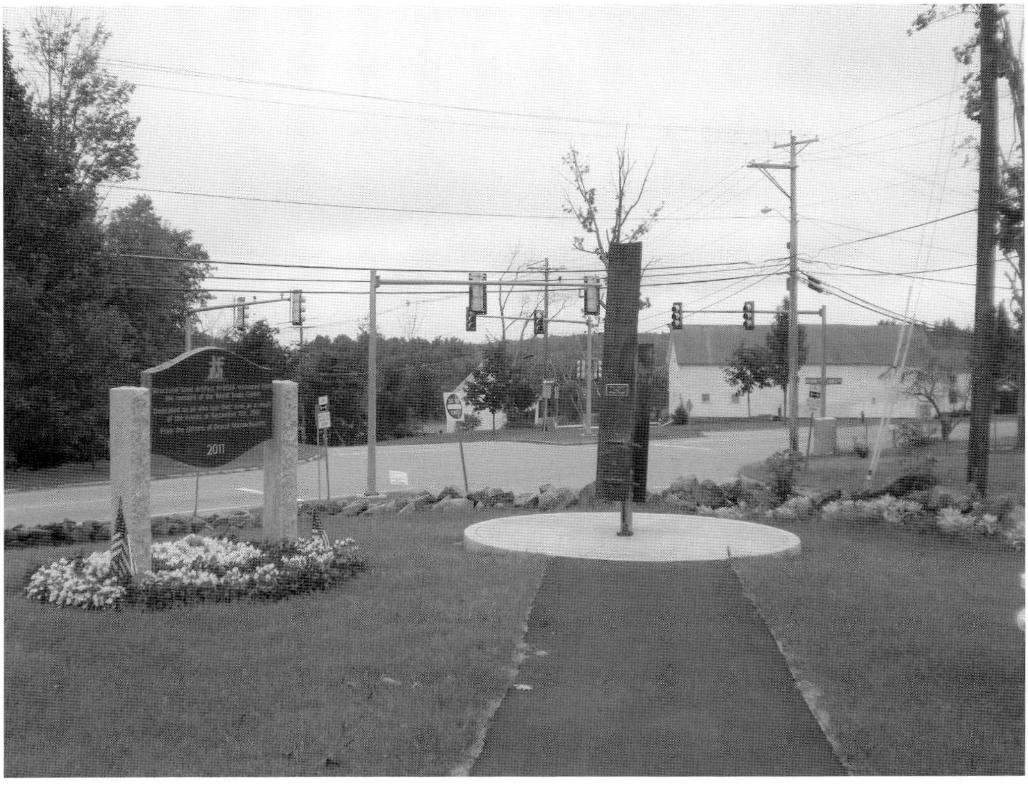

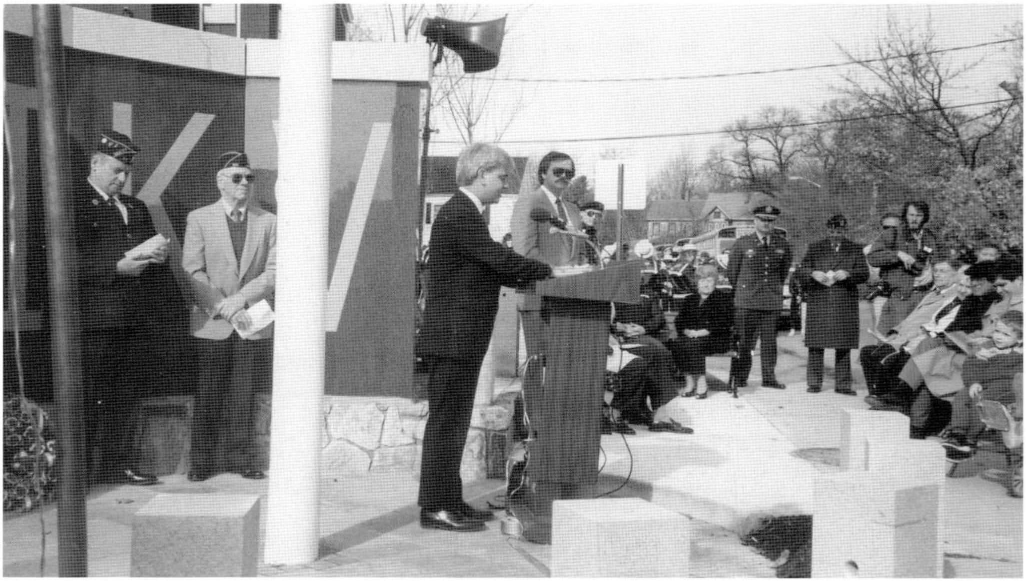

Frank Gorman

Frank Gorman has been actively restoring and revitalizing different areas throughout town for many years. Pictured above is the rededication ceremony of the war memorial at the corner of Pleasant and Sladen Steets on November 11, 1989. In 1943, the Navy Yard's World War II honor roll was erected at this location and dedicated to the memory of Clarence Nichols, who died in Africa on December 18, 1942. The honor roll deteriorated over time and was eventually torn down. Frank and Darlene Gorman rededicated the site to Clarence Nichols and his brother Edmund, who was killed in Korea, and erected a new memorial to them and all those from Dracut who served in both World Wars, Korea, and Vietnam. Below, the Beaver Brook Mills are pictured undergoing renovations, when Gorman was revitalizing the old mills. Today, it is the site of Owen and Ollie's. (Above, courtesy Dracut Historical Society; below, courtesy Frank Gorman.)

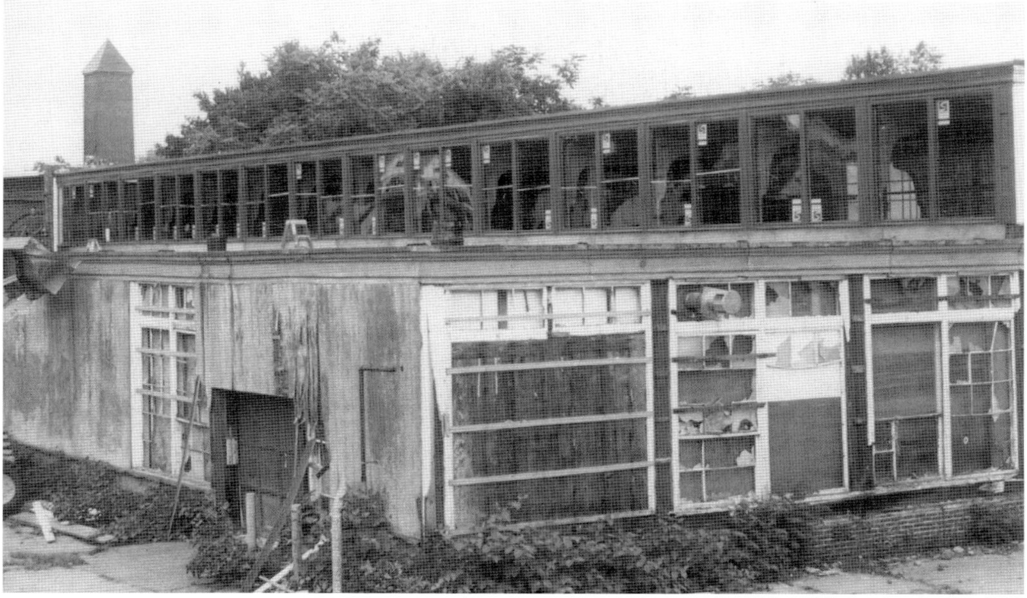

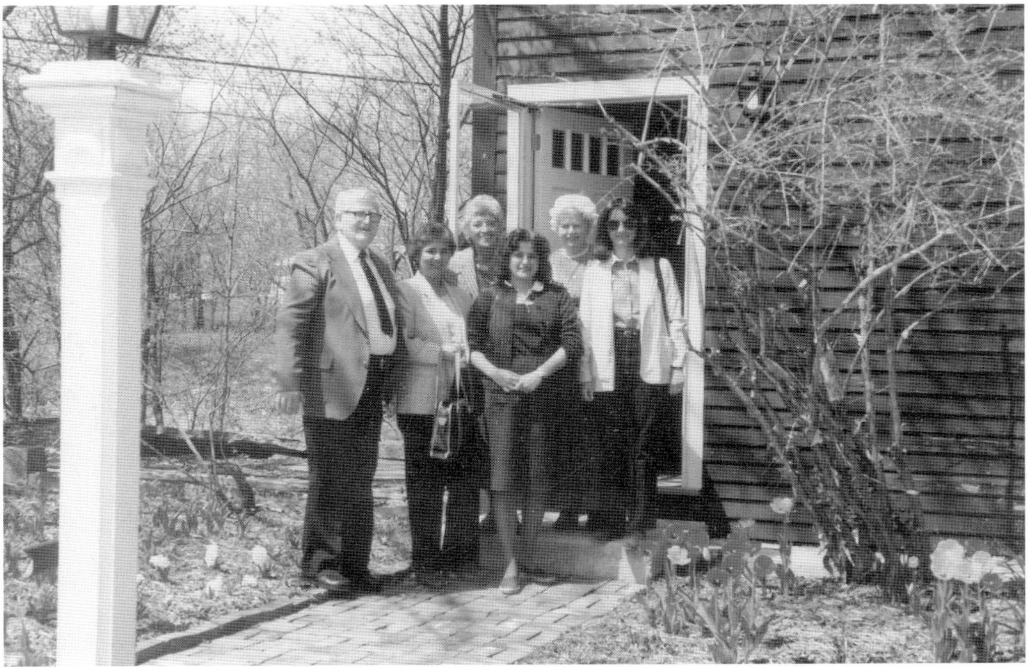

Donat Paquet

Born in St. Agapit de Beaurivage, Lotbiniere, Quebec, Canada, on May 13, 1919, Donat Paquet (far left), was a well-known English teacher at Dracut High School who had his students utilize primary sources to write their research papers. He authored the 1982 book *The Photographic History of Dracut*, an invaluable resource for all studying the town's history. The Dracut Historical Society has changed quite a bit since these photographs were taken in the early 1980s when Paquet was an active member. The photograph below shows the museum's grounds before Harmony Hall was moved there in 1994. Donat Paquet passed away in August 1997. (Both, courtesy Dracut Historical Society.)

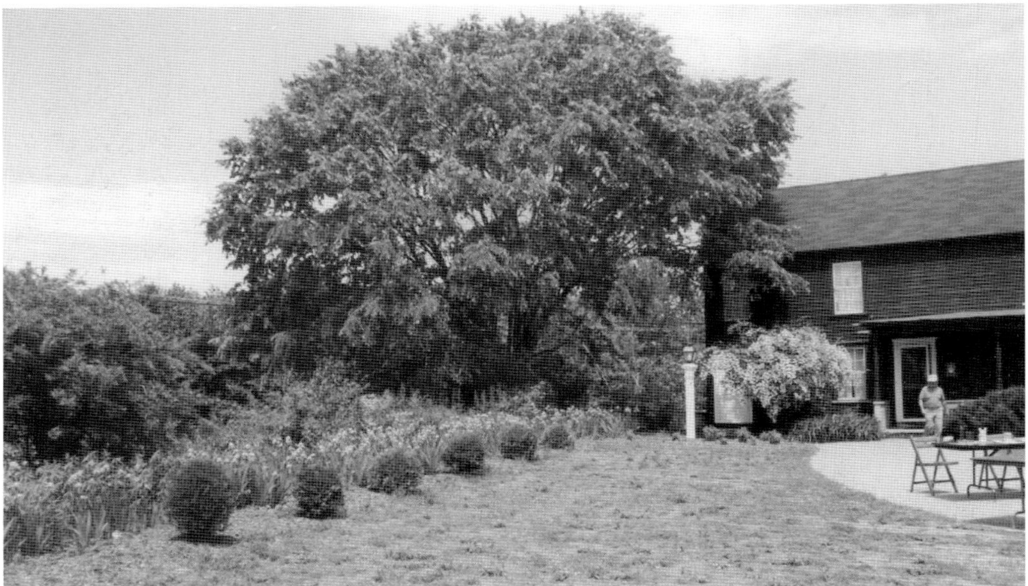

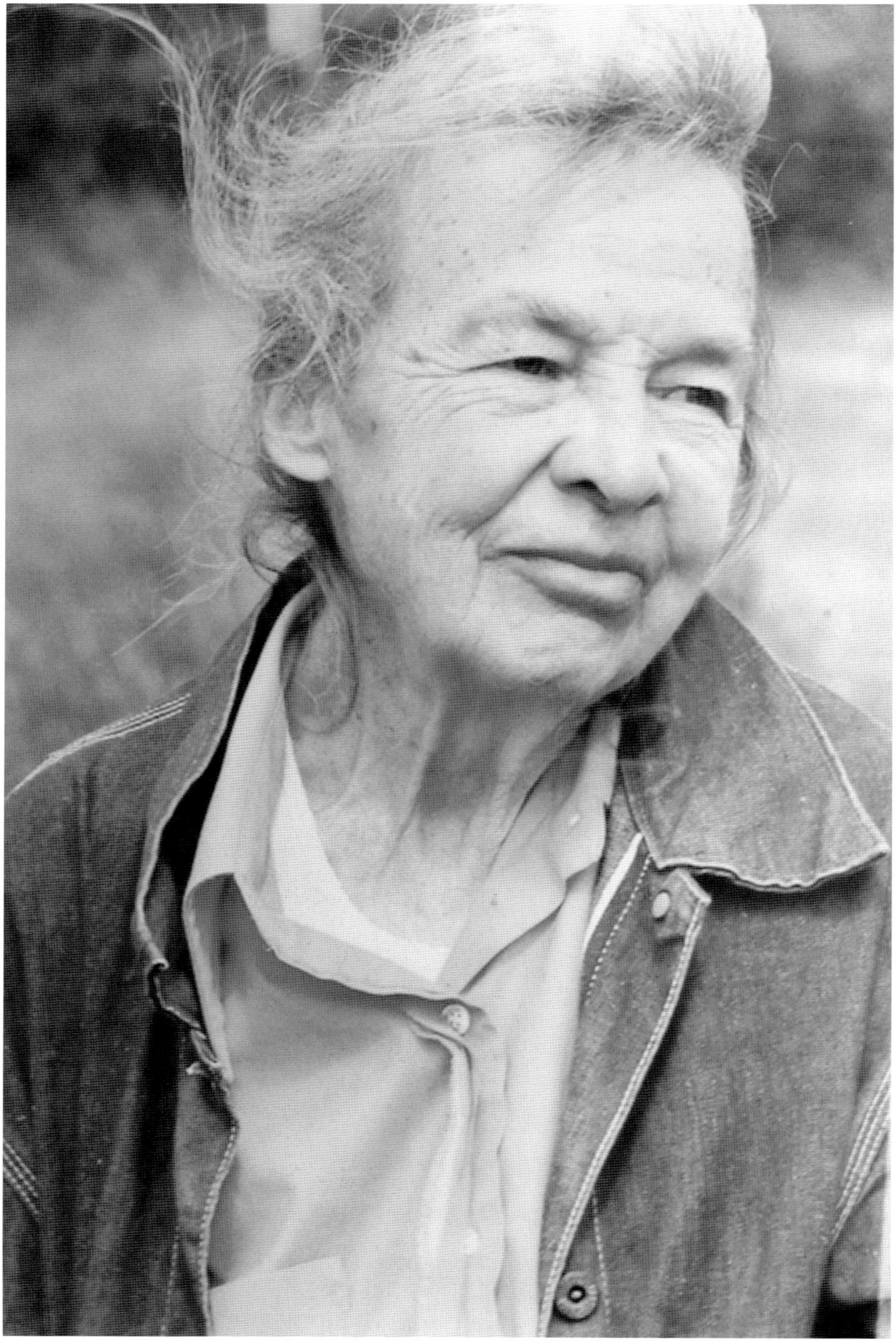

Marjorie Dunlap

Marjorie Dunlap, born in 1911, owned and operated a dairy farm with her husband, Bert, beginning in 1950. Located on Marsh Hill Road, the farm totaled 100 acres of beautiful fields, pastures, and wetlands. Dunlap's husband passed away in the early 1980s, at which time the fate of most farms in Dracut, and other communities throughout New England, was becoming clear. Thus she set her goal on preserving her much beloved farm. She first approached the Dracut Conservation Commission, which told her that it was "too late" to preserve farmland in town. Other organizations were not interested because they considered her farm too small to save. Undeterred, Dunlap went to her neighbor, then selectman Warren Shaw, who describes his first conversation with Dunlap: "As she climbed over the stone wall that ran between the properties she held up her finger for me to stop the tractor." Shaw did stop and listen to what she had to say. The idea was simple; she wanted to preserve her farm and protect it from future development. Looking into how the Dunlap property could be preserved, Shaw contacted attorney Joseph Hannon, who worked for the Northern Middlesex Area Planning Commission, for guidance. Hannon recommended, and helped with, the creation of a conservation restriction on the property, which would allow the Dunlap family to maintain ownership and use of the land without fear of future development. Because of the conservation restriction created in 1983, the land would remain a farm. Since her passing in 1997, a wooded area of the Dunlap property has been a favorite spot for hikers and nature lovers, and Boy Scouts made trails in this area known as Dunlap Sanctuary. Also due to Dunlap's efforts, the preservation of what is now White Gate Farm was made more likely, as conservation programs look favorably upon preserving contiguous parcels. For her efforts in land preservation, Earth Day in Dracut has been renamed Marjorie Dunlap Day. What began as a simple conversation would become a land preservation movement in Dracut that has seen over 400 acres saved. (Opposite page, courtesy Helen Dunlap; below, author's collection.)

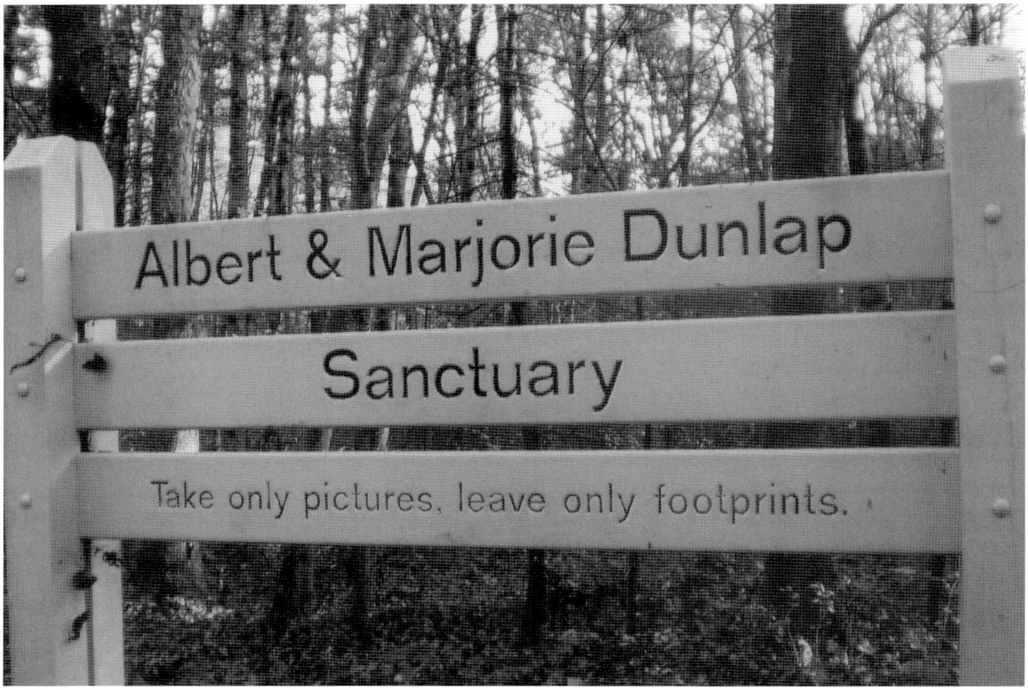

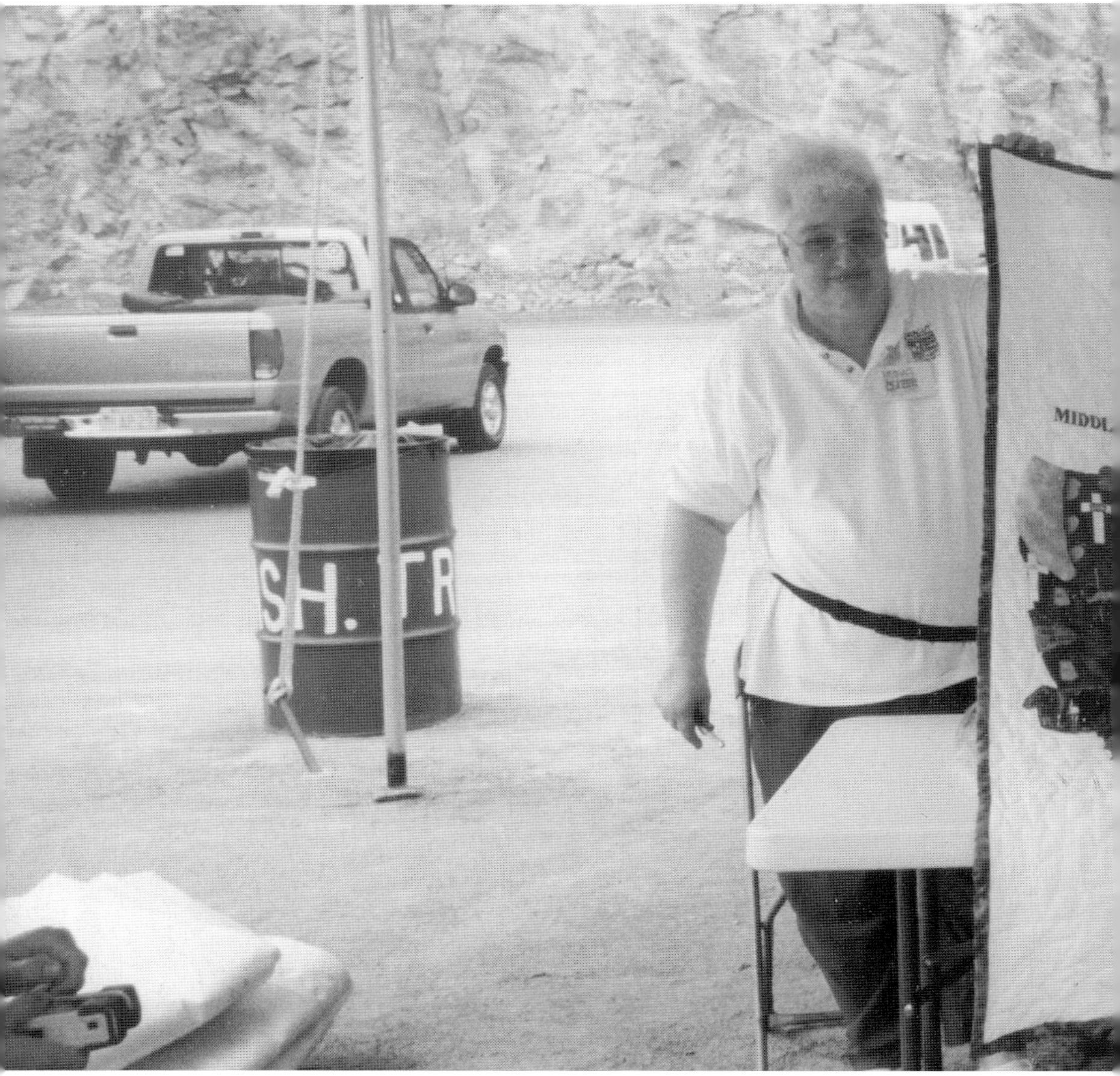

Tercentenary Quilters

Alma R. Reeves (left) and Barbara Agrella-Updyke hold a handmade quilt commemorating the tercentennial at the "Concert in the Quarry" in June 2001. This was one of the many activities planned during 2001—the year of the town's tercentenary. The tercentennial quilt was a group effort of many ladies, including Alma R. Reeves, Barbara Agrella-Updyke, Karen Merrill-Desrosiers, Pat Dadducci, Sharon Piendak, Nancy Gaudet-Martin, Kathleen Doiron, Annette Rondeau, Judy Bryand, Diana Coates, Lorraine Berard, Sandy D'Ascensao, and Roberta Briscoe. It was presented as a gift to the town at the Mill House Restaurant on February 26, 2001. The quilt was then taken to each tercentennial event, and more than 5,000 Dracut residents signed it. Currently, it is on display at the Parker Memorial Library. (Courtesy Dracut Historical Society.)

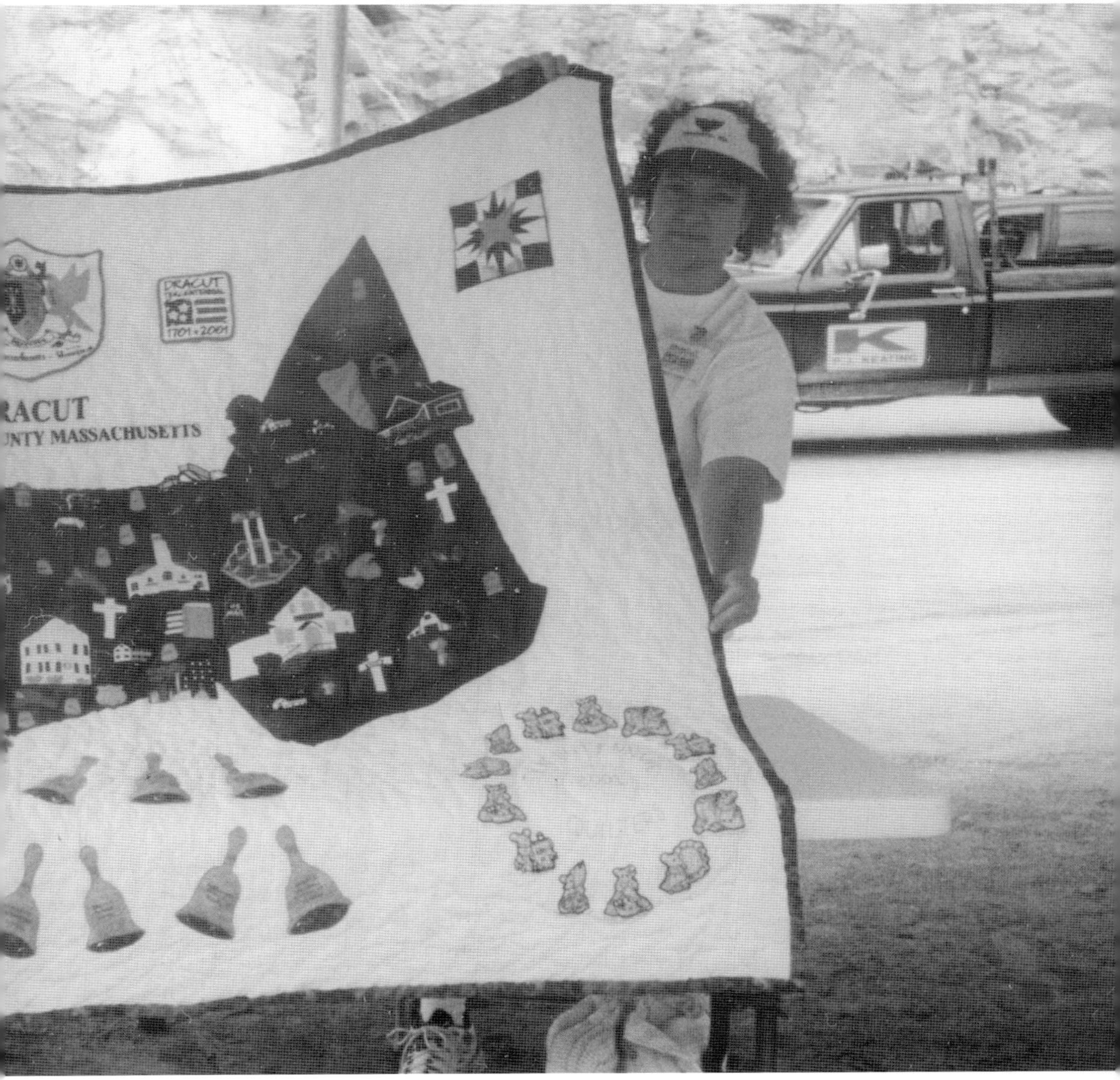
DRACUT
1701•2001
RACUT
UNTY MASSACHUSETTS

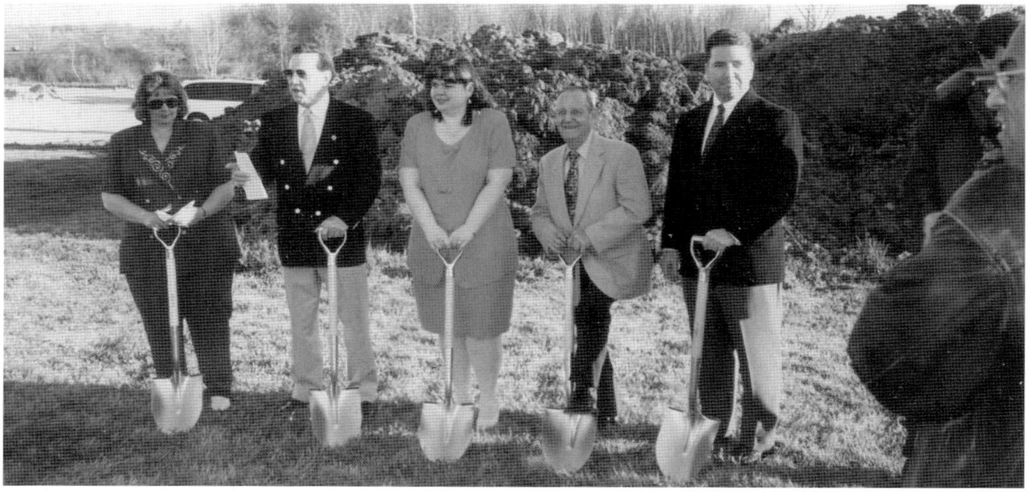

Marietta "May" Paquette

A lifelong resident of Dracut, May Paquette has served the town in numerous ways, but the time she spent working on Veterans Memorial Park helped to create a beautiful recreational area for the town. She served as chairman of the Veterans Memorial Development Committee (1996–2006) and chairman of the Veterans Memorial Concession Stand Committee (2006–2009). The origin of Veterans Memorial Park dates from 1996, when the Town purchased 23 acres along Broadway. Accounting for 68 percent of the purchase price, a grant of $462,400 from the state's Division of Conservation Services made this transaction possible. Once the land was purchased, the board of selectmen appointed a 47-member committee to help guide and advise on the development of the park. These 47 committee members created three subcommittees to accomplish their charge. By April 1999, enough fundraising had been done so that construction on the park could begin, and a ground-breaking ceremony took place. In 2007, the concession stand opened, and its sales help to support the park, which is now a total of 26 acres. Pictured above at the ground-breaking are May Paquet, William Zounes, Colleen Garry, Doug Willett, and Jack DiTillio. The image below shows the completed Veterans Park, a popular recreation spot for the town. (Both, courtesy Marietta Paquette.)

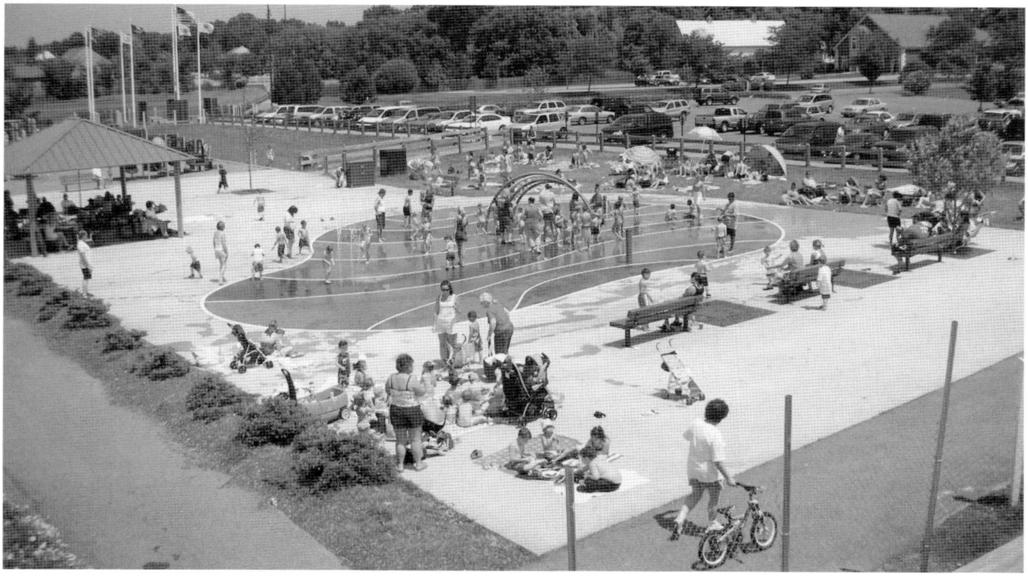

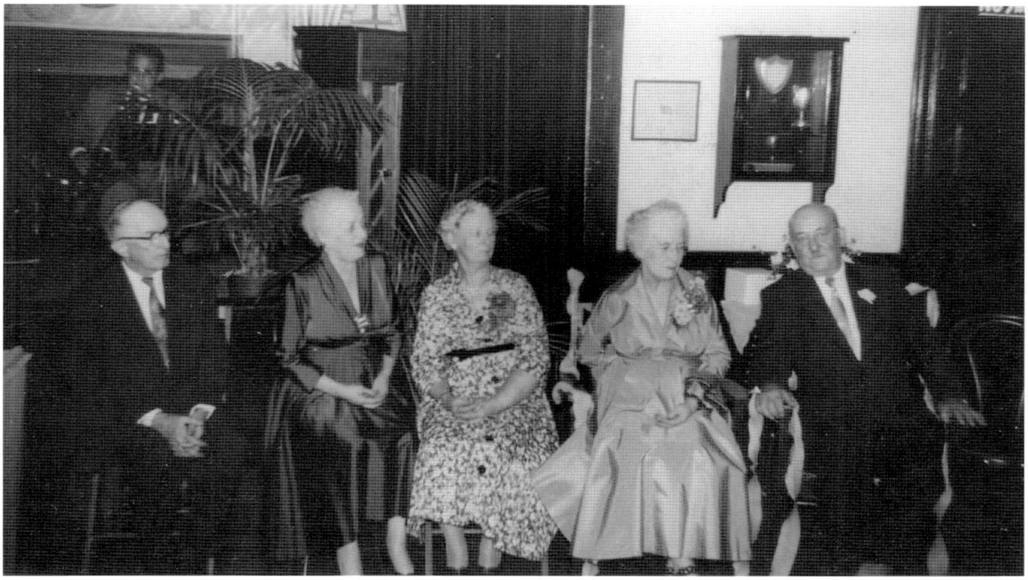

Arthur W. Colburn

Born in 1877, Arthur W. Colburn was educated in the one-room schoolhouse on New Boston Road. From there, he went directly to college, attending the University of New Hampshire. Upon graduation, he returned to Dracut and, in 1905, married Mabel Wilcox. Shown above celebrating their 50th wedding anniversary at the Dracut Grange, the Colburns (far right) lived on the family farm, pictured below in the 1870s. In the 1960s, Colburn helped to incorporate the historical society and wrote local history columns for the *Lowell Sun*. Colburn passed away at age 91 in 1969. (Above, courtesy Colburn family; below, courtesy Dracut Historical Society.)

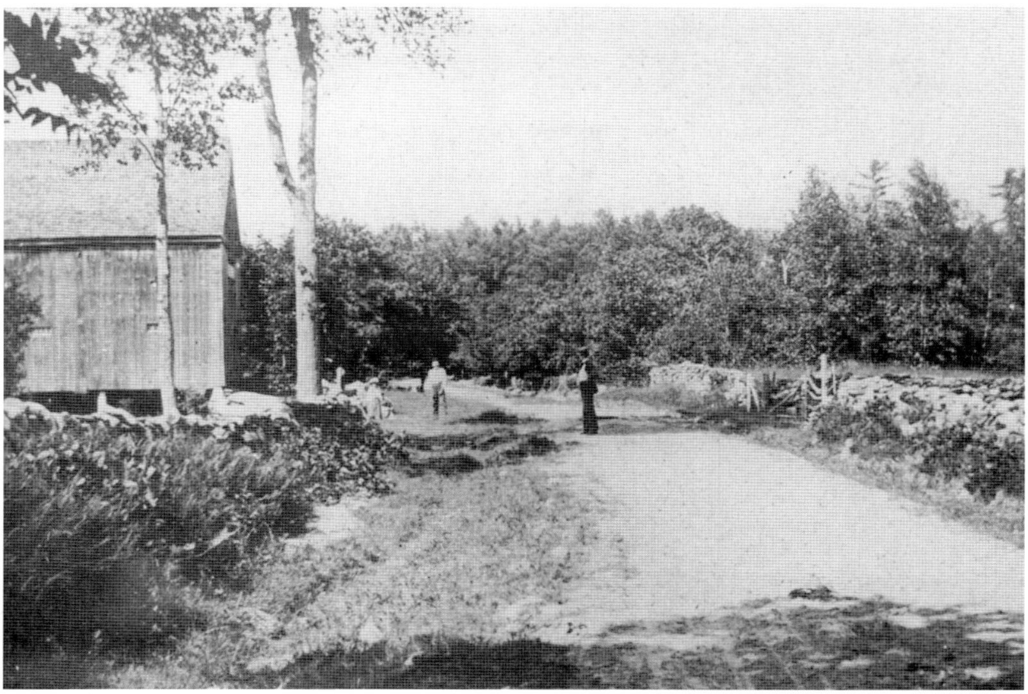

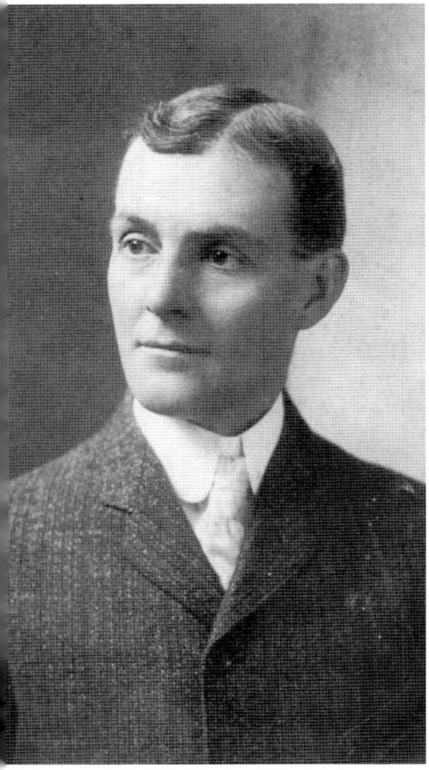

George H. Stevens

Born in Lowell on August 18, 1868, George H. Stevens moved to Dracut with his family when he was six years old. Active in town affairs, he served as selectman, town moderator, and town treasurer. Stevens also took an active role in preserving the town's history. In 1901, he served on the town's bicentennial committee, working closely with John Bailey to establish the Dracut Historical Society. Stevens was elected president of the society in 1935. (Courtesy Dracut Historical Society.)

Harmony Hall

Though not a person, Harmony Hall and its preservation are legendary about town. Harmony Hall was originally located on the corner of Lakeview Avenue and Mammoth Road. It was always a center of community activity in Collinsville. For example, in 1912 Collinsville residents attempted to get a branch library established for the neighborhood in Harmony Hall. It never materialized. In 1994, Harmony Hall was saved from the wrecking ball and relocated to its present location at the Dracut Historical Society, where it was refurbished and reopened in April 2007. Connected to the meeting room at the historical society, Harmony Hall is now used for community meetings and events. The photograph below shows Harmony Hall being moved down Lakeview Avenue. (Courtesy Dracut Historical Society.)

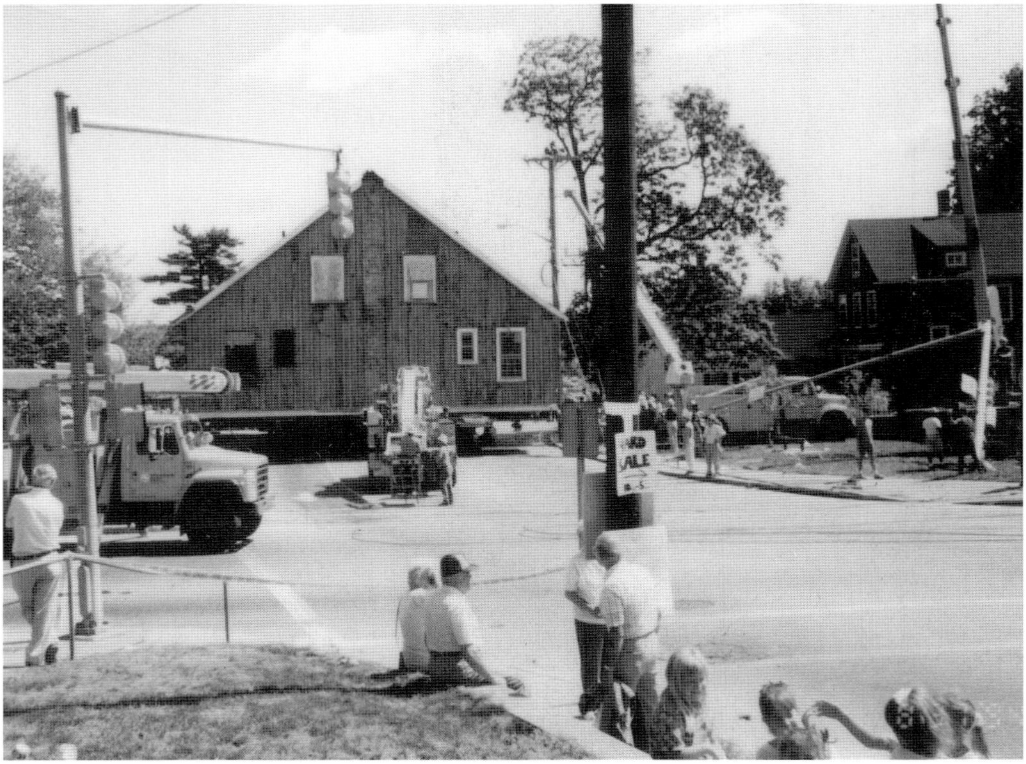

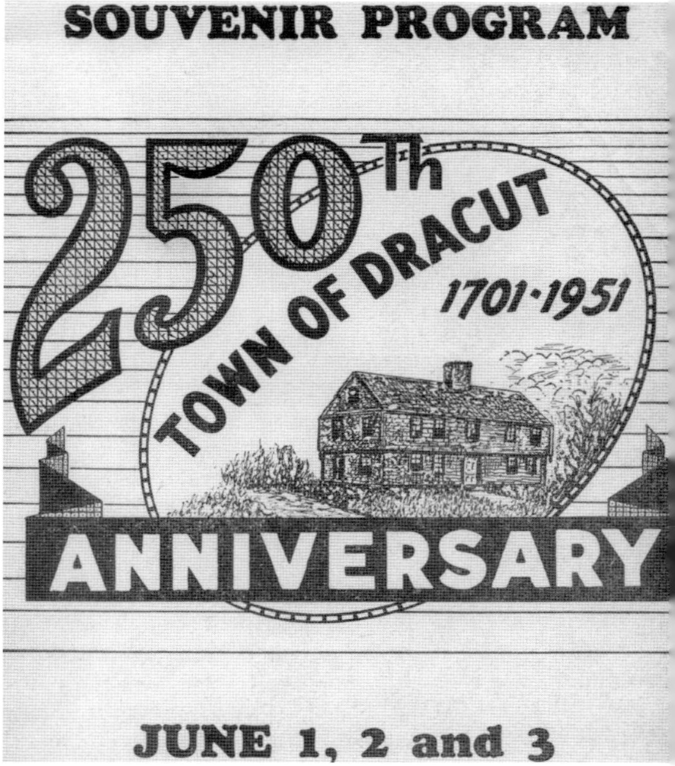

250th Anniversary Committee
In 1951, Dracut celebrated its 250th anniversary. On June 1–3 of that year, the town hosted an outdoor celebration with a parade, firefighters' muster, bean supper, sporting events, dances, concerts, and tours around town. The committee that worked to create the program consisted of the following members: Harry Fox, Agnes Vinal, Daniel Hanson, Valmore Cornellier, John Brox, Arthur White, Mary Dinley Howard, Joseph Swiniarski, Ernest Gunther Jr., Pauline Varnum, Nelson Fox, Christopher Lynch, Edward Dockett, Arthur Colburn, George H. Stevens, Oliver Richardson, Amedee Guimond, Wilfred Paquette, and Arthur Sheehan. (Author's collection.)

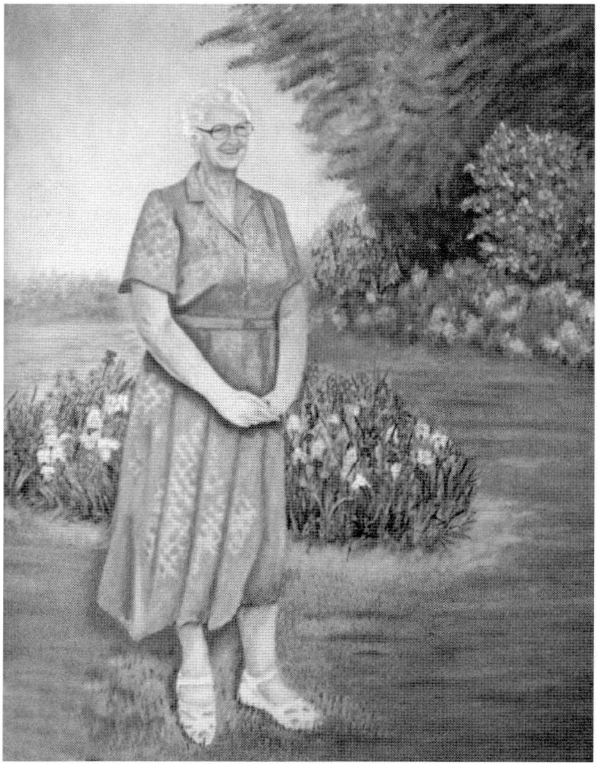

Orpha Coburn Fox
Orpha Coburn Fox was born in 1889. This painting of Fox was done by Betty Baroni and hangs at the Dracut Historical Society, where Fox worked tirelessly to record and write about Dracut's history. Today, those visiting the society pass the Orpha Fox Memorial Garden. The Fox family was one of the earliest families to settle Dracut. Fox passed away in 1980. (Courtesy Dracut Historical Society.)

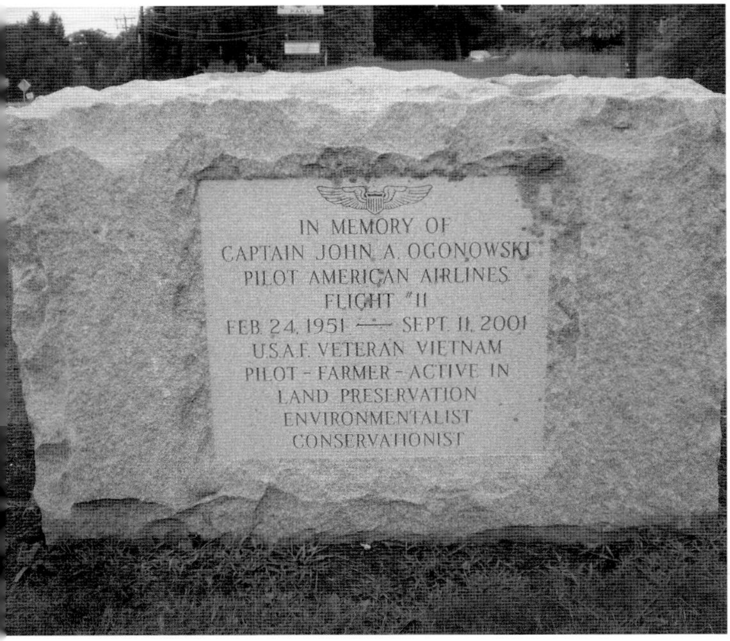

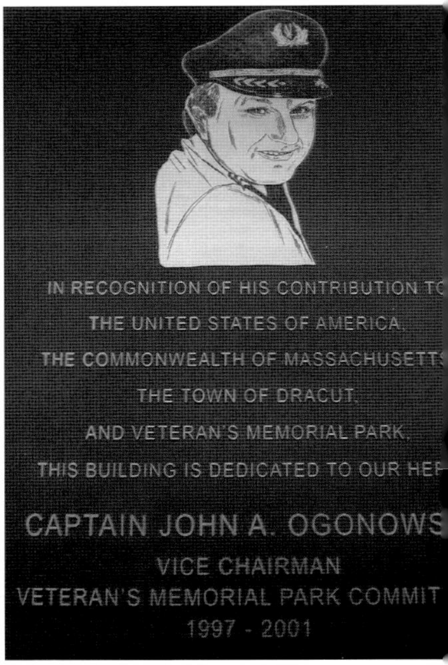

Capt. John Ogonowski

Born to Alexander and Theresa Ogonowski on February 24, 1951, John Alexander Ogonowski was a fourth-generation farmer. Polish immigrants, the Ogonowski family settled in Dracut around the turn of the 20th century. However, long before Captain Ogonowski was killed on September 11th, he had built a reputation as a well-respected resident of Dracut and a leader in land preservation and agriculture. After the Dunlap property had been protected, Ogonowski moved forward to acquire and preserve neighboring land owned by Textron. Ogonowski hoped to fund the purchase of the land with the Massachusetts Agricultural Preservation Restriction Program. With the program, he would still need $702,000 from the town. It went before town meeting on June 6, 1988, and was approved without opposition. This was due to the support of town manager Dennis Piendak, the Board of Selectmen, and hard work on Ogonowski's part. What is now known as White Gate Farm would be protected. In addition, Ogonowski was a longtime member of the Massachusetts Farm Bureau Federation and was deeply involved in the New Entry Sustainable Farming Project (New Entry), a joint partnership between Community Teamwork, Inc., and the Tufts University Freidman School of Nutrition. New Entry, which helps farmers to establish and grow their businesses, provided technical assistance to Cambodian immigrants who were farming on the land. Ogonowski rented 12 acres of his farm to seven families and worked with them as their mentor farmer. He immersed himself in the project. and it was highly successful. He then went on to help form the Dracut Land Trust in order to protect a 33-acre parcel, on Broadway Road and Jones Avenue, from development. After his death, members of Ogonowski's family asked Congressman Marty Meehan to help obtain funding to save this land. With the support of Senator Kennedy, the remaining $760,000 needed to purchase the parcel was secured. The land is managed through the Dracut Land Trust. As Ogonowski often said, "When you plant a building on a field, it's the last crop that will grow there." (Both, author's collection.)

BIBLIOGRAPHY

Chartier, Armand and Catherine Rivard Chartier. *Legacy.* Boston, MA: Works in Progress Press, 1985.

Coburn, Silas R. *History of Dracut Massachusetts.* Lowell, MA: Courier-Citizen Company, 1922.

Duda, Rebecca. *Dracut Revisited.* Charlston, SC: Arcadia Publishing, 2012

Paquet, Donat. *A Photographic History of Dracut.* Lowell, MA: Dracut Historical Society, 1982.

Pendergast, John. *Dracut.* Portsmouth, NH: Arcadia Publishing, 1997.

"Roth wins in primary." *Lowell Sun*: January 24, 1934, p. 3.

"Director of Special Education Receives Community Guardian Angel Award." *Dracut Dispatch*: April 24, 1997, p. 1.

"Great Activity in Eaton Case and Developments are looked for soon." *Boston Post*: March 14, 1913, pp. 1 and 9.

"Mrs. Eaton Charged with Murder." *Lowell Sun*: March 20, 1913, p. 1.

"Joseph A. Campbell Succumbs." *Lowell Sun*: April 28, 1974, p. 67.

"No Danger in Dracut Schools." *Lowell Sun*: September 25, 1928, p. 1.

"Mr. and Mrs. Zoel Houle Celebrate 38th Wedding Anniversary." *Lowell Sun*: August 7, 1939, p. 9.

"Collinsville Postmaster retires after long service." *Lowell Sun*: April 30, 1950, p. 50.

"Leo C. Roth Succumbs." *Lowell Sun*: February 9, 1958, p. 5.

"Trial of Francis E. and Miriam T. Heath for the Murder of their father at Dracut." *Boston Post*: June 4, 1858, p. 1.

INDEX

INDEX

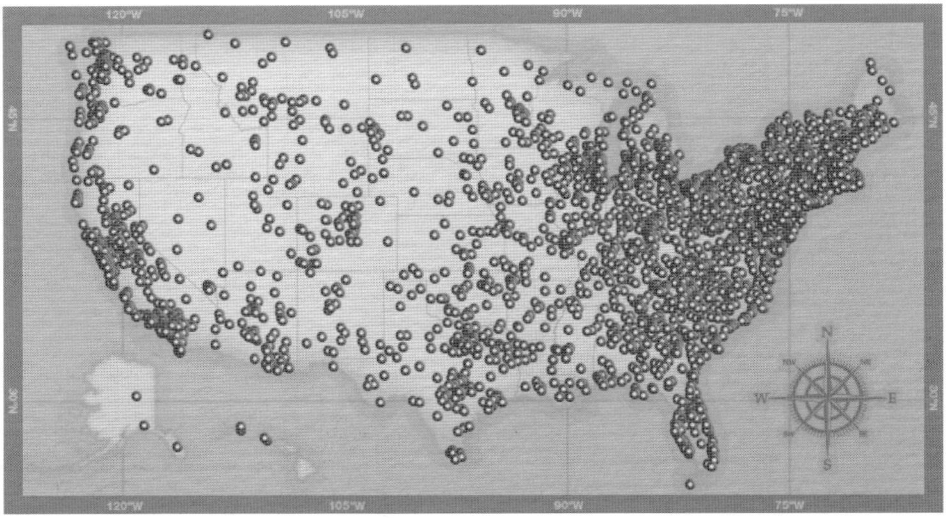

Consistent with our mission to preserve history on a local level, this book was printed in South Carolina on American-made paper and manufactured entirely in the United States. Products carrying the accredited Forest Stewardship Council (FSC) label are printed on 100 percent FSC-certified paper.